The Official Book of the Neapolitan Mastiff

Sherilyn Allen, VMD

REVODANA PUBLISHING

A Modern Molosser Book

REVODANA PUBLISHING
81 Lafayette Avenue, Sea Cliff, N.Y. 11579

Copyright © 2016 Revodana Publishing
All rights reserved

ISBN: 978-1-943824-26-7

www.revodanapublishing.com

Praise for *The Official Book of the Neapolitan Mastiff:*

"This reissue of Dr. Sherilyn Allen's important book on the Neapolitan Mastiff gives me the opportunity for some reflections, the first of which is that the author has a profound understanding of the breed, has bred Mastini for many years, and has gotten great results both in terms of morphology and character. Second, Sherilyn is a very well-versed veterinarian who knows very well all the problems that this very ancient breed has had, and still has, from a health perspective.

In long-ago 1995, in Contarina, Italy, the first international scientific conference on the Neapolitan Mastiff was organized by the ATIMANA (Associazione Tecnica Internazionale Mastino Napoletano), and it was Sherilyn who gave a presentation on hip dysplasia in the breed that is remembered even today. Since then, every year, in conjunction with the ATIMANA championship, which has been held in almost 15 countries and on three continents, that conference has been held with absolute regularity, and it reminds us of her role in the ATIMANA, which she served as a scientific consultant for many years.

I am very pleased that her important book is being republished, and I hope it will be read by many new Mastinari. It gave me the opportunity to remember just how much Sherilyn has done for the Mastino, and not just in the United States."

Giuseppe Alessandra
FCI judge, author, ATIMANA president and Mastino breed specialist
November 8, 2016

"You want to understand the Mastino Napoletano? The story behind this ancient breed? Its charisma and myth as much as its conformation, health and rearing? Then Sherilyn Allen's exquisite book is an absolute must-read for any Mastinaro, as nothing more educational has ever been written about the Neapolitan Mastiff. It will open the doors for readers to all that has been previously published in the Mastino's native land."

Christofer Habig
FCI judge and Mastino breed specialist, Germany
November 17, 2016

On the Front Cover
Magnificent lineup of three generations of Magnufi Neapolitan Mastiffs
in Australia. From left: Magnufi Romana, four and a half years; Gr. Ch.
Magnufi Favola and Ch. Magnufi Ferruccio, both 14 months; Magnufi
Giulietta, seven and a half years, and Gr. Ch. Magnufi Simpatica, four
and a half years. Owner and breeder: Lorene Cantarella. Photo: Lorene
Cantarella.

On the Back Cover
Neapolitan Mastiffs Bossa Nova (top) and Orso (bottom).

Contents

Quinto della Zacchera. Owner: S. Allen.

Foreword

It has been almost a quarter-century since I first started compiling information for the first edition of this book on Neapolitan Mastiffs. Many people who were avid promoters of the breed in the 1980s and '90s have since gotten out of the breed or simply died off. Now new people are coming into the breed, and they have new ideas and want to change things associated with the breed, sort of like what happens whenever government regimes, congress and presidents change. Sometimes new regimes get rid of the old because they feel it does not suite their agenda, or the types of dogs they are breeding. Sometimes new regimes think that "change" is good, and they want to change the breed (or society) to what they see as a better way.

Worldwide, I think many would agree that times have not changed for the better. The economy everywhere is worse, and our human rights are more compromised than they have ever been. And so it is with the Neapolitan Mastiff. Financially wealthy political activists were able to prevail over less wealthy dog organizations to stop the cropping of ears and docking of tails in Europe. As a result, we now see imported Neos without cropped ears and docked tails, and the attitude of the younger generation of Americans is that cropping the ears is cruel, while they themselves have all parts of their bodies pierced or tattooed or surgically altered for a look they think enhances their appearance or makes a statement. So today not as many people are cropping ears or docking tails on their Neos. This changes the entire expression and look of the dog, but the new entrants into Neos would not know the difference. It also makes for more ear infections in Neos, which is good for veterinarians.

Since new global societies embraced more "change" in the various dog breeds, citing their reasons as being beneficial for the health of the dog, they had to write down these changes and rules in the form of a new breed standard. The FCI adopted a new Neapolitan Mastiff standard effective November 13, 2015. The Neapolitan Mastiff Club of the United States is still arguing about what changes to make in the AKC standard. I have included the new FCI standard in an addendum to this book (see page 310), and will comment about the changes to the standard there. Here I will simply state that the changes they made basically have made it impossible create a Neapolitan Mastiff from the pool of genes that has defined the breed since the 1970s at least. (From 1946 until the late 1960s, the breed underwent phenotypic changes to make it more massive, more wrinkled and more unique in comparison with the other Mastiff breeds.) In my opinion, the 1970s to 1990s were the golden age of Neapolitan Mastiff breeding: At that time there was money and demand for the breed, and breeders were encouraged to produce more and more "exceptional" specimens. In the late 1990s, breeders began going overboard on type, which lead to a physically more degenerate dog. All the recessive genes that were responsible for Neapolitan Mastiff type led to dogs with many health issues, such as every orthopedic problem known to man, cardiomyopathy, eye problems in about every dog, skin problems galore, demodectic mange, and shy, fear-aggressive temperaments, just to mention a few of the problems.

Now I see that in America at least, there is vehement discussion among the newer players in the Neo game about how to make the breed sound again and get rid of the eye problems. When I addressed this issue in 1995 as veterinary speaker at the ATIMANA, I was practically thrown out of the country by the Italians, who called me a heretic to the breed. What I said then, I say now as I observe the dogs being bred in this country, and the Neos I see in other countries on the Internet. In this breed, you can have type, or you can have soundness, but you can't have both, according to the definition of type in the Neo and biomechanical soundness in dogs.

The AKC standard remains the same as the one adapted by me in collaboration with Peggy Wolfe and the AKC in 1996. The AKC is very specific on what it wants in its standard. It is not easy to change. But some people want to change it to make it more in keeping with the 2015 FCI standard of the Neapolitan Mastiff.

It is interesting to me that some changes, such as length of body versus height, are pushed through as they were in the FCI standard to fit the conformation of the dogs produced by certain breeders. Other changes, such as eliminating ear cropping and tail

docking, are pushed through by wealthy animal-rights groups. Some disqualifying faults and caveats are put into the standard in an attempt to create a healthier animal. And some disqualifying faults, which were in the earlier standards for a reason, have been eliminated in the 2015 FCI version, negating the standard's attempts at making a physically and mentally healthier dog.

What do I think has happened to the breed in the past 25 years? Like the world financially and socially, nothing. It has remained static, and gone downhill somewhat. There are very few active Neo breeders in the mid-Atlantic anymore, and not many people showing. It seems to me that there are more Neo breeders in the central part of this country than there were 20 years ago. I don't hear much from the West Coast. Some of the original people in the breed are still there. The Neos I see in show pictures seem pretty nice. They embody my compromise of just enough type with correct conformation, which should result in a sound gait. A lot of Neos I see in videos from all over the world are active, yes; exhuberant, yes; typey, yes; but sound – no.

Most all Neos I see in person or in photos or videos have eye problems, especially entropion. With the right kind of wrinkles on the forehead, the thick heavy ones in skin which is tightly attached to the skull, there will not be entropion. See the dogs Ironstone Atlas on page 12, Ironstone Islero on page 29 and Ms. Denger's dogs with Christofer Habig on page 131.

Since the introduction of excessively

Ironstone Hermes, one and a half years old. Breeder and owner: S. Allen. Photo: S. Allen.

wrinkled dogs with loose thin skin all over their bodies to the gene pools, it is now difficult to find a Neo without entropion. That loose skin, which is not tightly adhered to the skull, falls forward over the dog's face in abundant wrinkles, and mechanically makes the upper lids roll inward to the eyeball. If you want to eliminate entropion in Neos, you can't breed a dog that has entropion. If the parent has it, the puppies will have it.

Entropion leads to cherry eye, which is inflammation and infection of the gland of the third eyelid, because the eyelids are constantly irritating the eye. Then the dog rubs his face and eyes and scratches his cornea. So he rubs some more, making more tears and infection, which start to eat away the cornea, creating an ulcer. If the ulcer is caught early enough and treated, and the cause (the entropion) is surgically repaired at the same time, the eye might be saved. Otherwise, the dog becomes blind.

Since I have not seen much change with the Neapolitan Mastiff in the past 25 years, in spite of man's verbiage to change it, I think this book as published in 1995 is very relevant today. It is a tell-it-like-it-is with the breed. It is not politically correct, which is a no-no in today's society. I am not politically correct because animals are not, and if one is to deal with animals and animal husbandry, one cannot be politically correct with them. All animals know one thing: "He who makes another move is boss." The Neapolitan Mastiff, as a guard dog and protector of people, is innately dominant. All innately dominant beings try to be top gun in their pack or society. All Neos are happy to follow a leader, if the leader shows he is top gun. But if the human is submissive to the dog, the dog will take over. Once the Neo takes over, it is only a matter of time before he is sent to rescue or euthanized.

Because I am old, I can say that 42 years ago, when people came to my office, their children and dogs were mainly well behaved and under control of the " parents." Now, in 2016, I can say that for the past 20 years, maybe a handful of times per year have I seen well-behaved, under-control dogs of any breed or children in my office. "Change"

Quiet contemplation. Photo: S. Allen.

has brought parents who do not discipline their children and pet owners who do not discipline their dogs. It is a different world. And people in today's America who have Neos are playing with fire.

From the Neos that come to my office, I can state that they are mostly happier, not so shy, not so wary, and more outgoing with strangers than they were 20 years ago. However, they are no less dominant, and because I have not seen one Neo in my office, puppy or young adult, that was under control of its owner, I am not happy. The owners tell me their dog is wonderful at home while it is growling at them when they try to restrain it so that I can examine it. The dog may come up to me at first sniffing and jumping all over me as if happy (actually just totally disrespectful), but as soon as I try to examine it, the dog turns into Cujo.

Most owners bring their dogs to me for eye problems or lameness problems in young dogs. I rarely see old Neos anymore. I think they have long been gotten rid of. I always give them the same politically incorrect spiel on how they need to get their dog under control. They look at me with a blank stare, and they usually do not come back. Some of these dogs are very pretty. Some have pretty good conformation. They all have eye problems. They all are out of control. What more can I say?

I stopped breeding Neos right before the financial crash in the U.S. in 2008. Though I believed my dogs were sane and had good temperaments, I would not sell to the general American public. People in South America and parts of Europe and even in Asia know how to deal with large dogs. Americans in general do not.

Obviously American breeders of Neos know how to handle them. And the Neo breeders still showing in AKC shows certainly are experts in handling Neos. They are superb dog people, and I admire them totally. But I was not going to sell my Neos to the general American public, since everyone in America wants a guarantee on everything, and everyone thinks they can return something after a few days or weeks or months or years if whatever they bought does not work out for them. Selling Neos to the American pet owner who wants "another family member in our home" is not what Neos are about.

I still think the dogs are special. The properly bred ones have a neat personality and are good companions (outside the house – I can't deal with the drool inside). One could certainly feel safe in today's ever-so-not-safe world with a Neo on the property. As the years go by and new people decide what they want in the breed, I am sure the breed will be changed from what I was enthralled with. The special ones, the special owners who had them, the fun shows we had in the rare-breed circuit are good memories for me. Whatever happens to Neos in America, I am sure some Mastinari hidden in the countryside of Italy will preserve the breed, true to its ancient heritage. It is a special breed that should not be exploited or changed is its ways in an attempt to turn it into the family pet. It is an ancient-minded dog best kept by mature dog people. It is a marvel of nature, and if given a chance to propagate on its own, will keep the mix of genes needed to make it a robust dog

with special traits that are not excessive.

I hope that the access to this book again will be a fun and educational read for people interested in this unique breed of dog. I hope it will make them seriously think about whether they have the personality, talent and environmental facilities to handle such a special animal. Sometimes looking at art in pictures or in a museum suffices. You don't have to own it and take care of it. Neos are for looking at, but they are bred to do a job. They need to have a job. They need to have a master. At some point in time, the world has to get out of politically correct mode and people won't just be weak computer geniuses. If that happens, and survival of the fittest comes into play again, as it has always existed, then the Neo will be at home in the world again.

This edition of *The Official Book of the Neapolitan Mastiff* is being published with the original text from 1995, a time when the Neo was still a rare breed in the United States, and not yet recognized by the American Kennel Club. Keep that chronological dissonance in mind as you read. At the end of the original book is an addendum with pictures of modern dogs and also the new FCI 2015 standard of the Neapolitan Mastiff. I have made some pertinent comments to that standard which the people engaged in trying to change the current AKC standard of the Neapolitan Mastiff might want to take into consideration.

Sherilyn Allen
August 6, 2016

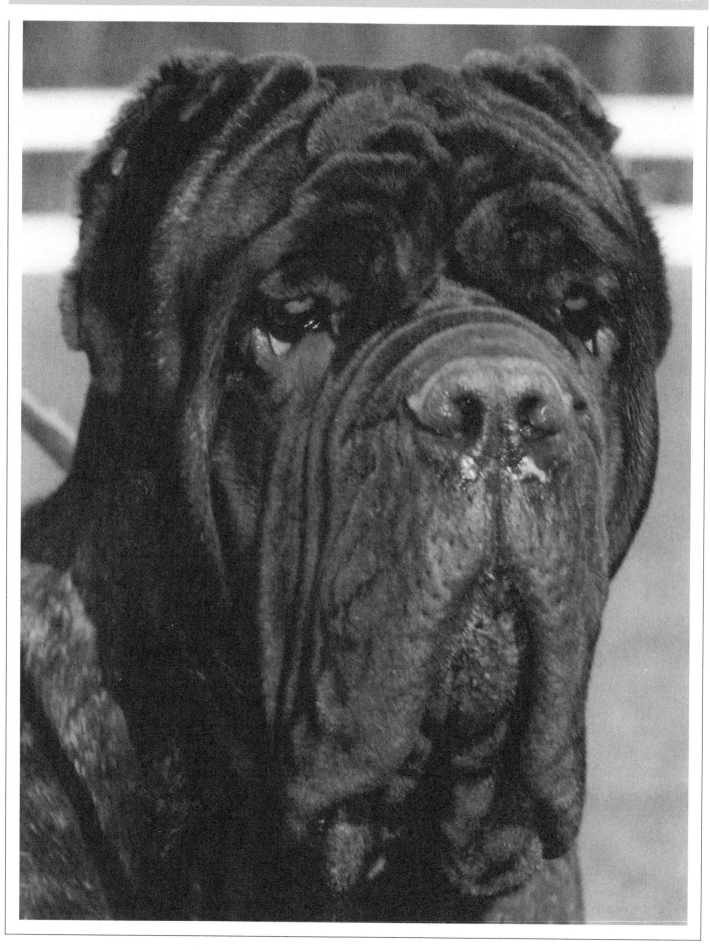

Preface

A short time ago, I attended a social gathering of dog fanciers where I had to give a brief presentation. After my address, the host, a very distinguished gentleman and avid dog lover, came up to me and said, "You are an educated and well-spoken person; why would you have those messy, dumb Neapolitan Mastiffs? They are hard headed, unattractive, and they slobber. Why do you like them? What do they do for you?"

"Why do you have that Dali painting on your wall?" I asked. To me, Neapolitan Mastiffs are awesome. There is no other dog in the world like them. They are an art form, a relic from the past, a primitive incongruity in today's world. Not only do they as a breed look different from other dogs, they as individuals each look different from one another. Each Neo is a 'one of a kind.' For the breeder who is engaged in the creation of a living art form, each Neapolitan puppy has the possibility of being that one chef-d'oeuvre.

"Your Dali and your Rodin just sit there," I told him. "My Neo sits there next to me when I want, but he also loves me back incredibly. It is born into them to love and protect that which is theirs, and they do those things better than any other dog I know. They are not stupid," I continued. "They simply have their own mind. If you were lying on the couch watching a football game, and your wife told you to get up and take the garbage

Left: **Ironstone Atlas. Breeder/owner: S. Allen.**

out – now – would you necessarily do it immediately? If you did not, would you then be classified as 'hard headed' or 'dumb'?

Do not try to compare a Neapolitan Mastiff's mind to that of other breeds of dogs. Most domesticated breeds have been modified to remain juvenile in personality throughout their lives. It is for that reason that we are able to control them. The Neapolitan Mastiff still retains its original nature. It grows up after puberty and has an adult dog mind. For this reason, the relationship between human and Neapolitan is very different from the relationship other breeds have with their owners. Just because the Neo's body does not look elegant, it does not mean that he does not act elegantly. To me, the serene majesty of the ancient, wise face of the Neo lying on the porch surveying his domain makes him among the most elegant of dogs. It is just a matter of how you look at him.

"As for the slobbering," I explained, "that is part of his defense mechanism. Would you, as an intruder, want to get near all that slime?"

To have expounded any more on a passion that has encompassed me for the past 10 years would have been a little long for a dinner-party conversation. So in answer to the question of "Why Neapolitans?" I thought it best to put it all down in a book. To be sure, as the dinner host noted, a Neapolitan Mastiff is not for everyone. The admirer of a Neapolitan Mastiff is someone who has an appreciation for the

Above: **Stonehenge Barabas, four-year-old male. Breeder and owner: R. Evans. Photo: S. Allen.**
Below: **Cindia della dea Partenopea, three-year-old female. Breeder: Mme. Le Méhauté. Owner M. and Mme. Patrick Salomon. Photo: P. Salomon**

unusual, a fascination for the history and the Mediterranean spirit of which the Mastino is a product. The owner of the Neo is someone who is emotionally moved by the mystique of this ancient breed, has been able to care for one, and has the ability to control it.

This book, therefore, is written as an explanation of Neapolitan Mastiffs. It is an explanation of why I like them and what they do for me. It is an explanation of how to care for and preserve these survivors from the past. Most of all, this book is written as an explanation of the duty each prospective Neapolitan owner must accept in order to maintain this ancient breed properly. Owning a Neapolitan Mastiff entails an enormous amount of responsibility. To preserve and perpetuate a living antique is a responsibility. To keep a breed of dog that has been exported to other countries true to its national heritage is a responsibility. To control in today's society an animal that was bred to be a hunter and a warrior is a responsibility.

I would like to thank all those Neapolitan Mastiff owners who so kindly sent me photos of their dogs; Rüdiger Schmalzbauer, who gallantly gathered a wealth of photos for me; Markus Rogen, who allowed me to use his professionally produced photos; The British Museum and the Oriental Institute of the University of Chicago, which provided photos of some of the ancient artwork depicting Molossoid-type dogs; René Evans for his beautiful drawings to illustrate the breed standard; Christopher Arts, for his research, resources and comments; my daughter, Lisa, who helped me sort and

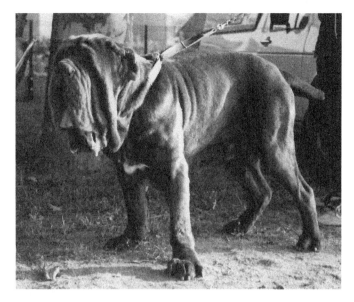

Slobbering as a defense mechanism. Fido Bravo Belli van Hadimassa, male. Breeder: B. Martens. Photo: Schumacher.

caption all the photos; Barbara Rivolta, who helped me procure photos of ancient artwork; ARBA and TFH Publications, for making this book possible; and the dogs themselves, who are a never-ending source of fascination and education for me.

Sherilyn Allen

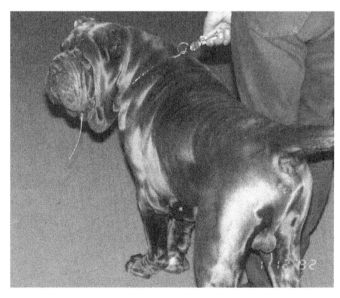

Drooling happily, Ch. Etrusco, two-and-a-half-year-old male. Breeder and owner: G. Iazetta. Photo: S. Allen.

Each Neapolitan puppy has the possibility of being that one chef-d'oeuvre. Marlena, seven-week-old female. Breeder: R. Evans. Owner: C. Kemp. Photo: S. Allen.

Introduction

There have been a number of excellent books written in the past 10 years on the Mastiff breeds, and specifically the Neapolitan Mastiff. Most of the books on the Neapolitan Mastiff are written in languages other than English. The only one in English is John Twinam's translation of Mario Zacchi's Italian-language book on the Neapolitan Mastiff.

Since more people are now becoming aware of the breed, more information on this dog is needed for availability to English-speaking people. My goal in writing this book is to emphasize how different the Neapolitan Mastiff is from other more familiar and "modernized" breeds of dogs. People who think they "know" dogs will find that they do not know the Neapolitan Mastiff. He is different in appearance, health requirements and personality from the normal "dog" with which people are familiar.

It is of utmost importance that people know what they are getting into when they buy that cute little wrinkled Neapolitan Mastiff puppy. It is amazing to me how resistant people are to believing what I have to tell them about the Neo. But just let me say that in more than 35 years of intense experience with dogs, and more than 20 years of that as a veterinarian, I have never met a domesticated dog that behaves like a Neapolitan Mastiff.

To comprehend the Neapolitan Mastiff, you must read the existent ancient descriptions of mastiffs. You will then understand that this breed has not changed materially for the past 2,000 to 5,000 years. When you understand what ancient instincts run in his genes, you will understand what the cute, wrinkly puppy is going to grow into. Then you will be more able to rationally decide whether the Neapolitan Mastiff is the animal for you and your lifestyle.

The earliest description I could find of the ancestors of the Neapolitan is by a Latin author of the first century AD, Lucio Giunio Mederato Columella. In his work *De Re Rustica*, Columella states that the house guard dog, which was the Roman Mastiff of that time, should be black, "*because a black dog has a more terrifying appearance; and during the day, a prowler can see him and be frightened by his appearance. When night falls, the dog, lost in the shadows, can attack without being seen. The head is so massive that it seems to be the most important part of the body. The ears fall towards the front, the brilliant and penetrating eyes are black or grey, the chest is deep and hairy, the shoulder wide, the legs thick, the tail short, the hind-legs powerful, the toenails strong and great. His temperament must be neither too gentle nor too ferocious and cruel; whereas the first would make him too apt to welcome a thief, the second would predispose him to attack the people of the house. He should be of solemn and not merry character and must always react with rage against all intruders. Above all, these dogs must demonstrate not only vigilance in guarding without making a mistake, but must be guarding out of diligence* and a questioning nature rather than because they are fearful. For the first type will give the warning only when they are sure something bad is happening, and the second type will get excited about every little noise or false suspect. It does not matter that house guard dogs have heavy bodies and are not swift of foot. They are meant to carry out their work from close quarters and do not need to run far. In fact, these dogs want to stay behind closed walls or at the house without even trying to run off. They do their work very well by their astute sense of smell, which informs them of who is coming, and they warn with their bark whomever is approaching not to come near. And if the person persists in approaching, they violently attack. Indeed, the most important quality in these dogs is that they are guards

Ironstone Andiama, two-year-old female. Breeder: S. Allen. Photo: S. Allen.

American Ch. Ironstone Authority, three-year-old male. Breeder: S. Allen. Photo: S. Allen.

and do not permit an attack. The second quality is that if provoked, they will defend and fight with vigor and tenacity."

Another description of only 400 years ago is by Conrad Heresbach as written by Conrad Heresbach in *Foure Books of Husbandrie* in 1586.

"In choosing a mastie that keepeth the house, you must provide such a one as hath a large, mightie body, a great shrill voice, that both with his barking he may discover and with his sight dismay the thief – yea, being not seen, with the horror of his voice, put him to flight. His stature must neither be long nor short, but well set. His head great, his eyes sharp and fierce, either brown or grey; his lips blackish neither turning up nor hanging too much down. His mouth blacke and wide, his .\

Ramon del Bonrampino, one-year-old male. Breeder: G. Maja. Owner: S. Allen. Photo: S. Allen.

Ch. D'Annunzio de Néropolis, 18-month-old male. Breeders and owners: M. et Mme. Beck. Photo: J.P. Beck.

neather jaw far, and coming out of it on either side a fang appearing more outward than his other teeth; his upper teeth even with his neather, not hanging too much over, sharpe, and hidden with his lips. His countenance like a lion's, his breast great and shag haired, his shoulders broad, his legs big, his tail short, his feet very great. His disposition must neither be too gentle nor too curst, that he neither fawn upon a thief, nor fly upon his friends. Very waking, no gadder about, nor lavish of his mouth, barking without cause. It maketh no matter that he be not swift, for he is but to

fight at home and give warning of the enemy. A black dog is best, because of the hurt he may do to the thief by reason of not being seen."

The two passages, one from first-century Rome AD, and the other from 16th-century England, are practically identical in their descriptions of the home guard dog. If we analyze both descriptions, we understand that the Neapolitan Mastiff of today is exactly what these people were describing 400 and 2,000 years ago.

To recapitulate, the Neapolitan Mastiff of today is categorized by the Fédération Cynologique Internationale (FCI) as a dog bred for protection and guarding. Its distinguishing trademark is its terrifying countenance so that "a prowler by day can see him and be frightened by his appearance." His typical color is black or gray, so that "when night falls, the dog, lost in the shadows, can attack without being seen." "The head is so massive that it seems to be the most important part of the body."

The body is thick, with a "short" tail, powerful feet and strong claws. "He is of solemn and not merry character," and the important point for all to remember is that it is bred into him to "always react with rage against all intruders." The dogs' bodies are heavy, so that they are big enough to bring down a man or other beast, and "it does not matter that they are not swift of foot. They are meant to carry out their work from close quarters and do not need to run far. In fact, these dogs want to stay behind closed walls without even trying to run off." They are not dogs bred for running. They are actually bred so that they will not run away. Therein may lie the reasons why their conformation is so different from that of other dogs seen and admired in show rings. If the dogs had been bred for running and beautiful movement, and therefore the conformation that goes along with "beautiful movers," the dogs would have run off.

Actually, in ancient days, proprietors used to purposely cripple their dogs by cutting off their toes so that they could not run off and catch game. This expeditating (also called lawing) forced their giant-bodied dogs to stay home and do the job of defending, instead of wandering off.

Right: **Ch. Hatrim della Grotta Azzurra, four-year-old male. Breeder: G. Siano. Owner: S. Di Micco. Photo: J.P. Beck.**

Below: **Ch. Claus del Nolano. Breeder/owner: M. De Falco Jovane. Photo: M. De Falco Jovane.**

Neapolitan Mastiffs are not noted for their correctness of conformation, and they often have orthopedic problems. But you will always notice that even the most cumbersome and apparently ungainly Neapolitan Mastiff can instantaneously jump up when aroused, and attack and hit its mark before a human being even has time to react.

Never touch a sleeping Neapolitan Mastiff. That was the first lesson I learned after getting Neapolitan puppies. One night in winter, I wanted to see if the dogs were warm enough in their dog houses outside. I stuck my hand inside the box where I could hear a snoring puppy. Luckily for me, it was only a puppy. If you want to wake a sleeping Neo, stand back and call to it.

Back to the original topic – a Neapolitan Mastiff is heavy and lumbering because it was bred to be that. There was a reason for it. To compare it with light-boned, swiftly moving dogs that we consider to be elegant is wrong.

"They do their work very well by their astute sense of smell, which informs them of who is coming." This sentence sums up what every owner of Neapolitans has observed – most of them do not see very well at all. They appear to be near sighted. Many do not recognize a person they are supposed to know until they smell that person, or see the person up very close. The ramifications of an attack dog who cannot recognize by sight as well as he can by scent are obvious.

"And if a person persists in approaching [the house guard dogs], they violently attack."

This is their nature, and it is what they always do. Do not expect them to recognize your mother-in-law coming to pay you a visit if they have never met her before and been socialized with her.

For "indeed, the most important quality in these dogs is that they are guards, and do not permit an attack" by anyone onto their property. And if they are provoked, "they will defend and fight with vigor and tenacity."

Their heads are bigger than yours, their teeth are longer than yours, and their jaws open wider than yours. Their feet are as large as your hands, and their claws are like a bear's. When they stand on their hind legs, they are taller than you, and they can jump off their hind legs while they are standing up on them to come down over a man six feet in height. Most of the time, they outweigh you, and if you weigh more than 175 pounds, they are still stronger than you. The only thing that can control them is for them to think that you are tougher and stronger than they are.

It is most important for people in today's society to realize that the Neapolitan Mastiffs of today have not changed at all from those dogs of 400, 2,000 and even 5,000 years ago. People today want dogs for protection, but expect that the dogs will not actually hurt anyone. Then society is outraged when the dogs act like dogs and do actually bite or attack someone.

People today also anthropomorphize animals and expect them to be able to reason like human beings. People think a dog has the ability to decide who is an enemy and who

Ironstone Ilythia, one-year-old female. Breeder and owner: S. Allen. Photo: S. Allen.

is a friend. Most times human beings cannot even tell which people are enemies and which are friends, as proved by spies and undercover FBI or other police agents. There is certainly no way a dog is going to be able to decide if he should or should not bite the meter reader, if he was bred for the past 2,000 years not to let anyone onto his designated property.

Doesn't this face alone tell you it has no desire to be petted? Ironstone Cassiopeia, 10-month-old female. Breeder/owner: S. Allen. Photo: S. Allen.

It is important to realize that humans have succeeded in changing and developing some breeds of dogs to fit into the mold dictated by our present-day Western society. The close bond that existed between human and animal when animals were used for work, and almost all people knew how to control them, has been replaced by a different human-animal bond. People today seek animals primarily for companionship and love. Dogs and cats are now referred to as "companion animals." People have forgotten

how to properly "master" a pack animal. The Neapolitan Mastiff still retains a strong sense of social hierarchy and needs to know who is boss on the place. No matter how much some people may have tried in the past 20 years to modify the behavior of the Neo to make it a gentler, more sociable dog, genes cannot be erased. They can be modified, by adding to them, and it is well understood by those who know Mastini that some breeders in other countries introduced other blood into the breed in an attempt to get more size, conformational soundness or a gentler personality. This is not a criticism, but it is an explanation of why the Mastino in other countries differs somewhat from the "Made in Italy" Mastino. Once you understand what you are dealing with in the pure Italian Mastino, you can take the proper precautions to protect the public from the dog you have acquired to protect you.

I am reminded of a recent incident in which a Neo owner had her two dogs in her car, and a person she was talking to reached through the open car window to pet them. The person was lucky to come away requiring only 30 stitches in his hand. The dogs were doing what they have been bred to do – protect their space. The owner was not aware enough of the personality of her dogs, or she would have told the person to stay away from the car. Part of the goal of this book is to teach you how to be aware, so that you can be a responsible Neo owner.

I love the Neapolitan Mastiff. Because I do love the breed, I feel it is my duty to present it so that anyone who deals with it has no surprises. I see the great possibility, as the

Neapolitan Mastiff becomes more popular in this country, for it to acquire a bad or incorrect reputation. Since the development and reputation of a breed lies primarily in the hands of the owners of the dogs, I feel that an educated person is better qualified to own a Neapolitan Mastiff than a person who does not know all there is to know about the breed. So, in this book, I will tell all that I know about Neapolitan Mastiffs. I will tell the bad as well as the good. I may be blunt, but I will be honest as I relate what this 10-year obsession with the breed has taught me.

Islero del Bonrampino dressed for the snow and looking very Italian. Photo: S. Allen.

I believe Mastini make great companions for those adults who are animal oriented and can control as well as care for a very powerful animal whose basic instincts are to guard, defend and attack if necessary.

Now that the warnings are out of the way, let me get on with some of the experiences I have had that make me love the breed. I believe educated owners, knowing what their Neapolitan Mastiff is capable of, can also

socialize and train their dog to behave in a way they would want them to behave. There are some individual dogs who are born just plain dear, and they are the ones for breeders to propagate if bringing some docility to the breed is a goal.

I have been lucky enough to own such a dog. It is in honor of him also that I write about his brethren. I bought him as a puppy from Giovanni Maja in Italy, then sold him twice in his life. (Everyone who sees him falls in love with him.) I bought him back again twice – the first time when he chewed his way out of his new owner's chain-link dog kennel and carried the professionally installed, 200-pound, expensive rubber floor mats out with him in shreds; and the second time when he atomized his new owner's MG top. He didn't like being in kennels or garages. He never demolished anything at my

Islero del Bonrampino, watching. Photo: S. Allen.

house except for stainless-steel food dishes and plastic detergent bottles. But, then, he is older and wiser now, and his teeth are more than worn. Also, I have given up trying to keep him apart from me.

He is the veterinary hospital mascot, and he spends his days as a watch dog – watching clients and their animals come in and out all day long. At 7 o'clock, he knows office hours are over, and he stops watching and realizes it is time to become ferocious. After 7 p.m.,

when someone comes onto the property, he races toward them, charging, his bass voice roaring. Some people have even been observed to jump for cover onto the trash dumpsters when they see him coming from 200 feet away. But when he finally reaches them, the tail starts wagging and he holds up his paw, which is his way of saying, "Pet me." Those unerasable genes within him remind him that he is supposed to be a ferocious guard, but his desire for love and attention always gets the better of him.

He is indeed the guardian – for puppies as well as other animals. He will sit for hours, just watching them, staying with them. A baby robin foundling I had to hand-feed adopted him as its mother. He sat with the bird vigilantly day after day, and protected it. Unfortunately, one day, it crawled under the fence into a pen with a French Bulldog, and was promptly eaten by that "little house dog."

When the children start screaming and racing around the yard like small prey, he does not run after them, pouncing on them and bringing them to the ground like most adult Neapolitan Mastiffs would do. He takes out his pent-up energy and frustration on the plastic detergent bottles, barking at them and chewing them to shreds. He teaches the puppies to travel well in automobiles (something most Neos hate), and he shows them how to behave in the house. He shows them how to fetch a ball. He keeps the puppies from wandering away, for he never leaves the immediate area around the house. He is the best dog trainer I ever had.

He is always at my side. One soon learns

Islero del Bonrampino with his robin buddy. Photo: S. Allen.

that doors mean nothing to Neapolitan Mastiffs. Being with their owner means more to them than anything, and doors are only a small encumbrance to a Neo who wants to be with his person. He would rather be with me than eat – unless, of course, the horde of guinea chickens who roam free on tick patrol start sneaking over to his food dish. Then, in a superb display of ferocity, he charges them till they scatter away. He proudly marches back to his food and meticulously eats, one eye on the

chickens as if to dare them to come near. He then shakes off all the slime he manufactured during his meal, and saunters off in search of me, to take up his position of watching.

In the uncanny way of Neapolitan Mastiffs, he knows several days in advance if I am planning to leave on a trip. He becomes anxious, won't eat, and chews up a greater than usual number of plastic detergent bottles. He also knows the day I am to arrive back, planting himself in front of the garage waiting for the car to return.

He fathers wonderful babies, imparting to them his outgoing temperament and gentler nature. Some of his sons have been known to eat through garage walls or chew up hard-plastic crates to get closer to their owners. But I haven't heard of any eating the hot tub like a nephew of his happened to do. As I said before, Neos are unbelievably strong. They are incredibly desirous of

companionship. When they are separated from the object of their affection, they take matters into their own jaws to change their conditions. One can't criticize them for this, and one mustn't call them hardheaded. I would call them awesomely devoted.

How many people do you know who would chew through a steel door just to be with you?

Islero has been a great source of pleasure and company to me. He has taught me a lot about his breed. He is a Neo, but he is also different from most other Neos. He has contributed to a gentling of the breed in America, if one considers that an attribute. He taught me a lot about genetics and a lot of veterinary medicine. He is, in my estimation, a great dog. I owe him a lot. And all he asks of me is a constant supply of plastic detergent bottles and to be next to me 24 hours a day.

Another great Mastino companion of mine, Orso, in 1999. His expression is iconic.

Ironstone Islero,
1½-year-old
son of Islero del
Bonrampino.
Breeder: S. Allen.
Owner: H. Booker.
Photo: S. Allen.

Lavinia del Bonrampino, two-year-old female. Breeder: G. Maja. Owner: S. Allen. Photo: S. Allen. "The only thing between you and him is me. Would you care to try to get past?"

History of the Neapolitan Mastiff

The Neapolitan Mastiff belongs to the group of large, heavy-bodied, heavy-boned, short-muzzled, wrinkled-browed, frightful-looking dogs that were used as fighters and protectors of persons and property. These types of dogs, which we know from ancient artwork and writings, existed at least 5,000 years ago. They were called Mastiffs, Molossians, Bandogs, Dogues, Mastini, etc. depending upon the period and region in which they were found. Their body types were in contrast to the sleek-bodied, light-boned, long-nosed, swift-footed sighthounds that existed at the same time and were used for chasing down game. Our Eurocentric history indicates that for thousands of years, these two basic types of dogs were bred and kept by people in western Asia and Europe, each for its own specific purpose. It has only been in the last 200 or so years that dogs have been bred for their looks in beauty contests rather than for their use as an aid to humans in their life's endeavors.

Because the body type of each dog was so dimorphic (i.e. the swift coursing hound type as opposed to the heavy, ferocious-looking guard-dog type, great care was taken throughout history to maintain the integrity of each type unmixed with the other. Purity of a breed was therefore defined by the extent to which its exaggerations of body type were maintained. Oppiano, a Greek poet of the third century AD, wrote about three different groups of dogs, categorizing them as to various types of hounds, the Egyptian

Al Hara's Yassi, seven-month-old Azawakh. Breeder: I. Aigledinger. Photo: S. Allen. Note the long neck, legs, tail and face. The body is very lean. The bones are long and light. These traits are characteristic of the swift-running sighthounds, which were used for running down game.

Rosco di Ponzano, male. Breeder: M. Querci. Owner: M. Mazzucconi. Photo: M. Massacconi. Note the immense head, short, wide muzzle with strong jaws capable of gripping onto game, and lots of loose skin over the head and neck, which serves as a protection of these areas. The front legs and shoulders are very muscular, for grabbing and bringing down prey. These traits are all characteristic of the Molossian dogs, which were used for gripping onto and killing large game after it had been run down.

Nineveh Terracotta, circa 850 BC. Copyright: The British Museum. Note the massive size of the dog with respect to the man. The short muzzle, wrinkles on the face and dewlap are apparent. The legs are thick and heavy in proportion to the dog's size. The shoulders and forearms are powerful.

dogs (greyhounds) and the Molossians. He mentions that people could interbreed the various hounds for experimental purposes of creating new breeds, but that the more handsome Greyhounds and Molossians should remain pure.

Assyrian Hunting Scene, 700 BC. Copyright: The British Museum, London.

Whereas many Molossian breeds have now evolved from the breeding of one race with another, it is the very heaviest and most ferocious guards, and the most streamlined and swiftest coursers, that appear to most closely resemble the most ancient breeds as described in the ancient literature and artwork.

Earlier, I cited Columella's description of the Roman house guard dog of the 1st Century AD. These dogs were most likely descendants of the Macedonian dogs, as they were called at the time of Alexander the Great around 350 BC, because his homeland was Macedonia. Alexander probably obtained the ancestors of these dogs from the peoples he had encountered in his conquests of the lands stretching from India to Macedonia. The dogs he brought back were called Indian Dogs or Assyrian Dogs, in accordance with the names of the peoples who inhabited the lands at that time. The Assyrians had taken over the lands around the Tigris and Euphrates rivers, now present-day Iraq and also Iran, but which were at that time referred to as Babylonia, Mesopotamia, Assyria and Persia.

What is so fascinating for Mastino fanciers is the amount of artwork from the Mesopotamian region that depicts mastiff-type dogs remarkably similar to the present-day Neapolitan Mastiff. These terracotta statues, bas-reliefs, cylinder seals and tiles depcting giant dogs with enormous heads, short muzzles, dewlaps, wrinkled foreheads, cropped ears and massive legs are common relics found in the Mesopotamian region, and they date from as early as 3000 BC.

Terracotta Dog from Mesopotamia, second millenium BC. Courtesy of the Metropolitan Museum of Art, Purchase, The Charles Engelhard Foundation Gift, 1989. (1989.233)

Above: **Follia di Ponzano, three-year-old female. Breeder and owner: M. Querci. Photo: courtesy S. Freeman.** *Below:* **Sumerian Molossian bitch suckling her pups, clay relief pressed from mold, ca. 2025-1763 BC. Courtesy of the Oriental Institute of the University of Chicago.**

It was around 3300 BC that the Sumerian peoples settled into the area between the Tigris and Euphrates rivers. This area came to be known as Babylonia, and a frequent finding in Babylonian molded clay reliefs or statues is the Molossian or mastiff dog. One of the earliest examples of these apparent ancestors to our Mastino is found in the Sumerian clay plate of the second millennium BC.

Another wonderful example of evidence of the relationship between our Neapolitan Mastiffs and the Sumerian dogs of at least 5,000 years ago is a 16¼ inch terracotta statue of a Mesopotamian mastiff dog dating from the second millennium BC. It is on exhibit at the Metropolitan Museum of Art.

This dog depicted by the statue has the same short, square muzzle and wrinkled forehead as our current Neapolitan Mastiff. The ears are the same shape as the cropped ears of our Neos. There is an obvious wrinkling on the muzzle, and loose skin and dewlap hang from the face. The forelegs have been broken off, but the legs that remain are very thick and powerful. The stance of the dog in a sitting position is characteristic of guard animals in the art of the period. The mouth is open, showing its ferocity and intentions to deter those who might approach it.

The Mastino fanciers has to be both excited and astounded by how closely this 4,000-year-old dog resembles our present-day Mastino in both form and function. It is practically absolute proof that our Neapolitan Mastiff is the living relic of 5,000 years ago. Other dogs have been changed in their appearance and nature by humans to suit special needs or lifestyles as times changed. Those who know the Mastino realize that he is an animal unlike other modern-day dogs, and the reasons, as proved by this statue in particular, are that the genes that determine both structure and temperament must be practically unchanged in our modern Mastino from what they were 5,000 years ago.

It is this contact with history and with civilizations that were our beginnings that the Mastino provides those of us who own him. I believe that this fascination with the past is one reason that certain people are attracted to this breed. Just owning a Neapolitan gives us the exoeruebce if what life had to be like thousands of years ago.

Going to the hunt. Assyrian, 700 BC. Copyright: The British Museum.

Being able to see for ourselves proof that our dogs are practically the same as the dogs that were used, prized and coveted in the cradle of Western civilization is a thrill that allows us to complete the puzzle of why our dogs are so unique.

Eventually, in the second millennium BC, the Sumerian civilization fell to other conquering peoples, among which where the Akkadians, and the region then came to be known as Babylonia. It is from this time that the Terracotta Dog probably came, as it is very similar to a steatite "mastiff" in the Louvre Museum, according to Prudence O. Harper, curator of the Ancient Near Eastern Art Section of the Metropolitan Museum of

Art. She has written an informative historical overview of mastiffs in Near-Eastern art, describing the different mastiff relics found in the region of Mesoptamia from the times of the Sumerians down to the Assyrians in the first millennium BC.

By the first millennium BC, another group of people known as the Assyrians had conquered the area of Mesopotamia and Persia. Assyrian bas-reliefs from these times show giant dogs with enormous heads, short muzzles, dewlaps and cropped ears. It is from Nineveh that many likenesses of mastiff dogs have been found. So it is obvious that, whereas different peoples in that fertile crescent area kept falling to other conquering peples coming into the area over the 3,000-year time period, the mastiff dogs were important enough to be maintained and propagated from one people to the next.

Prudence Harper describes one miniature Terracotta Dog found buried at the North Palace of Ashurbanipal (668-627 BC) at Nineveh. Its name was written on the body of the sculpture. The name of the dog was "Enemy Catcher."

Another example of a giant mastiff dog is shown in another Nineveh bas-relief of 850 BC, now in the British Museum.

The relationship of our modern-day mastiffs to the Persian and Assyrian dogs of 1,000 years ago is again apparent in the two examples of artwork from the seventh century BC. The dog's feet are very large in proportion to their body. Their snarling faces and open mouths illustrate their ferocious nature. Their courage is shown by their willingness to latch on to wild horses, which are much larger than they are.

It is logical to conclude that the dogs depicted in these Assyrian works were the ancestors of the dogs Alexander the Great found when he conquered Mesopotamia and western Asia in the fourth Century BC. Alexander treasured these ferocious war dogs. It is said that he pitted them against many types of wild animals, including lions, bulls and elephants. In a time when lawsuits were not the solution for obtaining money, a person's power, and therefore his ability to acquire wealth and prestige, were dependent upon his degree of ferocity, strength and cunning. Conquering nations was the key to a better life. Alexander, therefore, wanted to possess those things that would make him more powerful.

These strong, ferocious, powerful and awesome-looking Molossian dogs were a status symbol. When Alexander died, and Macedonia and Eastern Europe fell to the Romans, the great war dogs were seized and propagated by the Romans. Since the Roman men, especially under the Caesars, were always going off fighting and conquering more lands, they needed someone besides slaves to stay at home and protect their families. A slave would tend to run away if given the opportunity. The proper guard dog would not.

Hence, the development of the Roman house guard dog came about. When the paterfamilias (father of the house) was able to leave behind such a dog, he could feel secure that his family was being guarded by the best deterrent to intruders that he could hope for.

Through the legacy of the artwork and literature from these ancient civilizations, we are able to trace the lineage of our mastiff dogs from one conquering people to another up to more modern times. The nationalities of the people owning the dogs change, but the physique of the massive, gigantic, broad nosed, dewlapped guard and fighting dog remains the same.

Following the Molossian dogs from the Roman empire through another 1,650 years

Enemy Catcher:
Make my day!
Owner: S. Allen.
Photo: S. Allen.

Rosco di Ponzano, six-year-old male. Breeder: M. Querci. Owner: M. Mazzucconi. Photo: Mazzucconi.

to 350 years closer to our time, we find a *German Natural History of 1650*, which describes the mastiff dogs of this time:

"This kind of dog called a Mastiff or bandog is vast, huge, stubborn, ugly and eager, of a heavie and bourthenous body, and therefore but of little swiftness, terrible and frightful to behold and more fierce and fell than any Arcadian cur. They are appointed to watch and keep farm places and country cottages, sequestered from common resourse and not abutting upon other houses, when

there is any fear of thieves, robbers or night wanderers. They are serviceable against fox or badger, to drive wild and tame swine, to bait and take the bull by the ear, one dog or two at most is sufficient for that purpose be the bull never so monstrous and fierce. It is a kind of dog capable of courage, violent and valiant, striking cold fear into the hearts of men but standing in fear of no man. No weapons will make him shrink nor abridge his boldness. The fast hold which they take with their teeth exceedeth all credit, three against a bear, four against a lion." (Baxter and Hoffman, *The History and Management of the Mastiff*)

As the Roman Empire broke up, and the peoples of Europe organized their lands into separate countries, the descendants of the Roman Molossian evolved into the different mastiff breeds of today. Each breed acquired its name and its characteristics from the country in which it remained. There is the English Mastiff, the French Dogue de Bordeaux, the Spanish Mastiff, the Swiss St. Bernard, the German Rottweiler. But it was the Italian Molossian that still today remains practically the same as described by Columella during the Roman Empire. It has survived the ages along with the Colosseum and all the history and feelings and remains of the mighty empire that was Rome. Hidden during more recent times in the Italian countryside, and almost unchanged in appearance and personality, the Italian Mastiff is a living relic of a time when man had to rely on only himself for his needs and his safety.

When, after World War II in 1949, Piero

Scanziani reintroduced this canine monument to antiquity, it was named the Mastino Napolitano, or Neapolitan Mastiff.

Now, in the 1990s, some still find the need for a protector of property. And like the peoples of the past 3,000 years who wrote about and depicted the most perfect protector, modern man (and woman) want that most ferocious-looking deterrent they can get to do their protecting for them. The dog that fits that bill the best for many is the Mastino, because he looks to be the most primitive and scary. He looks the most ancient of the mastiffs, and his personality seems to be the most primitive. It is as if the Italian Mastino has been able to transcend time and come to the 21st Century from another time zone. He is the embodiment of all the apparitions conjured up by storytellers and religions to inspire fear for the purpose

Ramon del Bonrampino, one-year-old male. Breeder: G. Maja. Owner: S. Allen. Photo: S. Allen.

of keeping people in line.

The Mastino evokes the power of the Roman armies, the strength of the Roman architecture, the massiveness of the Roman Empire, the glory of a strong and conquering nation. The Mastino evokes the grey solemnity of the Middle Ages, of a time when people were shrouded in superstition and fear of the unknown. The Mastino's face was the face of the gargoyle that was used on churches and buildings to ward off evil. For thousands of years the Molosser turned into mastiff or Italian Mastino has been preserved and propagated for his ability to scare away

Mastino in Naples, early 1980s. Photo: courtesy S. Freeman.

and do away with evil. This personality, which has been so cultivated for thousands of years, is what the Neapolitan Mastiff is still today.

Trying to trace the lineage of the Neapolitan Mastiff from the time of the Romans up to 1946 is sketchy. We find mention of the mastiff guard dogs in writings and paintings of various authors and artists all over Europe. As stated earlier, we know that as conquering Roman armies moved across Europe, dogs issuing from the Macedonian and Roman stock were mixed with native dogs of the various regions. Those mastiff dogs that developed further from the region of the original source of the Molossian developed more diverse traits. Those dogs that stayed in the original region most likely retained the original features and traits of the Roman guard dogs.

It was in the region of Naples and the surrounding countryside of Mt. Vesuvius that certain dogs fitting the description of Columella's Roman house guard dog were conserved and bred. These dogs were highly prized by the people who had them, whether they were wealthy landowners or the

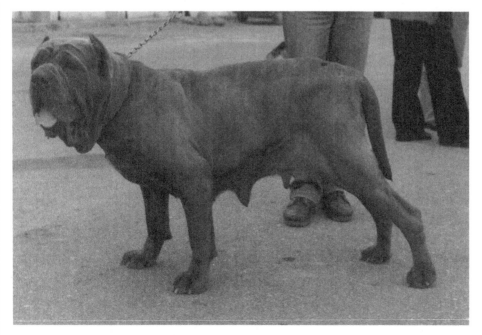

Top left: **Mario Querci and Tazio di Ponzano. Photo: Schumacher.**

Left: **Ch. Giada, three-year-old female born 1979. Breeder: E. Di Tomasso. Owner: M. Querci. Photo: courtesy S. Freeman.**

Toscano di Ponzano, aged male champion of reproduction. Breeder: M. Querci. Owner: G. Mira. Photo: S. Allen.

poorer farmers. But the dogs were so highly prized that they were not openly traded or marketed. They were something special, a relic of the past to be treasured. It was as if they were being kept a secret on purpose. There were no written documents of the various lineages.

It was these Roman Molossers that Piero Scanziani, a well-known writer and journalist, discovered and was able to promote in the late 1940s. He was aided in his efforts to reconstruct the breed by Dr. Ruggero Soldati and other dog fanciers. They publicized the breed, wrote a standard to which the dogs should be bred, christened it with the name Mastino Napoletano, and made it a recognized breed allowed to be shown at the Italian Kennel Club shows. There was apparently debate among the founders of the breed on what to name it. Some wanted the dogs to be called Molosso Romano in honor of the breed's ancestors. Others opted for Mastino Napoletano, in honor of those people in the environs of Naples who silently but diligently carried

Ch. Caligola di Ponzano, four-year-old son of Toscano and Astarte di Ponzano. Breeder: M. Querci. Owner: A. Pegoli. Photo: Schumacher.

Ch. Carina di Ponzano, three-year-old daughter of Toscano and Astarte di Ponzano. Breeder: M. Querci. Owner: G. Mira. Photo: S. Allen.

Ch. Zeta di Ponzano, four-year-old daughter of Toscano and Ch. Eufemia di Ponzano. Breeder: M. Querci. Owner: G. Mira. Photo: S. Allen.

on their work to maintain this ancient dog. Mastino Napoletano won out.

The promotion of this ancient breed in 1946-49 came at a significant time in Italy's history. It is as if this newly revived Italian treasure had become symbolic of a reviving Italy. Both had emerged from World War II changed and ravaged, but both were still mighty and noble in their substance. It may be because of the concurrent revival of the dog and the nation that the image of the Neapolitan

Mastiff evokes such a feeling of national pride in the Italian people. The Neapolitan Mastiff represents power, courage, strength, might. He represents the fragility of life, and how easily it may be lost if not nurtured. He is the essence of all that is Italian, and he is symbolic of how a great nation, even though it may be battered and neglected, can be brought back to all its glory, if given the opportunity.

The Mastino is the embodiment of the history of a great nation and a great people. He is earthiness, power, eccentricity and

Ch. Ombrone di Ponzano, five-year-old son of Toscano and Edera. Breeder: M. Querci. Owner: Photo: E. Crepaldi.

class all rolled into one. His countenance transcends the ages. His gaze looks through us to something else he is trying to perceive. The Mastino Napoletano is all the ancient glory that was Italy. It is his unique Italian qualities that we breeders in other countries must preserve if we are to perpetuate the Italian Mastino in foreign lands.

Development of the Neapolitan Mastiff since 1946

One of the most renowned breeders and nurturers of the Mastino was the late Mario Querci. He was persistent in his art of Mastino breeding, and he and his dogs have made a great contribution to the evolution of the breed. He lived in the region of Florence, and bred Neapolitan Mastiffs from the early 1950s until his untimely death in 1990. His kennel name, Di Ponzano, is in the pedigrees of most of the great dogs of today. Querci's stud dog Toscano was small and not much to look at, but he sired more champions than any other Italian Neapolitan Mastiff to date.

By the 1970s, Mastino breeding had reached an apogee in Italy. It was at that time that some of the best remembered dogs were born. It was also then that some of the best known Mastinari of today were engaged in fruitful Mastino production. Mastinaro is the Italian term for a breeder of Neapolitan Mastiffs who has undertaken insurmountable amounts of work for the sheer passion for this breed of dog. Mastinaro is not a name applied lightly to any would-be breeder of Neapolitan Mastiffs. Mastinaro is reserved only for those

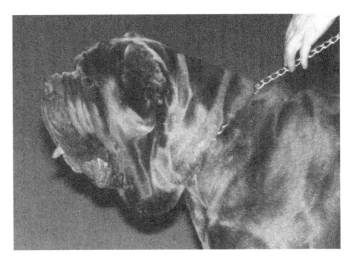

Ch. Gaio di Ponzano, three-year-old son of Toscano and Boumpie di Fossombrone. Breeder: M. Querci. Owner: Fossombrone Kennel. Photo: S. Allen.

Zero di Ponzano, son of Toscano. Breeder: M. Querci. Owner: G. Iazzetta. Photo: G. Maja.

Ch. Durano, four-year-old son of Toscano and Marchesina. Breeder: G. Iazzetta. Owner: A. van Doremalen. Photo: Schumacher.

Ch. Leone, born 1971. Owner: A. di Lorenzo. Photo: courtesy A. Di Lorenzo.

methods that allows him to be successful, where the less cunning would-be breeder is not. A mastinaro is to be highly respected for his abilities and his creations, but do not expect him to give away any of the secrets.

Back to the 1970s: A list of the great Mastinari would be meaningful to those readers truly desirous of learning about the Mastino. Unfortunately, it would most likely be deficient in names of those people who were instrumental to the breed, but who

dedicated artists and connoisseurs of mastini who have paid their dues in time spent, tribulations, disappointments and loss of money, and yet have persisted in bringing to creation that certain astounding dog.

A mastinaro is gifted with an indomitable constitution and a talent for outwitting Mother Nature, for the breeding of excellent Mastini is an endeavor bordering on the impossible. For the mastinaro, breeding Mastini is the ultimate challenge. To win the game, each breeder has his own secrets and

Ch. El Gavilan dell'Altafiumara, four-year-old male. Breeder: A. Di Lorenzo. Owner: G. Beta. Photo: courtesy A. Di Lorenzo.

were not in the forefront of showing and presenting the dogs. So I will mention just a few of the great dogs of this era that had an impact on today's individuals and the evolution of the Neapolitan Mastiff.

Ch. Leone, born in 1971, obtained and raised by Antonio di Lorenzo, was the sire of many excellent dogs, among which were Ch. Sansone I di Ponzano, born 1973, and Ch.

Left: **Ch. Falco della Grotta Azzurra, born 1973. Owner and breeder G. Siano. Photo: courtesy of J.P. Dupuis.**

Socrate di Ponzano, born 1974, father of the beautiful Argo di Ponzano, born 1977, who in turn sired Toscano di Ponzano.

Falco della Grotta Azzurra, owned and bred by G. Siano, was born in 1973. His offspring became foundation sires of Michele De Falco's Del Nolano line. Many of the Neapolitan Mastiffs in France trace their lineage back to Falco through his son Ch. Madigam della Grotta Azzurra, sire of champions in Albin Aiello's San Basile kennel.

During the late 1970s, many good Neapolitan Mastiffs were being produced and presented in Italy, and soon the rest of Europe began to take an interest in them. Some excellent individuals such as Oro and

Ch. Gazzania di Ponzano, three-year-old daughter of Toscano and Astarte di Ponzano. Breeder: M. Querci. Owner: F. Vilardo. Photo: B. Vilardo.

Monzon della Grotta Azzurra were sent to Germany, where, for some reason, the breeding endeavors were halted, and very few excellent dogs were produced. Better

Ch. Mosé, five-year-old male. Breeder: P. Turci. Owner: A. Dionizi. Photo: J.P. Beck.

Zimbo della Zacchera, two-year-old male. Breeder and owner: R. Barani. Photo: courtesy R. Barani.

success was had in France, where the culture of the Mastino was carried out meticulously, with quite nice results today. In the United States, where there had been a few scattered dogs brought over by Italian emigrants, the Neapolitan Mastiff was introduced primarily by Michael Sottile and Jane Pampalone.

The 1980s saw a large exodus of puppies and older breeding stock from Italy to foreign countries as Neapolitan Mastiff fever started spreading. Some very high prices for dogs in the Far East plus parvovirus epidemics depleted quite a lot of the Italian stock, so that the early 1990s saw a hiatus in Italy in the production of sufficient numbers of exceptional individuals.

Many of the offspring of some of the excellent Italian dogs born in the 1980s did get brought over to the United States. It may

be that the gene pool now reduced or in some cases lost in Italy will be found here in the U.S. in the descendants of such great dogs as Antonio di Lorenzo's El Gavilan dell'Altafiumara, A. Dionisi's Mosé, Michele De Falco's Squarcione, G. Mira's Frazier della Grotta Azzurra, A. Sorbo's Gic, R. Barani's Zimbo della Zacchera, L. Sorbao's Turid, S. Di Micco's Hatrim della Grotta Azzurra, and many others.

Since the importation in the 1980s of numbers of Neapolitan Mastiffs into the States, a general awareness of the breed has increased dramatically. With the greater popularity of the breed has come an enormous increase in breeding of the dogs. There are a number of individuals who are really trying to breed quality dogs in the United States. It is too early to tell whether any of them will earn the name mastinaro,

Ch. Frazier della Grotta Azzurra, five-year-old male. Breeder: G. Siano. Owner: G. Mira. Photo: Schumacher.

Ch. Hatrim della Grotta Azzurra, three-year-old male. Breeder: G. Siano. Owner: S. Di Micco. Photo: P. Salomon.

but at least they are starting out with the idea of making a mark in the breed.

The rest of Europe has also experienced a heightened interest in the Italian Mastino. Again, since the importation of fine stock into the Netherlands, Belgium, Hungary and Yugoslavia in the 1980s, some excellent dogs are being produced in these countries. A great interest in the breed has suddenly arisen in Australia and in England. In these latter countries, however, the six- to nine-month quarantine of dogs imported into the country is quite a deterrent for people in search of good foundation stock.

In the past 50 years, the Neapolitan Mastiff has evolved from a few individuals preserved in the Italian countryside to a breed recognized and sought after all over the world. Interestingly, but not surprisingly, each country is molding the Italian dog to its own standards of what a constitutes a canine. As such, the Neapolitan Mastiff is taking on a different body type and character in each country, in accordance with the standards placed upon it by the people in each different country.

Those would-be Mastinari in countries other than Italy will have a difficult time in many instances adhering to the dictates of their country while maintaining the flavor and appearance of the Neapolitan Mastiff in the dogs that they produce. The Mastino type will fare better in those countries such as Hungary and France, where a sense of flair, style and romance runs strong in the people's souls. It will be easier in these countries to create the aesthetic being that is a Mastino than in the countries more concerned with measurements and precision of body parts, such as in Germany or the United States. When too much emphasis is placed on only several aspects of the dog, such as having complete sets of teeth and perfect hips, as in Germany, or in being a great moving dog, as required by the health- and athletic-conscious society in the United States, we end up with dogs with good hips, all their teeth and beautiful movement. The problem is, they may not look like the Italian Mastino. Dogs bred near to the equator, where it is very hot and humid, will not survive unless their body type is of a slimmer, less massive animal that is able to endure tropical conditions. Dogs in places like Russia and Alaska will tend to develop heavier, thicker and possibly longer coats in order to survive. It will be a challenge to those breeders in other countries to breed the Mastino true to his type.

Turid, four-year-old male. Breeder: A. Sorbo. Owner: L. Sorbo. Photo: courtesy O. Le Méhauté.

Standard for the Neapolitan Mastiff

ILLUSTRATIONS BY RENÉ EVANS

As showing of dogs became a formalized activity back in the 1800s, dog owners created organizations to keep tabs on the breeding and recording of events associated with the many different breeds of dogs. In England, the Kennel Club became the governing organization for the dog industry. In the United States, the American Kennel Club was the mother organization that had jurisdiction over all the individual breed clubs in the country. In Europe and other countries of the world, each country developed its own primary kennel club, akin to the AKC. Additionally, however, the European countries, South American countries and most of the countries in the rest of the world joined a worldwide organization called the Fédération Cynologique Internationale, or FCI. This organization governs the rules of showing dogs in most parts of the world except the United States and Great Britain. It has final say over the organization of the individual country kennel clubs.

The Neapolitan Mastiff is regulated in Italy by its national breed club, known as SAMN (Societá Amatori del Mastino Napoletano). SAMN is in turn regulated by the Italian Kennel Club, known as ENCI (Ente Nazionale della Cinofilia Italiana). This national kennel club is regulated by the FCI. The FCI recognizes about 342 breeds of dogs. The AKC recognizes about 140 breeds of dogs in the breed classes and a few more breeds in the Miscellaneous classification.

The Neapolitan Mastiff is not yet recognized by the AKC. (Editor's note: Since this book was first published, the Neapolitan Mastiff achieved AKC recognition, in 2004.) The FCI does not recognize any breed clubs in the U.S., even though these breeds that are not recognized by the AKC may be recognized by them in other countries. The Neapolitan Mastiffs born in the U.S. are, therefore, not recognized by any official worldwide organization. For this reason, the only official worldwide standard for the Neapolitan Mastiff is the FCI standard as submitted by ENCI, which, in turn, should get the standard from SAMN.

The FCI states that the standard for a breed belongs to the country of origin of that breed. In accordance with this policy, I recommend that those people breeding, showing or trying to learn about Neos in the United States adhere to the FCI standard for the breed. If the Neapolitan Mastiff necomes accepted into the AKC, the standard will have to be written according to an AKC-formatted model. Until such time, I recommend that the FCI standard be employed.

The standard of the Neapolitan Mastiff has a rather complicated, ongoing history. The controversy that exists today in Italy over the fine-tuning of the standard is a reflection of the continuing evolution of the Mastino in today's world. The original standard, written in 1946 by several of the early Mastino lovers, was rather brief. In 1949, Scanziani and others elaborated on the standard previously engineered by Dr. Soldati, and, due to their efforts, ENCI accepted the new breed.

The 1946 ENCI standard remained in force until 1968. At that time, the SAMN created a longer, more explicit standard, which was not accepted by the ENCI. ENCI contracted another individual to draft a Neapolitan Mastiff standard in 1968. This standard, #197B, was adopted by the FCI in 1971.

When the FCI, in 1987, decided that the standards for all their recognized breeds should be revised into a specific format, the standard was changed again. This time, it was changed without the total approval and suggestions of the Mastino circles. It was accepted anyway by ENCI and by the FCI in 1991.

This story of the complications associated with the authoring of a standard that fits the Italian Mastino lover's concept of the Neapolitan Mastiff explains the discrepancies between the standard and the actual dogs chosen in dog shows to be champions by those judges who truly know the breed.

Fédération Cynologique Internationale Standard for the Neapolitan Mastiff

I believe it is important to present both the 1971 standard and the 1991 standard so that the reader can better comprehend the special characteristics of the Neapolitan Mastiff. The 1971 standard is specific, and by its detailed descriptions distinguishes the Neapolitan Mastiff from other mastiff breeds. The 1991 version in its shortened form is more vague. A reading of the 1971 standard will clarify the shortened 1991 version, though a few differences exist in the 1991 standard.

FCI Standard #197B of the Mastino Napoletano

December 20, 1971
Translated from the Italian by Sherilyn Allen, VMD

SCIENTIFIC CLASSIFICATION:
Dog belonging to the Mollossoid Group (according to the classification of Pierre Megnin)
An ancient, rectilinear, smooth-coated breed (according to the classification of Dechambre).

CLASSIFICATION ACCORDING TO USE:
Guard dog, defense dog, police dog and tracking dog.

ORIGIN:
Italian, and specifically Neapolitan.

GENERAL CHARACTERISTICS THAT TYPIFY THE BREED:
General Appearance, Conformation, Balance and Disposition:
The Neapolitan Mastiff is a guard dog and denfese dog par excellence. He is massive, powerfully built, strong, of coarse and at the same time majestic appearance. He is robust and courageous, with an intelligent expression, gifted with an even temperament, of a docile nature, not

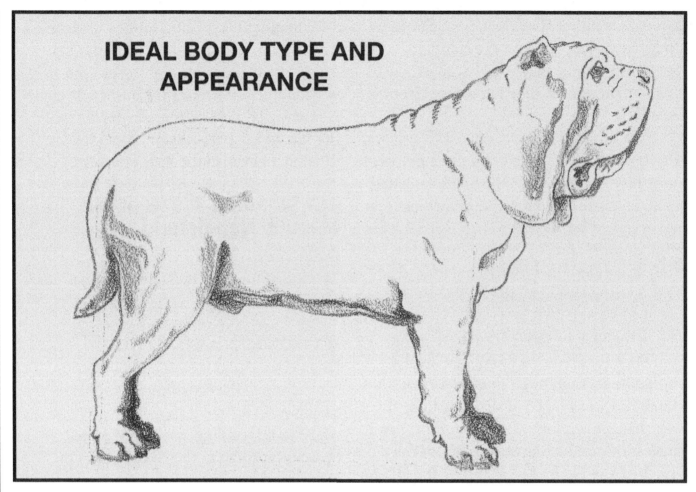

IDEAL BODY TYPE AND APPEARANCE

aggressive, but an unsurpassed defender of persons and property.

The general conformation is that of a heavy brachymorph, whose body is longer than its height at the withers. The body is in proportion with respect to its substance (massiveness, power, strength of bone) and relatively in proportion with respect to its outline (the way the body parts fit together). The skin is not adherent to the underlying tissue, but is copious, with lax connective tissue all over the body, especially on the head, where it forms wrinkles and folds, and on the neck, where it forms a dewlap.

Head:
Brachycephalic, massive; a short skull which is wide between the zygomatic bones (cheekbones).

The total length of the head should equal about three-tenths the dog's height at the withers. The length of the muzzle must equal one-third of the total length of the head. (In a dog that is 70 cm high at the withers, the total length of the head would be 21 cm. Therefore, the skull would be 14 cm long and the muzzle, 7 cm.)

The width of the skull between the zygomatic bones is greater than half the total length of the head and is almost equal to the length of the skull.

Author's note: The cephalic index is about 66. The cephalic index is a ratio of the width (between the outer edges of the cheekbones)

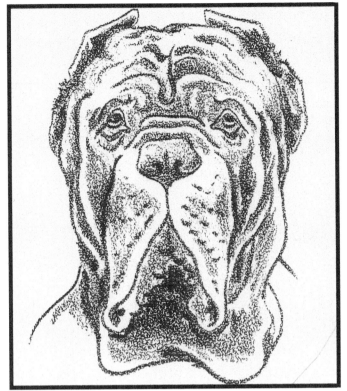

to the length (from the occipital crest to the end of the nose) of the head. It is calculated:

$$\text{Cephalic Index} = \frac{\text{Width of the head} \times 100}{\text{Length of head}}$$

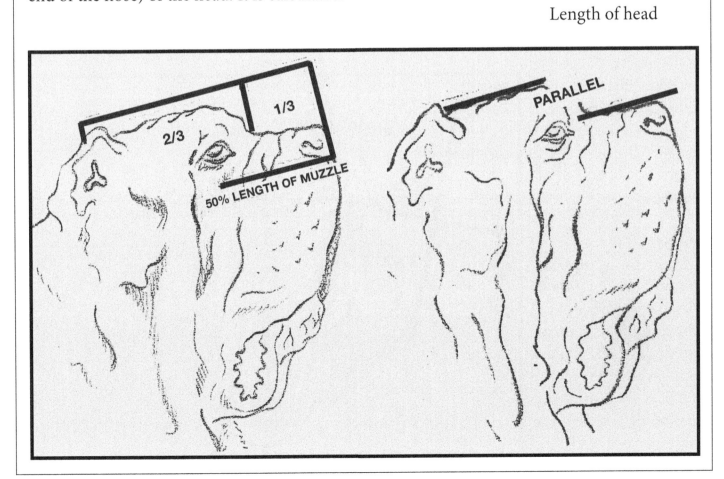

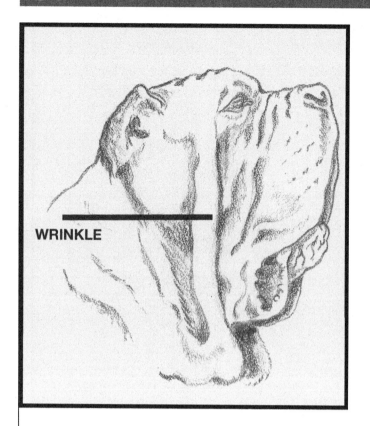

WRINKLE

the same vertical plane as the anterior face of the muzzle.

The nose must be large, moist and cold, with well-open, large nostrils.
The color must be consistent with coat color: black in the black coat, brown in the mahogany coat, dark in all the other coat colors.

Bridge of the Nose:
Straight. For its length and its relationship to the axis of the skull, see "Head."
The width, as measured at the midpoint of the muzzle, must equal about 20 percent of the total length of the head and about 50 percent of the length of the muzzle.

The longitudinal axes of the top of the skull and the top of the muzzle are parallel.

The skin is copious, with wrinkles and folds. A characteristic wrinkle falls from the outer corner of the eyelid in a posteriorly convex direction to the homologous corner of the lips.

Lips and Muzzle:
The lips are made of thick tissue; they are copious and heavy.
The upper lips, seen from the front, form by

Nose:
The top of the nose is a continuation of the line of the bridge of the muzzle. As seen in profile, it shall not stick out beyond the anterior vertical plane of the lips; rather the anterior face of the nose must be in

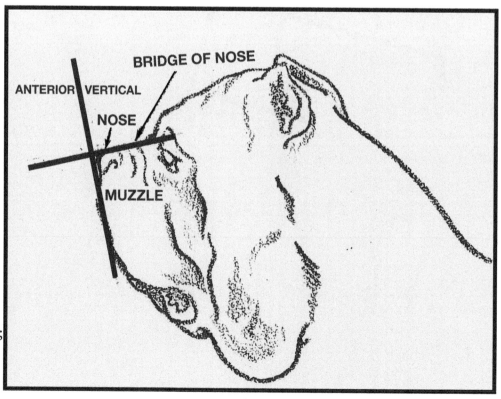

BRIDGE OF NOSE

ANTERIOR VERTICAL

NOSE

MUZZLE

the junction of their lower edges, an inverted V.

They are copious, and for this reason, the anterior face of the muzzle is well developed in both height and width. In addition, because the lateral faces of the muzzle are parallel, the anterior face of the muzzle looks flat, thereby creating the squareness of the muzzle.

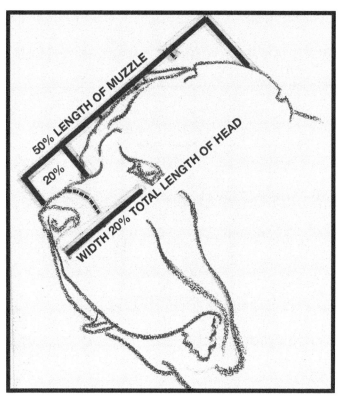

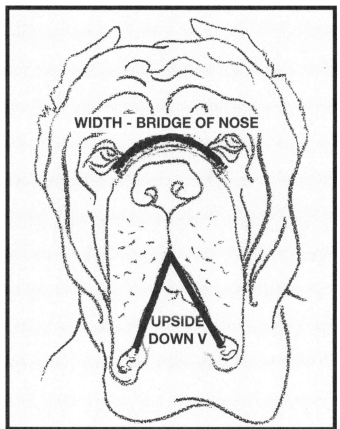

an almost closed semicircle. The length of the muzzle corresponds to the length of the nasal bridge. The buccal slit is long, in that the labial commissures must meet a perpendicular line drawn from the outer corner of the eye.

The lower lateral profile of the muzzle is made by the lips, and the lowest point of the profile is made not by the lips, but by the commissures of the lips. The labial commissure is obvious, and its mucosal surface is very visible; that is, the mucosa in the folds where the upper lip and lower lip join together should be visible. The frontal, lower profile of the muzzle is shaped like

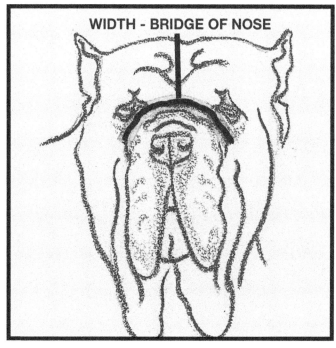

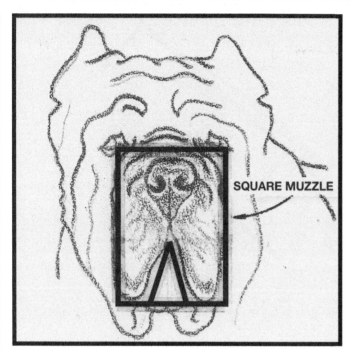

SQUARE MUZZLE

Jaws:
Powerful, well developed, and with dental arcades meeting each other perfectly; that is to say that either the maxillary incisors must barely overlap the mandibular incisors (scissors bite), or that the biting surfaces of the maxillary incisors must perfectly meet the biting surfaces of the mandibular incisors (pincer bite). The branches of the

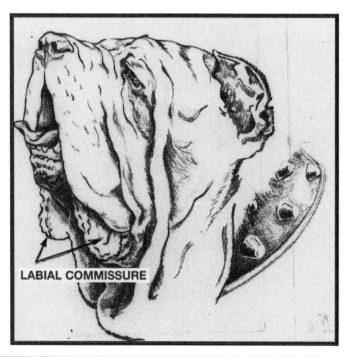

LABIAL COMMISSURE

very powerful mandible tend to be curved in profile, especially at their most posterior part. The body of the mandible must be very well developed anteriorly, to form a prop or support for the lower lips to rest against; never receding.

Teeth are white, in straight alignment, and complete as to the development and number.

Stop (Naso-frontal depression)
The naso-frontal depression or stop is made up by the following boundaries: the anterior portion of the frontal bone, the top lines of the two nasal bones, and the upper boundaries of the two maxillary bones.

The stop should create a 90-degree angle as measured from the bridge of the nose to the forehead, and an angle of 120 to 130 degrees as measured from the point of the nose to the forehead.

Cranium (Skull):
Its length must be equal to two-thirds of the total length of the head, and its width as measured between the cheekbones is approximately the same as its length.

The zygomatic arches (cheekbones) are accentuated and situated far apart, offering an adequate insertion fr the masseter and temporal muscles.

Viewed from the front, the skull is spherical. Seen in profile, it approaches this shape, except at the very top part of the skull between the insertion of the ears, which is flat. The eyebrows are very developed. The medio-frontal suture is evident. The

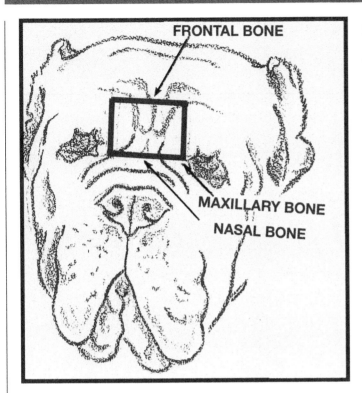

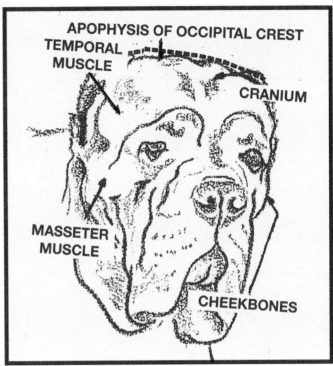

apophysis of the occipital crest is barely pronounced.

Ears:
Small in comparison to the size of the dog, triangular in shape, attached well above the zygomatic arches (cheekbones). If

left uncropped and hanging, they are flat, adhering to the cheeks and parotid region, and in length should not go past the margin of the throat.

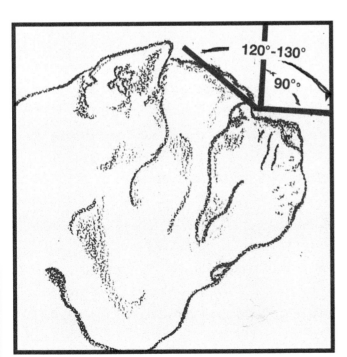

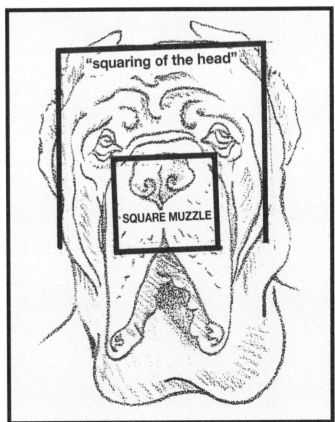

At its insertion, the ear sticks out a little and then falls abruptly. If the ear is cropped, it is cut almost all the way off and to a point so as to form an equilateral triangle.

Eyes:
The eyelids should adhere normally to the eyeball (neither ectropion nor entropion). The eyes, situated in a subfrontal position, are well separated from each other with a palpebral opening that is almost round. But

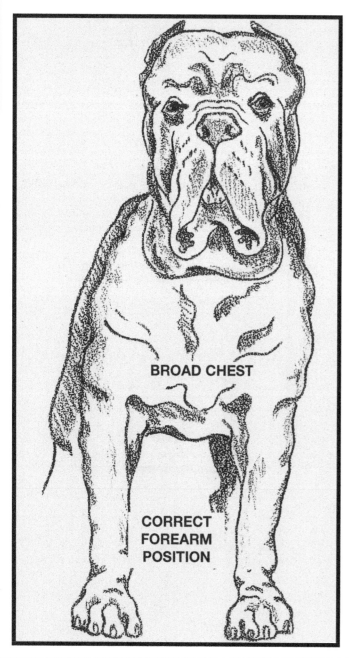

BROAD CHEST

CORRECT FOREARM POSITION

because of the heavily hanging skin on the eyebrows, thy are not open very wide, and so appear oval. The eyeball us slightly sunk back. The pigmentation of the eyelids is the same as the coat color – black, gray or brown. The color of the iris is the same as, but lighter than, the coat color.

Neck:
Short, stocky, very muscular. Its length, measured from the base of the skull to the cranial margin of the withers, is about 28 percent of the height of the withers. Its perimeter, measured in the middle of the neck, is about eight-tenths of the height at the withers. The top line, at the anterior third of the neck, is slightly convex. The lower line of the neck has a great deal of loose skin which forms the dewlap. The dewlap should not be too long and, most importantly, must be divided into right and left sides. The dewlap begins at the branches of the mandible and ends about halfway down the neck.

Body:
The length of the trunk is 10 percent greater than the height at the withers, as measured from the point of the shoulder (external angle made by the scapula and humerus) or from the manubrium of the sternum (point of the breast) to the posterior point of the ischium (point of the rump).

Chest:
Wide, very open, with very well-developed pectoral muscles. Its width, which is in direct proportion to the rib cage, as measured between its lateral boundaries (the upper anterior margins of the arms), should attain

40 to 45 percent of the height at the withers. The manubrium of the sternum should be positioned at the same level as the point of the shoulder.

Rib Cage:
Ample, descending to the level of the elbow or slightly below it -- well convex midway down its span – the transverse diameter diminishing slightly toward the sternum, without forming a keel.

The ribs, are long, well rounded, oblique; the intercostal spaces are wide; the last false ribs are long, oblique and well open. The circumference of the rib cage must be about one-quarter greater again than the height at the withers; as measured at the costal arches, it is about 10 cm (3.9 inches) less. Its transverse diameter should reach at least 32 percent of the height at the withers.

The depth should measure 50 to 55 percent of the height at the withers. The thoracic index should not be greater than eight, and preferably less.

The sternal region is long. In profile, its ventral outline is shaped in a long semi-circle which curves up slightly toward the abdomen and then forms a straight line.

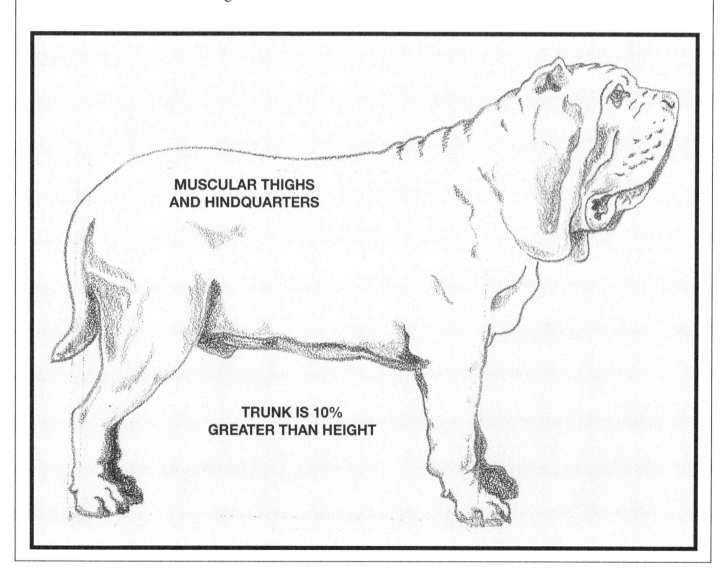

MUSCULAR THIGHS AND HINDQUARTERS

TRUNK IS 10% GREATER THAN HEIGHT

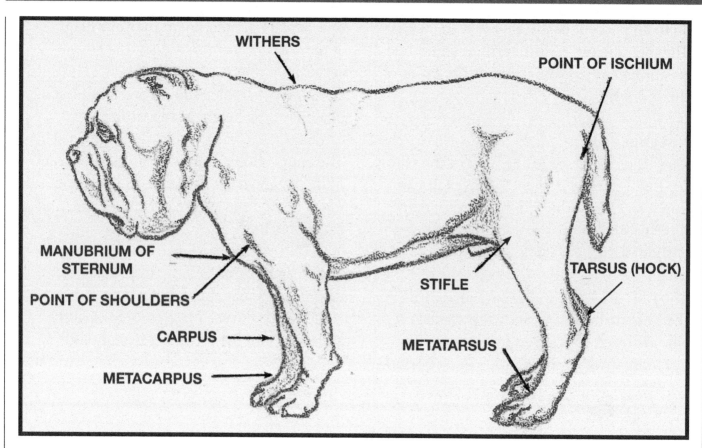

Back:
The topline of the back is straight, with only the withers rising anove this straight line. The back is wide, and is length is equal to about 32 percent of the height at the withers.

Loin and Kidneys:
Well blended into the line of the back. In profile slightly convex, with musculature well developed along its entire width. Its length is a little less than one-fifth of the height at the withers. Its width approaches its length in a ration of about 14.5 to 16.

Abdomen and Flanks:
The ventral line of the abdomen, extending from the sternum, is practically horizontal. The flanks must be almost equal in length to the lumbar region (loin). The abdomen appears voluminous, and the tuckup of the flank should be as small as possible.

Croup:
The croup, which is formed by a continuation of the convex line of the loin towards the rearm shoud be wide, strong and muscular. The transverse length between the two hips should be 15 percent of the height of the withers. The hips should project out to meet the top line of the loins.

The length of the croup is almost three-tenths of the height at the withers. The croup slopes down, and the slant of the line which joins the anterior external corner of the ileum (hip joint) with the ischiatic tuberosity is about 30 degrees from horizontal.

Sexual Organs:
Perfect, complete and equal development of the two testicles which must be situated within the scrotum.

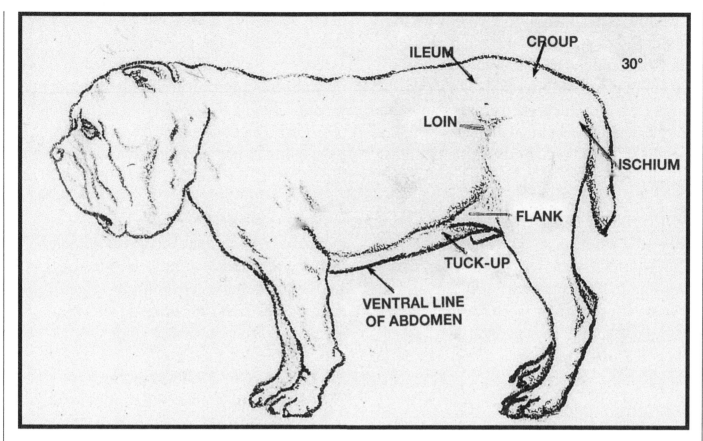

Tail:

The tail attaches to the croup with a large base. It is thick at the root, strong, tapering slighty toward the tip. When the dog is at rest, the carriage of the tail should be scimitar-like, that is to say, hanging for its first two-thirds, and slightly curved at the end third. It is never carried straight up or rolled over the back. It must be carried horizontally or a little higher than the back when the dog is in action. Its length when the puppy is born reaches or slightly exceeds the hock joint. (It has been cut to two-thirds of its original length.)

Shoulder:

The shoulder should be long, slightly sloping, comprised of long muscles, well developed, and clearly divided one from the other. It should move freely. Its length is about three-tenths the height at the withers. Its slope is 50 to 60 percent from the horizontal. With respect to the median plane of the body, the points of the scapulae are fairly well separated from each other and tend toward the vertical.

Forelegs:

UPPER ARM:

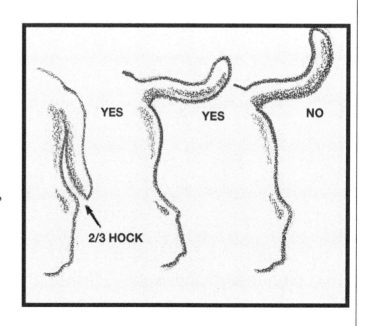

The arm, well adherent to the body for the upper three-quarters of its length, should, like the shoulder, be endowed with strong, prominent and well-developed muscles. Its angle is 55 to 60 degrees from the horizontal, and its length is about 30 percent of the height at the withers. Its direction is almost parallel to the median plane of the body.

FOREARM:
Very heavy boned, straight and vertical to the ground. Its length is almost equal to the length of the upper arm. At the carpus (wrist), the groove between the ulna and the radius should be evident. The height of the forearm at the elbow is 52 percent of the height at the withers.

The elbows, covered with abundant, slack skin, must be parallel to the median plane of the body; that is, they must not be too close to the rib cage, thereby eliminating the axillary cavity (causing the so-called elbows-in condition); nor must they be held too far out (causing the elbows-out or Bulldog position). The point of the elbow should meet a line drawn perpendicular to the ground from the caudal edge of the scapula.

CARPUS (WRIST):
It should be in straight vertical alignment with the forearm. It should be wide, lean, smooth, without visible bony protuberances except at the posterior margin, where the accessory carpal bone sticks out.

METACARPUS (PASTERN):
The metacarpus should be flat from front to back, and viewed from the front should follow the vertical line if the forear. From

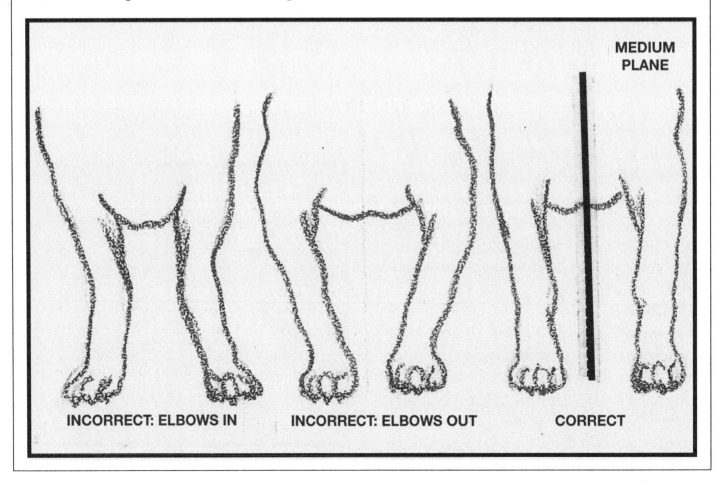

INCORRECT: ELBOWS IN   INCORRECT: ELBOWS OUT   CORRECT

a side view, the meacarpus should extend forward at a 70 to 75 degree angle. It should not be longer than one-sixth of the length of the entire lumn to the elbow.

FEET:
The feet should be round and large, with toes close together and well arched. The pads should be dry and hard, well pigmented. The nails are strongly curved and well pigmented.

Hindquarters:
THIGH:
Long, wide, covered with heavy muscles which are prominent and well delineated from each other. The posterior margin is rather straight. The length should not be less than on-third of the height at the withers; in other words, it should be 33 percent of the height at the withers. It should be inclined

from back to front at a 60-degree angle, and shold make almost a right angle with the hip bone. The thigh should fall in a vertical plane with the median plane of the body.

LEG:
Heavy boned and very muscular. The length is a little less than that of the thigh, and its angle from back to front is about 50 to 55 degrees. The stifle joint angle is about 110 to 115 degrees. The groove between the gastrocnemius tendon and the tibia is well delineated and noticeable.

TARSUS (HOCK):
The sides of the hock can never be broad enough. Because of the slope of the tibia, its anterior angle is open. The distance from the ball of the foot to the point of the hock is about a quarter of the height at the withers.

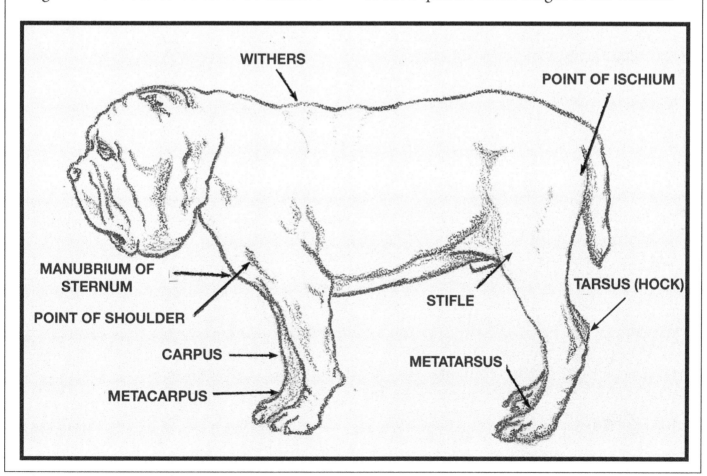

As seen from behind, the posterior line descending from the point of the hock to the ground should be vertical and a continuation of the line of the buttocks. The anterior angle, that is the tibio-metatarsal angle, is open, as already syayed, and about 140 to 145 degrees.

METATARSUS:
Strong and lean, almost cylindrical in shape. Its length is about a quarter of the height at the withers. Seen either from behind o from the side, it should be vertical, that is, in a perfect plumb line. Any dewclaws, single or double, are removed.

FEET:
Like the front feet, and with all their characteristics, but not as large.

Hair/Coat:
The hair should be thick, the same length all over, uniformly smooth, fine, short, no longer than 1.5 cm. There should be no sign of a fringe, even at the outermost edges of any part of the body, the legs or the tail. Coat textire is hard and shiny.

COLOR OF THE COAT:
The preferred colors are black, lead gray, gray, mahogany, tawny and fawn, sometimes with small white spots on the chest and on the tips of the toes. All coats may be brindled.

Skin:
Copious all over the bidym particularly the head, where is forms numerous folds and wrinkles, and at the ventral margin of the neck, where it forms a dewlap. The color of the mucosae and the epidermis must be black or brown, according to the darker hairs of the coat. The nails and digital cushions should be dark in color.

Height at the Withers:
In the males, 65-75 cm (25.5-30 inches). In females, 60-68 cm (23.5-27 inches), with a tolerance of 2 cm (1 inch) either way.

Weight:
From 50-70 kg (111-155 lbs.).

Gait:
The walking gait is one of the typical characteristics of the breed; lanky and slow, like that of a bear. The trot is slow with long, ground-covering strides. The Neapolitan Mastiff rarely gallops.

DEFECTS IN TYPE AND CONFORMATION

General Characteristics, Appearance, Symmetry:
The overall impression being one of light build, light or soft bone structure, lack of harmony.

Head:
The upper cranio-facial axes diverging or converging (most serious fault).

Nose:
Lower or higher than the line of the nasal bridge; protruding beyond the vertical line of the anterior plane of the muzzle; with traces of depigmentation. Nostrils not well open, small, with deficient coloration.

Nasal Bridge:

Long or too short, narrow, the lateral lines converging, the top of the nasal bridge not straight.

Lips and Muzzle:
Muzzle too short or too long; lips under or over developed, hanging lower than the labial commissure, flaccid. Fold of the commissure over-accentuated, hanging too low, reversed or lacking. From a side view, lips appearing to recede. Narrowing of the sides of the muzzle toward the front, forming a pointed muzzle; so that the front plane of the muzzle would not be flat. The junction of the upper lips forming a semi-circle instead of an upside-down V.

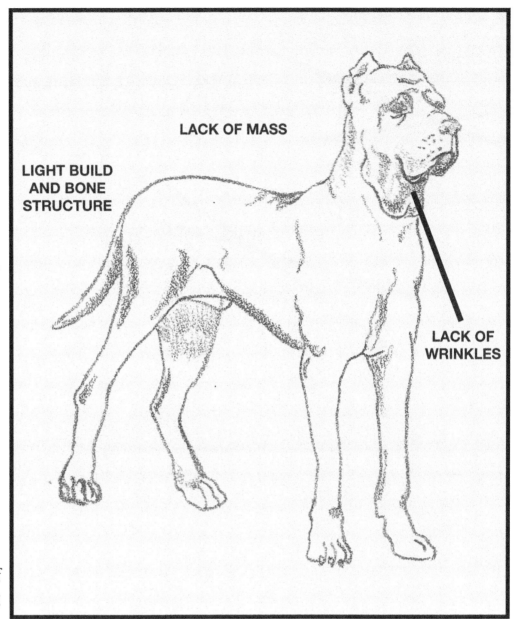

LACK OF MASS

LIGHT BUILD AND BONE STRUCTURE

LACK OF WRINKLES

Horizontal erosion of the teeth.

Jaws:
Weak; prognathism (undershot jaw) if it deform the outward appearance of the muzzle; parrot mouth (overbite jaw) – whether caused by a deficiency in the length of the mandible (this is a disqualification), or caused by a defect in the direction of the teeth (a fault). Branches of the mandible too curved. Teeth not correctly aligned or deficient in number.

Skull:
Small, short, found narrow at the sides, i.e., at the level of the zygomatic and parietal bones; domed, flat supraorbital (eyebrow) ridges; masseter muscles poorly developed; lack of occipital crest or overdeveloped occipital crest. Underdeveloped forehead. The stop not sufficiently accentuated – i.e., flattened. Direction of the upper longitudinal cranio-facial axes not parallel.

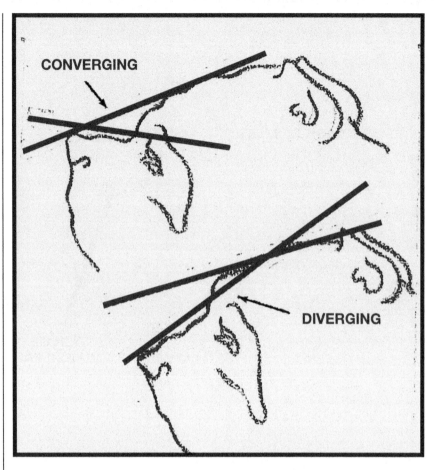

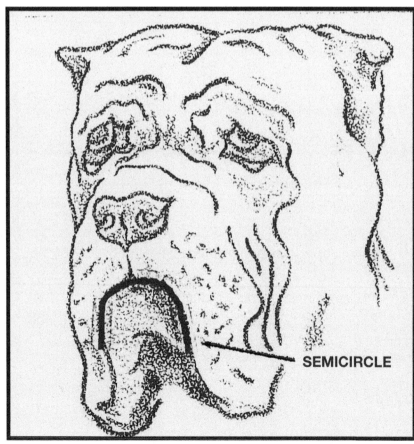

Eyes:
Small; prominent; iris too light in relation to coat color; not in subfrontal position; ectropion; entropion; eyes too close together; strabismus (cross-eyed). Partial depigmentation of the eyelids.

Ears:
Too long or too short; attached too low; tip of the ear narrow and pointed; poorly carried and poorly cut; hair not short.

Neck:
Weak; too long or too short; flattened sides; lacking dewlap or having too much or undivided dewlap. Dorsal margin of the neck (crest) insufficiently arched, lacking definition at the nape, not well blended into the shoulder.

Shoulder:
Straight;heavy; short; with poorly developed muscles; not moving freely; edges of the scapulae too close to one another.

Forelegs:

UPPER ARM:
Too angled or too straight; short; deficient muscular development; weak bone structure.

FOREARM:
Bone structure weak or spongy; round bones; deviation from the vertical line; elbow too out or too

in; armpits too low. Height (from ground to the elbow) less than half the height to the withers, or considerably more than half.

CARPUS (WRIST):
Obvious hypertrophy of the carpal bones, spongy, small; accessory carpal bone not very pronounced, lameness.

METACARPUS (PASTERN):
Short or too long; weak; too slanted or straight; deviating from the plumb.

FEET:
Oval; flattened; fleshy; with splayed toes; insufficiently arching of the toes. Feet turned out or in (splay-footed or pigeon-toed), i.e., not plumb; the digital cushions too fleshy; the skin of the pads too thin; deficient pigmentation in nails and pads. Incorrect position of pads; pads too long.

Body:
Length equal to height at withers, or too long.

Chest:
Narrow; not deep enough; insufficiently developed muscles. Manubrium of the sternum situated too low.

Rib cage:
Deficient in depth; too narrow or too wide; decidedly keeled; Xiphoid cartilage curved inward; sternal region short; costal arches not open enough.

Ribs:
Not properly sprung; intercostal spaces not wide; false ribs short, not well sprung, not open and low.

Back:
Short; sway back (lordosis); roach back (kyphosis); break in the topline at the 11th vertebra; withers not elevated.

Loins:
Long; flat; narrow.

Abdomen and Flanks:
Abdomen tucked up; flanks very curved and long.

Sexual Organs:
Incomplete development of one or both testicles; one or both testicles not contained within the scrotum (ectopic testicle) – see "Disqualifications." Monorchid or cryptorchid.

Croup:
Narrow; deficient in length; not sloping enough; horizontal.

Hindquarters:

THIGH:
Short; deficient in muscular development; narrow; carried splayed outward at the stifles; too straight or too slanted.

LEG:
Weak bone structure; groove between tendon and tibia not well delineated; short; too straight or too angled.

HOCK:
High; not wide; hock angle too open or closed because of forward deviation of metatarsus. Out of plumb.

METATARSUS:
Long, weak; out of plumb; dewclaws present.

FEET:
See "front feet."

Tail:
Too long or too short.
Congenital lack of tail or short tail; tail attached too low or too high; not wide at the root; carried higher than the line of the loin; carried curved over the back or straight up; lateral deviation; flaccid, hanging; mouse tail.

Hair/Coat:
Not short or hard.

COLOR OF THE COAT:
Partially white.

Skin:
Adhering closely to the body in all areas – not loose enough. Lacking wrinkles on the head; lacking dewlap.

Height at the Withers:
Deficient or exaggerated.

Defects of Character:
Timidity; fractiousness; tendency to bite; ferocity (disqualification).

DISQUALIFYING FAULTS
Head:
Markedly diverging or converging longitudinal axes of the top of the cranium and top of the muzzle.

Nose:
Total depigmentation.

Bridge of the Nose:
Markedly Roman nose or concave.

Eyes:
Sky-blue; total depigmentation of both eyelids; bilateral strabismus (cross-eyed).

Jaws:
Exaggerated prognathism (undershot jaw); enognathism (parrot mouth).

Neck:
Lacking dewlap.

Sexual organs:
Monorchid; cryptorchid.

Tail:
No tail; congenital short stumpy tail; carried curved in a horn shape over the back.

Color of the Coat:
All white; extensive white markings.

Height at the Withers:
Over 76 cm (31 inches) at the withers; more than 3 cm (1.2 inches) short of the specified minimum height.

SCALE OF POINTS
General conformation and stature – 30
Skull and muzzle – 20
Eyes and ears – 10
Rib cage – 15
Loins and croup – 10
Front and hind limbs and feet – 20
Tail – 10
Fur and color of coat – 15
Expression and character – 20

GRADING SYSTEM
Excellent – total marks not less than 140
Very good – 130
Good – 110
Satisfactory – 100

REVISIONS TO THE FCI STANDARD

The 1971 FCI standard of the Neapolitan Mastiff was revised in November 1989, and again in November 1991. As part of an FCI resolution in 1987 to uniformally format all the standards, the Neapolitan Mastiff standard was abbreviated from the 1971 version and put into less technical language. There are a few changes in the newer versions regarding gait and disqualifications. The 1991 version is also more vague in its description of the Neapolitan Mastiff. This abbreviation of the standard means that it will be harder for a neophyte to understand what a Neapolitan Mastiff is supposed to look like. At present, a group of Mastino fanciers in Italy are trying to institute more revisions of the standard. For the present, however, it is appropriate to present the 1991 standard as the FCI worldwide accepted standard of the Neapolitan Mastiff

New FCI Standard #197 of the Neapolitan Mastiff *as revised*
November 19, 1991
Translated from the Italian by Sherilyn Allen, VMD

COUNTRY OF ORIGIN: Italy

UTILIZATION: Dog for guard and personal protection

FCI CLASSIFICATION: Group 2 – dogs of the type Pincher, Schnauzer, Molossian, and Swiss Cattle Dogs. Section 2.1--Molossians, type – Dogue. Not required to do a working test.

Brief Historical Notes:
The Neapolitan Mastiff is a descendant of the large Roman Molossian described by Columella (1st century AD) in De Re Rustica. It was disseminated throughout Europe by the Roman Legions, with whom the dogs fought during their battles. In this way, the breed contributed to the formation of numerous other Molossian breeds in other European countries.

Having survived for many centuries in the countryside around Vesuvius and the environs of Naples, the Neapolitan Mastiff was reconstructed after 1947 by the devoted efforts of a group of Italian dog lovers.

General Appearance:
A heavy, massive and stocky dog of great size, whose length of the body is greater than the height at the withers.

Important Proportions:
The length of the body is 10 percent greater than the height at the withers. The length of the head is equal to three-tenths of the height at the withers. The proportion of the cranium to the muzzle is 2 to 1.

Behavior and Character:
The character of the Neapolitan Mastiff is steady and loyal, not aggressive or apt

to bite without reason. As protector of his property and persons, he is always watchful, intelligent, noble and majestic.

Head:

Short and massive, with the cranium being very wide at the level of the zygomatic arches (cheekbones). The length of the head is about three-tenths the height at the withers. The skin is abundant, with wrinkles and folds, the most typical and the best delineated of which is the fold which extends from the external angle of the eyelids to the external angle of the lips. The upper longitudinal axes of the skull and the muzzle are parallel.

Cranial Region:

The cranium is wide, flat in particular between the ears, and slightly convex at the frontal part. The width between the cheekbones is greater than half the length of the head. The zygomatic arches (cheekbones) are very prominent, but covered with flat muscles. The brow is very developed. The frontal furrow is marked. The occiput is barely apparent.

Stop:

Very defined.

Facial Region:

NOSE:
As an extension of the top line of the muzzle, it should not protrude beyond the anterior vertical plane of the lips. It should be voluminous, with well-opened, large nostrils. The color is in rapport with that of the coat color; i.e. black in black subjects, dark gray-brown in dogs of other colors, and brown in mahogany coats.

MUZZLE:
It is very wide and deep; its length corresponds to that of the bridge of the nose, and should be equal to one-third of the total length of the head. The lateral borders are parallel so that from the front, the muzzle appears to be practically square.

LIPS:
Heavy, thick and abundant. The upper lips, viewed from the front, make at their point of junction, an upside down "V." The lower lateral border of the muzzle is formed by the upper lips. The lowest part of the lower border is the labial commissure, with its visible mucosa, and situated in line with the vertical drop from the external angle of the eye.

JAWS:
Strong, with jawbones which are sturdy, and dental arcades which meet perfectly. The mandible (lower jaw) must be well developed in width.

TEETH:
White, properly developed, well aligned, and complete in number. They should meet either in a scissors bite (that is, the upper incisors overlap the lower incisors with a close contact), or they should articulate in a pincer bite (that is, the upper incisors contact the lower incisors with the free borders of the upper and lower teeth meeting end to end). The teeth are rooted evenly in the jaws.

EYES:
Situated in the same frontal plane, they are set wide apart. The palpebral opening is

almost round. The eyeball is set back slightly. The color of the iris is normally a little darker than the coat color. The eye color may, however, be lighter with coats of a diluted color.

EARS:
Small in comparison to the build of the dog, and triangular in shape. They are flat, held tight to the cheeks, and attached above the zygomatic arches (cheekbones). When they are cropped, they have the shape of an almost equilateral triangle.

Neck:
PROFILE:
The top border of the neck is slightly arched.

LENGTH:
Rather short, the neck measures about 2.8/10 of the height at the withers.

SHAPE:
It is cone shaped and well muscled. At mid length, the circumference of the neck is equal to about 8/10 the height at the withers.

SKIN:
The lower border of the neck is replete with loose skin which forms a double dewlap which is well divided but not too abundant. The dewlap extends from the lower jaw to the middle of the neck, but no further.

Body:
The body is approximately 10% longer than the height of the dog at the withers.

Topline:
The topline of the back is straight. The withers are wide, long and barely rise above the topline.

Back:
The back is wide, and its length is about 1/3 the height at the withers. The lumbar region must be harmoniously joined to the back, and the musculature must be very developed in width. The thorax is ample, with ribs that are long and well sprung. The circumference of the thorax is about 1/4 more than the height at the withers.

Croup:
The croup is wide, strong, and well muscled. From the hip bone, it is slanted about 30 degrees from the horizontal. Its length is equal to 3/10 the height at the withers. The haunches protrude at the point of attachment to the upper lumbar area.

Chest:
It is wide and open, with well developed pectoral muscles. Its width is in direct proportion to that of the thorax, and attains 40-45% of the height at the withers. The manubrium of the sternum (breast bone) is situated at the level of the point of articulation of the scapulo-humeral joint (shoulder).

Tail:
It is wide and thick at the root. Strongly built, it narrows gradually toward the tip. In length, it originally reaches the hock at birth, but it is normally docked to 2/3 its length. At rest, it is carried hanging like a scimitar. When in action, it is raised to the horizontal or a little higher than the back.

Forequarters:
As a whole, the front legs, when viewed from the side or the front, are vertical from the ground to the elbow. The bone structure is massive and thick in proportion to the body type of the dog.

Shoulders:
The length of the shoulder is about three-tenths the height at the withers with a slope of 50-60 degrees from the horizontal. The musculature is well developed, and the muscles are long and well defined. The angle of the scapulo-humeral (shoulder) joint is 105-115 degrees.

Arm:
The arm measures about 30 percent of the height at the withers. Its slope from the horizontal is from 55-60 degrees, and is comprised of a strong musculature.

Elbows:
Covered with abundant and loose skin, the elbows are not held too tightly against the thoracic walls.

Forearm:
Its length is almost equal to that of the arm. It is held in a perfectly vertical position, and is comprised of heavy, massive bone and tight, well-developed musculature.

Carpus:
Wide, tight and smooth, it is an extension of the vertical line from the forearm.

Metacarpus:
It is oval shaped, flattened from front to back, and follows the vertical line of the forearm.

It is angled forward at a 70- to 75-degree angle. Its length is equal to about one-sixth of the length of the leg from the ground to the elbow.

Foot:
Its shape is round and voluminous, with arched, tight toes. The digital pads are dry, hard and strongly pigmented. The nails are strong, curved and of dark color.

Hindquarters:
As a whole, they must be powerful and strong, in proportion with the body type of the dog, and capable of creating the impulsion desired in the movement.

Thigh:
In length, it measures one-third of the height at the withers, and its slope from the horizontal is about 60 degrees. It is wide, with large, protruding muscles that are clearly demarcated from each other. The femur and the hip bone form a 90-degree angle with one another.

Leg:
In length, it is a little shorter than the thigh, and it is angled at about 50-55 degrees. The bone is massive and the musculature is pronounced.

Knee (Stifle):
The tibio-femoral (knee) angle is about 110-115 degrees.

Hock:
It is very long with respect to the length of the leg. Its length is about 25 percent of the height at the withers. The tibio-tarsal (hock) joint form an angle of 140-145 degrees.

Metatarsus:
Comprised of massive bone, its shape is almost cylindrical. It is perfectly plumb in its position, and its length is about 25 percent of the height at the withers. Any dewclaws must be removed.

Foot:
Smaller than the front feet, it is round, with tight toes. The digital pads are dry, hard and pigmented. The nails are strong, curved and of dark color.

Movement:
The movement is one of the characteristics typical of the breed. At the walk, the movement is feline, like that of a lion. The trot or amble is slow and resembles that of a bear. The trot is characterized by a strong push from the hindquarters and a good extension of the forelegs. The Neapolitan Mastiff rarely gallops. The normal gaits are the walk and trot. Pacing is allowed.

Skin:
Thick, abundant and loose over all the body, particularly on the head, where it forms many wrinkles and folds, and on the lower border of the neck, where it makes a double dewlap.

Hair/Coat:

NATURE OF THE HAIR:
Short, stiff, hard and dense, of uniform length and smoothness all over the body, it is glossy, and measures 1.5 cm (one inch) maximum in length. There must not be any trace of fringe anywhere.

COLOR OF THE HAIR:

The preferred colors are: gray, lead gray and black; but also mahogany, tawny and dark tawny (stag), with, sometimes, white patches on the chest and on the tips of the toes. All the colors may be brindled. Also tolerated are light brown, turtle-dove gray and Isabelle.

Height and Weight:
HEIGHT AT THE WITHERS: Males 65-75 cm. (26-30 inches)
　　　　　　　　　　　　　Females　　60-68 cm. (24-27 inches)
A tolerance of 2 cm (1 inch) plus or minus is allowed.

WEIGHT: Males 60 kg. and greater (135 pounds and greater). Females　　50 kg and greater   (110 pounds and greater)

Faults:
Any deviation from the characteristics indicated in the description constitutes a fault which must be penalized according to its severity and its amount.

Severe Faults:
Pronounced prognathism (undershot lower jaw); tail held curved over the back; heights more than or less than the tolerated limits. Faults Which Result in Elimination: Enognathism (overshot upper jaw); marked convergence or divergence of the cranio-facial axes; bridge of the nose concave or convex, or very aquiline; total depigmentation of the nose; total depigmentation of the borders of the eyelids; sky-blue eye; strabismus (cross-eyed); absence of wrinkles, folds, or dewlap; short tail whether congenital or artificial; extensive white patches; white marks on the head.

NB: Males must have two testicles of normal appearance, completely descended in the scrotum.

PHOTOGRAPHIC GUIDE TO THE 1991 FCI Standard WITH COMMENTARY

Country of Origin:
Italy

The romance of the Neapolitan Mastiff is in his heritage. His charisma is created by the feelings he arouses in us when we look at him. His massiveness evokes the Colosseum and days of Roman predominance. His expressive face with its stolid gaze transports us back to times of primitive mystery. The correct Neapolitan Mastiff is one who by his very appearance seems to take us back in time to a different world.

Utilization:
Dog for guard and personal protection.

General Appearance:
A heavy, massive and stocky dog of great size, whose length of the body is greater than the height at the withers.

The important word in describing the Neapolitan Mastiff is "massive." He is not as large as the English Mastiff or as tall as the Great Dane. The massiveness comes from the heavy, thick bone structure and the wide, stocky body. For all his heavy bone structure, he is surprisingly quick in short bursts of energy. If he were bred for larger size, he might lose the quickness and agility that he had being

of substantial but not excessive height.

Important Proportions:
The length of the body is 10 percent greater than the height at the withers. The length of the head is equal to three-tenths of the height at the withers. The proportion of the cranium to the muzzle is 2 to 1.

At present, some Italian Neapolitan Mastiff connoisseurs question the accuracy of these measurements. They note that most of the Mastini are longer than 10 percent greater than the height at the withers. They would like the standard changed to read 10 percent to 15 percent greater than the height at the withers, as they feel this is a more accurate measurement.

The measurement of the head as equal to three-tenths the height of the dog at the withers is also an understatement, according to the knowledgeable Italian fanciers. The head of a normal dog may be three-tenths the height at the withers, but the Mastino head is larger in proportion to his body. They state that the head is closer to four-tenths the height of the dog at the withers, and they would like the standard changed to reflect this.

The measurement of the muzzle as being one-third the total length of the head is correct and an important characteristic of the head.

Behavior and Character:

The character of the Neapolitan Mastiff is steady and loyal, not aggressive or apt to bite without reason. As protector of his property and persons, he is always watchful, intelligent, noble and majestic.

This description of the Mastino's temperament differs from the 1968 standard, which states, "[The Mastino] is particularly adapted as a guard and personal defender. He is steady and calm, but aggressive with strangers, especially when commanded to be so." The newer description reflects the values of a more modern society, which tends to disparage ferocious people or animals. It mollifies the temperament in contrast to the ancient descriptions of the home guard mastiff. But even in downplaying the aggressive nature of the Mastino, the 1991 standard qualifies its description by stating, "not apt to bite without reason."

Head:
Short and massive, with the cranium being very wide at the level of the zygomatic arches (cheekbones). The length of the head is about three-tenths the height at the withers. The skin is abundant, with wrinkles and

Ch. Cinna della Dea Partenopea. Breeder: O. Le Méhauté. Owners: M. et Mme. Dupuis. Photo: Dupuis.

folds, the most typical of which, and the best delineated, is the fold which extends from the external angle of the eyelids to the external angle of the lips. The upper longitudinal axes of the cranium and the muzzle are parallel.

As stated earlier, the head of the Neapolitan Mastiff is larger than three-tenths of the dog's height at the withers. The head is the crowning glory, for the essence of the Mastino is in that extraordinary face and head. The copious wrinkles create the Mastino expression, which is actually

Adone, two-year-old male. Breeder and owner: M. Mazzucconi. Photo: M. Mazzucconi.

Above: **Teodata del Vittoriale, two-and-a-half-year-old female. Breeder: G. Mira. Owner: R. Barani. Photo: S. Allen.** *Below:* **Marcantonio della Nuova Fattoria, eight-year-old male. Breeder: V. Allocca. Owner: K. Marxer. Photo: M. Rogen.**

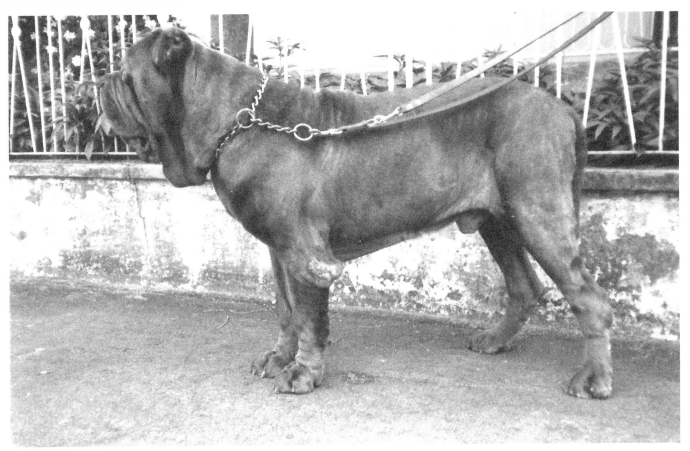

Above: **Ch. El Gavilan dell'Altafiumara, four-year-old male. Breeder: A. Di Lorenzo. Owner: G. Beta. Photo: A. Di Lorenzo.** *Below:* **Ch. Frazier della Grotta Azzurra, four-year-old male. Breeder: G. Siano. Owner: G. Mira. Photo: Schumacher.**

Above: **Altero v. Hadimassa, four-year-old male. Breeder and owner: Martens. Photo: K. Zimmerman.** *Below:* **Stonehenge Barabas, four-year-old male. Breeder and owner: R. Evans. Photo: S. Allen. This photo shows the proportion of the muzzle to the cranium as 1:2.**

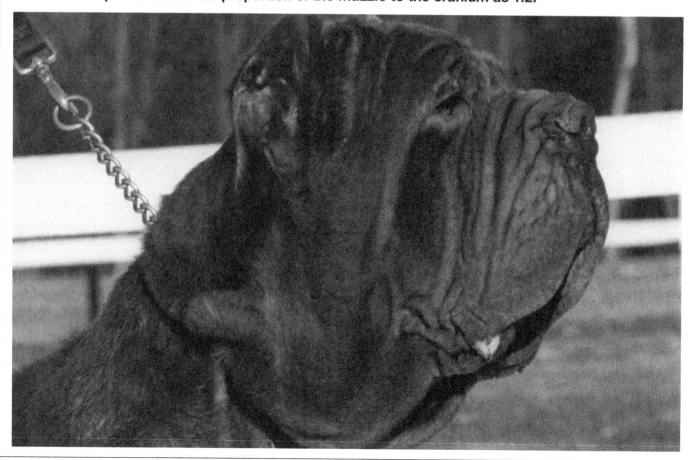

different in each individual. The source of many thrills and disappointments in breeding Neapolitan Mastiffs is the development of that incomparable head and its facial expression. Which dog is going to have that masterpiece of a head which evokes feelings of awe in every person who looks upon him? The head is the primary goal of the Mastino breeder artist in his endeavor to create the perfect specimen.

Of primary importance to the Mastino head is the parallelism of the longitudinal axes of the muzzle and cranium. The axis of the muzzle corresponds to the top border of the muzzle from the stop to the tip of the nostrils. The axis of the top of the cranium is an imaginary line which extends from the occiput to the brow, or the upper border of the stop. If the breeder allows the development of faces which have converging axes, the mastino will look too much like a boxer. If the axes are diverging, the face will look more like that of a Bloodhound. In either case, the expression will be totally incorrect from that of the Mastino.

CRANIAL REGION

The cranium is wide, flat in particular between the ears, and slightly convex at the frontal part. The width between the cheekbones is greater than half the length of the head. The zygomatic arches (cheekbones) are very prominent, but covered with flat muscles. The brow is very developed. The frontal furrow is marked. The occiput is barely apparent.

The 1991 standard specifies that the cranium must be wider than half the length of the total head. Ideally, the cranium should be as wide as it is long, or almost two-thirds

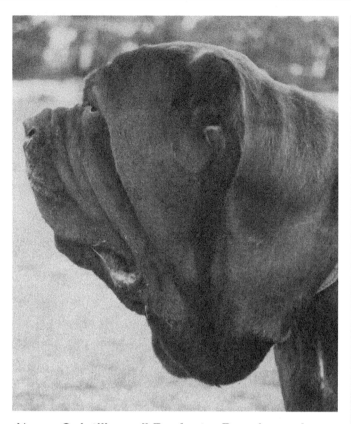

Above: **Quintiliana di Royfonte. Breeder and owner: Roy Anglada, Spain. Photo: Schumacher.** *Below:* **Ch. Caligola di Ponzano. Breeder: M. Querci. Owner: A. Pegoli. Photo: Schumacher.**

Above left: **Chemais della Dea Partenopea, young male. Breeder: O. Le Méhauté. Photo: courtesy O. Le Méhauté.** Another example of the prominent fold that extends from the eyelids to the outer corner of the lips on this very beautiful Mastino. *Above right:* **Fruit d'Amour Baronessa, one-and-a-half-year-old female. Breeder and owner: A. Spiriev. Photo: A. Spiriev.** The fold that extends from the external angle of the eyelids to the external angle of the lips is very apparent on this excellent dog.

the total length of the head. The older type Neapolitan Mastiffs tended to have very wide heads with not as much wrinkle on the top of the head. The trend in more recent times has been towards a head with more wrinkling on the top, not quite as wide, but with a wider muzzle. Either head type is excellent, and the goal of the breeder is to get as wide a head as possible with a lot of wrinkling. The following are examples of excellent heads:

Right: **Ch. Mosé. Breeder: P. Turci. Owner: A. Dionizi. Photo: A. Dionizi.** An example of an ideal Mastino head showing proper wrinkling of head and muzzle; proper width of skull and squaring of the muzzle; proper positioning of nose and eyes; correct stop and dewlap; proper expression.

Right: **The cranial axes of this dog are converging, giving it a Boxer-like appearance.**

STOP:
Very defined.

Facial Region:

NOSE:
As an extension of the top line of the muzzle, it should not protrude beyond the anterior vertical plane of the lips. It should be

This dog's muzzle is too long, the stop is too flat, and the head is insufficiently wrinkled.

voluminous, with well-opened, large nostrils. The color is in rapport with that of the coat color; i.e. black in black subjects, gray-brown in dogs of other colors, and brown in mahogany coats.

MUZZLE:
It is very wide and deep; its length corresponds to that of the bridge of the nose, and it　　should be equal to one-third of the length of the head. The lateral borders are parallel so that from the front, the muzzle appears to be practically square.

The shape of the muzzle is very important. It should be wide and "square" in appearance from the front. A muzzle that narrows to a pointed muzzle at the front is bad. Below are pictured two dogs with excellent wide muzzles.

LIPS:
Heavy, thick, and abundant. The upper lips, viewed from the front, make at their point of junction, an upside down "V." The lower lateral border of the muzzle is formed by

The cranial axes of this dog are diverging, giving it a Bloodhound-like appearance.

Older style head, very wide and flat between the ears. There are not many wrinkles on top of the head except for the frontal furrow, which is very marked, but there are a lot of wrinkles on the face. Very classic head. Regina, 10-month-old female. Breeder and owner: A. Panico. Photo: courtesy S. Freeman.

the upper lips. The lowest part of the lower border is the labial commissure, with its visible mucosa, and is situated in line with the vertical drop from the external angle of the eye.

JAWS:
Strong, with jawbones that are sturdy, and dental arcades that meet perfectly. The mandible (lower jaw) must be well developed in width.

TEETH:
White, properly developed, well aligned and complete in number. They should meet either in a scissors bite (that is, the upper

incisors cover over the lower incisors with a narrow contact), or they should articulate in a pincer bite (that is, the upper incisors contact the lower incisors with the free borders of the upper and lower teeth meeting end to end). The teeth are rooted evenly in the jaws.

The question of dentition is an ongoing controversy among Neo breeders and judges. It is well recognized that in brachycephalic breed dogs and short-muzzled animals such as cats, that there is little room for the three smaller premolars in the upper arcade and the four smaller premolars in the lower arcade. A decade or so ago, a Neo having a complete set of teeth was not all that important in the show ring. Hypertypical or very short muzzles came into vogue, and it was not uncommon for Neos with excellent type to be missing premolars. Then certain international judges, particularly those of the German school, began demanding that all the teeth be present in order for the

Excellent wide, flat head with moderate wrinkling, but still maintaining the deep frontal furrow. Spartacus de San Basile. Breeder: A. Aiello. Photo: Schumacher.

Excellent head, wide, flat, lot of wrinkling. Emir della Grotta Azzurra, two-year-old male. Breeder: G. Siano. Owner: A. Spiriev. Photo: A. Spiriev.

Right: **Beautiful head of a more recent type, more wrinkling on the forehead, wider muzzle with respect to the cranium. This is Ch. Vilardo Arké Kunon Ebe, three-year-old female. Breeder: G. Vilardo. Owner: S. Marletta. Photo: O. Le Méhauté.**

dogs to receive a rating of excellent. Panic reigned for a while, and breeders began producing dogs with slightly longer muzzles in order to fulfill the tooth requirement. The reality of Mastino breeding has prevailed now however, in that judges are beginning to realize that there are more important things to be bred into and out of Neapolitan Mastiffs than a few premolars. So now, the trend in judging is to give full points if all the teeth are present in a correct jaw, to not penalize much

Above left: **Magnificent head, wide, moderate wrinkling, deep frontal furrow, wide muzzle with perfect parallel borders giving it a square appearance. Zingaro della Zacchera. Breeder and owner: R. Barani. Photo: R. Barani.** *Above right:* **More recent head type common to the Di Ponzano line. Slightly narrower cranium with profuse wrinkling, very developed brow, very marked frontal furrow, wide muzzle with respect to the cranium. Ch. Carina di Ponzano, three-year-old female. Breeder: M. Querci. Owner: G. Mira. Photo: K. Zimmerman.**

This beautiful head shows a perfect stop, corner wrinkle from the eye to the lip, and proper muzzle to cranium ratio of 1:2. It also demonstrates proper positioning of the nose on the muzzle, as described next. Dewlap length is perfect. Corleone de Can Rayo, mature male. Owner: P. Van Melis. Photo: K. Zimmerman.

Top of cranium is too round. Eyes are too large. Lips make an inverted "U" instead of an inverted "V." Photo: S. Allen.

Very wrinkled head all over. Cranium could be a little bit wider. This is a young dog, however, and the head continues to develop and widen up to five years of age. Ironstone Ebony Oxide, one-year-old male. Breeder and owner: S. Allen. Photo: S. Allen.

Gray nose, gray rims of the eyelids and hazel eyes in gray (blue) dog. Ragna di Colosseo Avallu, male. Breeder and owner: L. Denger. Photo: Schumacher

The profile of this puppy is totally incorrect. The stop is barely defined. The angle of the stop is greater than 90 degrees. The muzzle is greater than one-third the length of the head. The ears are attached too low. Photo: S. Allen.

Brown nose, brown rims of the eyelids in mahogany dog. The eyes, which are blue in the puppy, will change to amber when the dog is mature. Carpe Diem Daphne, nine-week-old female. Breeder: E. Schiavo. Owner: Denise Rappaport. Photo S. Allen.

if at all if a couple of premolars #1 are missing, but to penalize more heavily if premolars #2, 3 or 4 are missing.

The Neapolitan Mastiff is a catch dog. Its original name was Cane é presa. Most catch dogs are prognathic, i.e. the lower jaw protrudes in front of the upper jaw (undershot). Again, all brachycephalic breeds tend to be prognathic. Whereas the standard calls for a level bite or a scissors bite, prognathism is not heavily penalized unless it is excessive or distorts the profile of the face.

Enognathism or overshot jaw is written into the standard as a disqualification. However, the lower jaw of Neapolitan Mastiffs in America keeps growing throughout their life. Many puppies with perfect scissors bites at eight weeks to six months old, go on to have a level bite at a year, and then become prognathic at one and a half to two years. On the other hand, puppies born with an overshot jaw, as long as it is not a pointy, deformed upper jaw, usually end up with a perfect scissors bite by the time they are two years old.

In Europe, Neos are not really judged seriously until they are 18 months old. Here, we start judging at six months old. I would not weigh an overshot jaw in a six-month-old puppy very heavily. An undershot jaw in an adult is not of much concern either, unless it is excessive. An overshot jaw in an adult over 18 months of age is a disqualification in the show ring.

EYES:
Situated in the same frontal plane, they are set wide apart. The palpebral opening is

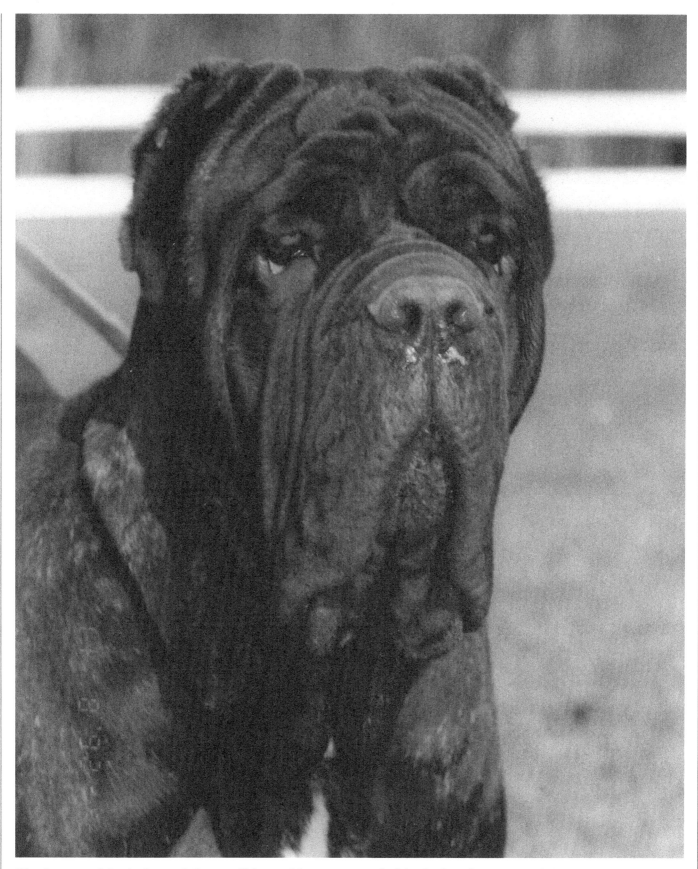

Black nose, black rims of the eyelids and brown eyes in black dog. Ironstone Atlas, 18-month-old male. Breeder and owner: S. Allen. Photo: S. Allen.

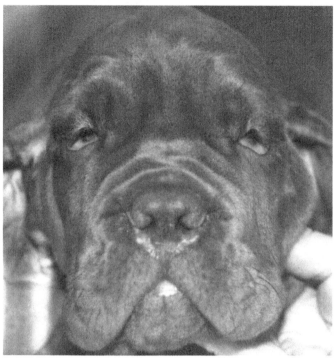

Above left: Tawny or isabelle nose, rims of the eyelids, and tawny eyes in tawny (isabelle) dog. Ch. Neptune de la Grande Vanousch, three-and-a-half-year-old male. Breeder: C. Wingel. Owners: Zimmerman, Klein, Weber. Photo: Zimmerman. *Above right:* Nostrils constricted, not well opened. Head domed. Ears set too low. Photo: S. Allen.

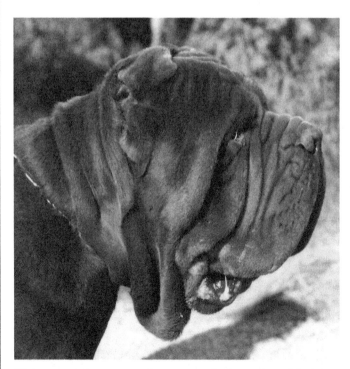

This dog shows perfect muzzle length, which is one-third the length of the total head. Emir della Grotta Azzurra, two-and-a-half-year-old male. Breeder: G. Siano. Owner: A. Spiriev. Photo: S. Allen.

The muzzle on this excellent head is very wide and correct. Eax des Mines du Roi, male. Breeder and owner: M. et Mme. Salomon. Photo: Salomon.

This dog has magnificent and correct wrinkling of the cranium and muzzle. The parallelism of the muzzle is perfect, and it is wide in proportion to the head. Lisandro, four-year-old male. Owner: R. Barani. Photo: J. Yarmush.

almost round. The eyeball is set back slightly. The color of the iris is normally a little darker than the coat color. The eye color may, however, be lighter with coats of a diluted color.

EARS:
Small in comparison to the build of the dog, and triangular in shape. They are flat, held tight to the cheeks, and attached above the zygomatic arches (cheekbones). When they are cropped, they have the shape of an almost equilateral triangle.

Neck:
PROFILE:
The top border of the neck is slightly arched.

LENGTH:
Rather short, the neck measures about 2.8/10 of the height at the withers.

SHAPE:
It is cone shaped and well muscled. At mid-length, the circumference of the neck is equal to about eight-tenths the height at the withers.
SKIN:
The lower border of the neck is replete with loose skin which forms a double dewlap, which is well divided but not too abundant. The dewlap extends from the lower jaw to the middle of the neck, but no further.

Body:
The body is 10 percent longer than the height of the dog at the withers.

In actuality, the body is 10 to 15 percent longer than the height of the dog at the withers.

The lips on this lovely Neo are exceedingly copious. This is a very difficult feature to attain in the dogs. Rumina di Colosseo Avallu. Breeder and owner: L. Denger. Photo: Schumacher.

Notice in this beautiful dog the heavy, ample lips, forming the upside down "V," and the labial commissure with its visible mucosa situated in line with the vertical drop from the external angle of the eye. Fruit d'Amour Baronessa, one-and-a-half-year-old female. Breeder and owner: A. Spiriev. Photo: A. Spiriev.

Topline:
The topline of the back is straight. The withers are wide, long and barely rise above the topline.

Because of the massiveness of Mastini, their topline, designated as "straight" is not as uniformly straight as in a Doberman, Great Dane or other lighter breeds of dogs.

Back:
The back is wide, and its length is about one-third the height at the withers. The lumbar region must be harmoniously joined to the back, and the musculature must be very developed in width. The thorax is ample, with ribs that are long and well sprung. The circumference of the thorax is about one-quarter larger than the height at the withers.

Croup:
The croup is wide, strong and well muscled. From the hip bone, it is slanted about 30 degrees from the horizontal. Its length is equal to three-tenths the height at the withers. The haunches protrude at the point of attachment to the upper lumbar area.

Chest:
It is wide and open, with well-developed pectoral muscles. Its width is in direct proportion to that of the thorax, and attains 40 to 45 percent of the height at the withers. The manubrium of the sternum (breast bone) is situated at the level of the point of articulation of the scapulo-humeral joint (shoulder).

Tail:
It is wide and thick at the root. Strongly

Above left: **Magnificent lips, head, wrinkle on this multiple internationally titled champion dog. Ch. Caligola di Ponzano, four-year-old male. Breeder: M. Querci. Owner: A. Pegoli. Photo: Schumacher.**
Above right: **The junction of the lips in this dog makes an inverted "U" instead of an inverted "V." This gives the dog a different, more pugnacious expression, and is not correct. Photo: S. Allen.**
Below: **This dog does not have enough lip. The muzzle is also too long and the cranial axes are converging. There is not sufficient wrinkle on the head. It is not a good specimen. Photo: S. Allen.**

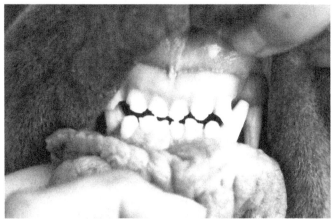

Pincer bite. The upper and lower incisor teeth meet end to end evenly. Photo: S. Allen.

Prognathic or undershot jaw. This is excessive. Photo: S. Allen.

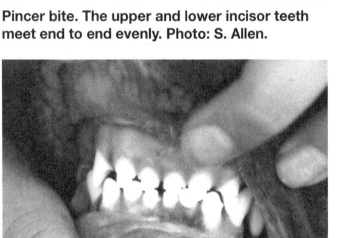

Scissors bite. The upper incisors cover over the lower incisors with a narrow contact. Photo: S. Allen.

Enognathic or overshot jaw in a puppy. Some lines are noted for producing puppies that are born with an overshot jaw, which will correct as the dog grows. In some cases, the overshot is a defect that crops up in some puppies and never corrects itself. Photo: S. Allen.

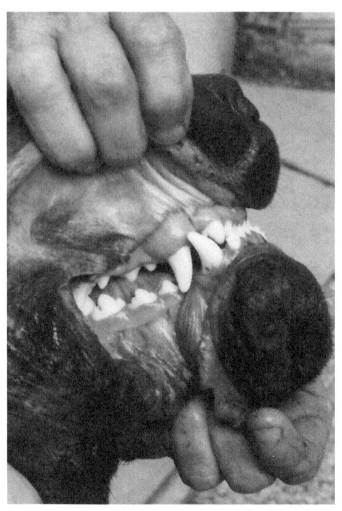

Reverse scissors bite in an adult. The lower teeth are only slightly in front of the upper teeth. This is perfectly acceptable. Photo: S. Allen.

Correct placement of ears in an uncropped dog. Lupra v. Vagantenhof. Breeder: W. Weisse. Owner: M. Mnig. Photo: M. Rogen.

Another example of a correct ear set in an uncropped dog. Note also the perfect inverted "V" at the junction of the lips, the large nose, and the shape of the palpebral openings due to the weight of the heavy wrinkles. Apollo, two-year-old male. Breeder and owner: M. Mazzucconi. Photo: S. Allen.

Illustration of the deep-set eyes and the palpebral opening, which would be round except that the weight of the skin pulls down the lower lid, exposing the red conjunctiva or haw. Ch. Dolli de Néropolis, three-year-old female. Breeder and owner: Mme. Beck. Photo: J.P. Beck.

Ears cropped to an equilateral triangle and standing up. Note the facial characteristics of this beautiful dog. Frasier des Molosses d'Or, three-year-old male. Breeder and owner: Mme. Galiment. Photo: S. Allen.

Note how in this magnificent dog, the weight of the wrinkles causes the upper lid to droop down over the eyeball, and the lower lid to be pulled down away from the eyeball. Note also the mucous and crusting around the eyes. This is normal in Neos because of the eyelids. An owner of Neapolitan Mastiffs must be prepared to deal with this. Igri. Breeder: G. Siano. Owner: A. Di Lorenzo. Photo: A. Di Lorenzo.

built, it narrows gradually toward the tip. In length, it reaches the hock, but it is normally cut to two-thirds its length. At rest, it is carried hanging like a scimitar; when in action, it is raised to the horizontal or a little higher than the back.

Front Legs:

As a whole, the front legs, when viewed from the side or the front, are vertical from the ground to the elbow. The bone structure is strong and thick in proportion to the body type of the dog.

Shoulders:

The length of the shoulder is about three-tenths the height at the withers with a slope of 50 to 60 degrees from the horizontal. The musculature is well developed, and the muscles are long and well defined. The angle of the scapulo-humeral (shoulder) joint is 105 to 115 degrees.

Arm:

The arm measures about 30 percent of the height at the withers. Its slope from the horizontal is from 55 to 60 degrees, and is comprised of a strong musculature.

Elbows:

Covered with abundant and loose skin, the elbows are not held too tightly against the thoracic walls.

Forearm:

Its length is almost equal to that of the arm. It is held in a perfectly vertical position, and is comprised of heavy, thick bone structure and tight, well-developed musculature.

Ch. Lumeloris, four-year-old male. Breeder: Pouwels. Owner: P. van Melis. Photo: Schumacher.

Longer ear crop with ears held over the head – more prevalent in the Naples area. Turillo, one-and-a-half-year-old male. Breeder: Panico. Owner: G. Travers. Photo: S. Allen.

Shorter ear crop more prevalent in northern Italy. Aronne, three-year-old male. Breeder: M. Blam. Owner: S. Allen. Photo: S. Allen.

Febla, two-year-old female. Breeder and owner: G. Iazzetta. Photo: G. Maja.

Mastino in Naples, regrettably unidentified. A beautiful dog.

Another gorgeous male showing dewlap, neck and wonderful head type. Note correct placement of nose with respect to the anterior plane of the lips. Don Corleone van Bennato. Two-year-old male. Breeder: Mrs. Bleijenberg. Owner: A. Van Doremalen. Photo: S. Allen.

The body of this dog is too long. Photo: S. Allen.

Ironstone Electra Blue Mao, one-and-a-half-year-old female. Breeder and owner: S. Allen. Photo: S. Allen.

Ch. Ironstone Honky Tonk Woman, two-year-old female. Breeder: S. Allen. Owners: Dr. and Mrs. Schiavo. Photo: Schiavo.

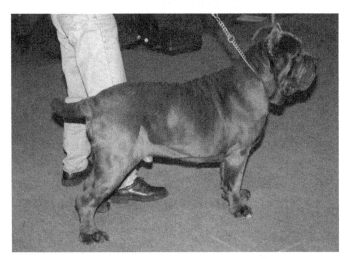

Oliver, three-year-old male. Owner regretfully unidentified. Photo: K. Zimmerman.

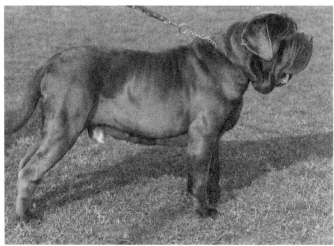

Well-balanced dog with good croup. Apollo, two-year-old male. Breeder and owner: M. Mazzucconi. Photo: M. Mazzucconi.

Another excellent chest. Unidentified male dog in Naples. Photo: Welscher.

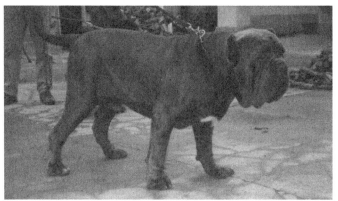

Great chest on this dog. Ivan, one-and-a-half-year-old male. Breeder and owner: R. Barani. Photo: G. Maja.

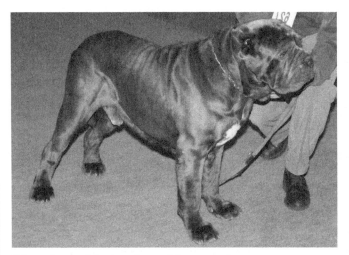

Showing wide back and harmonious proportions. Vilardo Arkè Kunon Menelao, two-and-a-half-year-old male. Breeder: Vilardo. Owner: A. van Doremalen. Photo: K. Zimmerman.

The topline of this dog is very swayed. The croup is higher than the withers. This is not correct. Photo: S. Allen.

Above: Correct tail as well as correct conformation on this young dog. *Right:* Excellent front legs on this female dog. The bone is heavy. Ch. Bella della Grotta Azzurra, three-year-old female. Breeder: G. Siano. Owner: A. Spiriev. Photo: A. Spiriev.

This is an excellent example of correct shoulders, front legs, back, topline, tail, head, etc. Vilardo Arké Kunon Ebe, three-year-old female. Breeder: G. Vilardo. Owner: S. Marletta. Photo: J.P. Dupuis.

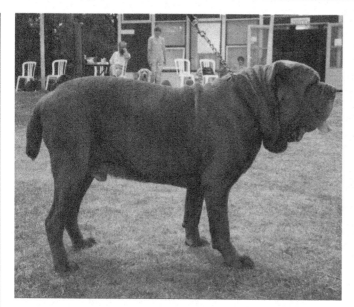

Tail cut a little short on this magnificent dog, but still acceptable. Altero van Hadimassa, mature male. Breeder and owner: B. Martens. Photo: K. Zimmerman.

Correct tail as well as correct conformation on this young dog. Frack del Cannae, two-and-a-half-year-old male. Owners: Weber and Klein. Photo: Zimmerman.

Tail cut a little long on this young dog, but still acceptable. Caracalla del Bonrampino, nine-month-old male. Breeder: G. Maja. Owner: S. Allen. Photo: S. Allen.

Carpus:
Wide, tight and smooth, it is an extension of the vertical line from the forearm.

Metacarpus (Pastern)
It is oval shaped, flattened from front to back, and follows the vertical line of the forearm. It is angled forwards at a 70- to 75-degree angle. Its length is equal to about one-sixth of the length of the leg from the ground to the elbow.

The dewclaws on the front legs are not removed. There is no reason to remove them, as they are both functional and aesthetic on this heavy breed of dog. The dewclaw is the equivalent of the dog's thumb. Neos especially use their "thumb" when holding onto toys or things they are chewing.

Foot:
Its shape is round and voluminous, with arched, tight toes. The digital pads are dry, hard and strongly pigmented. The nails are strong, curved and of dark color.

In most all Neapolitan Mastiffs, the front feet turn outwards slightly. The front feet in the puppy may start out pointing directly forward and plumb with the forearm as viewed from the front. When the dog grows and becomes heavier and more massive, the front feet invariably begin to turn out from the pasterns. As one becomes more familiar with the breed,

Right: **Note the elbows, covered by loose skin; the forearm, which is about equal in length to the upper arm; the heavy, thick bone of the forearm; the pastern, angled forward; the round, voluminous feet. Ch. Mosé, four-year-old male. Breeder. P. Turci. Owner: A. Dionisi. Photo: K.Rossé.**

The shoulder angle is too acute, about 90 degrees, making the dog look like it is crouching. In addition, the topline is sagging, and the body appears too long. The muzzle is too long. The face does not have enough wrinkle, and there is not much dewlap. The tail is good in shape and length. Photo: S. Allen.

Note the loose skin draping back toward the elbow of this good puppy. Stonehenge Barabas, six-month-old male. Breeder and owner: R. Evans. Photo: S. Allen.

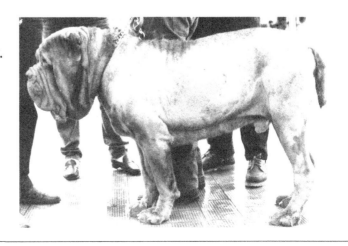

Above: **This young dog shows the growth typically associated with elbow dysplasia, which is common in the breed. Elbows are held into the body. Front feet are turned out and angled laterally at the carpus (valgus defect).** *Below:* **The bone in this dog's front legs is too fine for a Neapolitan Mastiff. Photo: S. Allen.**

namely by constant observation, one can distinguish a normal turnout which appears to be functional in that it gives the massive dog a wider base of suppot. This is opposed to pathological turnout, which is a result from aberrant bone growth of the radius and ulna. In this latter instance, the turnout is excessive, and the carpus (wrist or ankle) is bent in a valgus deformity. A valgus angulation is one in which the body part is bent outward away from the midline of the body.

Hindquarters:
As a whole, they must be powerful and strong, in proportion with the body type of the dog, and capable of creating the impulsion desired in the movement.

Thigh:
In length, it measures one-third of the height at the withers, and its slope from the horizontal is about 60 degrees. It is wide, with large, protruding muscles that are clearly demarcated from each other. The femur and the hip bone form a 90-degree angle with one another.

Leg:
In length, it is a little shorter than the thigh, and it is angled at about 50 to 55 degrees. The bone is massive and the musculature is pronounced.

Knee (Stifle):
The tibio-femoral (knee) angle is about 110 to 115 degrees.

Hock:
It is very long with respect to the length of the leg. Its length is about 25 percent of the height at the withers. The tibio-tarsal (hock)

joint form an angle of 140 to 145 degrees.

Metatarsus:
Comprised of massive bone, it is almost cylindrical in shape. It is perfectly plumb in its position, and its length is about 25 percent of the height at the withers. Any dewclaws must be removed.

Foot:
Smaller than the front feet, it is round, with tight toes. The digital pads are dry, hard and pigmented. The nails are strong, curved and of dark color.

Movement:
The movement is one of the characteristics typical of the breed. At the walk, the movement is feline, like that of a lion. The trot or amble is slow and resembles that of a bear. The trot is characterized by a strong push from the hindquarters and a good extension of the forelegs. The Neapolitan Mastiff rarely gallops. The normal gaits are the walk and trot. Pacing is allowed.

Neapolitan Mastiffs do not move like other breeds of dogs. Their bones and bodies are heavier for their size than other breeds of dogs, so they move in a slower, more lumbering fashion. They do not prance. They move with a very deliberate forward motion, head held outstretched and level with the back, and eyes fixed straight ahead. At the walk, their whole body undulates, much like that of lions and panthers stalking a prey. They hold their heads down very low when they walk, and constantly want to sniff the ground.

Above: **This dog's forearm is too long. The stifle is also very straight. Photo: S. Allen.** *Below:* **Ten-week-old puppy with good conformation of the front legs. The bone is heavy, the feet are tight. There is a slight hint of turnout beginning at the front feet. If the puppy grows to be thick and heavy, the turnout will increase. If the puppy grows to be leaner and lighter boned, the turnout will be less. Photo: S. Allen.**

Above left: **This champion Neo exhibits a normal turnout of the front feet. This conformation is so typical in the Neapolitan Mastiff that it appears to occur for structural reasons. This particular dog is very massive. Ch. Etrusco, three-year-old male. Breeder and owner: G. Iazzetta. Photo: S. Allen.** *Above right:* **This beautiful dog also shows correct front leg and feet stance of a Neo. The turnout of the front feet is a little less than that of the previous dog because this dog is a little slighter in build. Frasier des Molosses d'Or, three-year-old male. Breeder and owner: Mme. Galiment. Photo: S. Allen.**

Above left: **A typical, heavy female showing excellent bone and leg structure, with the typical turnout of the front feet. Photo: S. Allen.** *Above right:* **Another excellent Neo, slightly broader than the previous two dogs, showing typical conformation of the front legs and feet. Jade v. Vagantanhof, adult male. Breeder: Walt Weisse. Owner: D. Christman. Photo: Schumacher.**

Above: **A six-month-old male with excellent front legs, manifesting heavy bone and still quite straight. As he gets older and more massive, the feet may begin to turn out. Whether breeders should strive to produce dogs with straight front legs (because that is what the dog world is used to) or whether they should go with what seems normal at this time for the Neapolitan Mastiff is a philosophical question for those entrusted with the development of the breed. Orso, six-month-old male. Breeder: R. Blasio. Owner: S. Allen. Photo: S. Allen.**

Above: **An enormous male from England. Note shape of front legs. He is more massive than present-day English Mastiffs, and as such, shows a slight turnout of front legs. Trends with AKC English Mastiffs have been toward leaner dogs to produce better movement. With the leaner specimens comes the ability to produce dogs with straighter front legs. Ch. Kwintra's Hercules. Breeders and owners: Jean and Allister Clark. Photo: Clark, and courtesy of G. Travers.**

Right: **Correct foot for a Neapolitan Mastiff. The feet are round and very large. The pastern is angled forward correctly. The bone of the forearm is heavy and thick. Ch. Califf della Dea Partenopea, three-year-old male. Breeder: O. Le Méhauté. Owner: G. Oliviero. Photo: courtesy S. Freeman.**

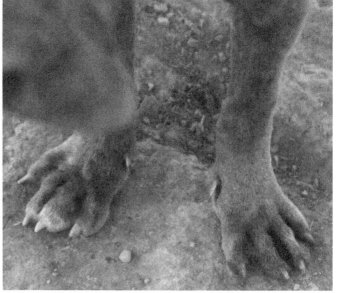

Above: **Incorrect feet are turned outward too much and have loose, splayed toes. In same cases, young growing dogs will go through a phase where their toes splay out, and then the foot will correct itself when the dog matures. Photo: S. Allen.**

Above left: **This dog's front feet are turned out excessively. This is a valgus deformity due to incongruous growth of the bones of the forearm. Photo: K. Rossé.**

Right: **This impressive dog shows overall powerful body type and especially strong hindquarters. Ch. Arno de la Fouinerie, male. Breeders: M. et Mme. Dupuis. Owners: M. et Mme. Salomon. Photo: courtesy M. Dupuis.**

An excellent dog showing correct proportions of leg (tibia) and thigh bone (femur). Fonzo du Pré au Clair, three-year-old male. Breeder: M. Guillox et Mme. Rouvarel. Owner: A. Aiello. Photo: S. Allen.

Nice rear on nine-month-old female Neapolitan. The bone structure is harmonious though the musculature is lacking. Photo: S. Allen.

The hindleg angulation of this dog is too straight. The legs are too long, making the dog taller than it is long. This is due to the forearm and leg being too long with respect to the arm and thigh. The back is roached, and the tail is kinked. Photo: S. Allen.

The back of this puppy is roached, and the tail is set on too low. He is high in the rear due to the excessive length of the leg bone (tibia and fibula). Photo: S. Allen.

Galloping Neo. Looks alone tell you that he has no intention of stopping (nor the ability to do so). Photo: S. Allen.

This dog's rear legs appear light and poorly muscled for his body. The angulation of the hindlegs is also too straight. Photo: S. Allen.

Caracalla del Bonrampino, three-month-old puppy. Breeder: G. Maja. Owner: S. Allen. Photo: S. Allen.

As a Neapolitan Mastiff increases his speed from the walk, he will usually begin to pace. The pace is characterized by a rolling, rocking movement in which both the front and back legs on the same side move forward at the same time, while the corresponding legs on the other side remain on the ground. Many large, heavy animals, such as bears, elephants, camels, and some horses, pace naturally. It is not an unsoundness, and it is allowable in the breed. It is simply ungainly looking for those who are not used to watching an animal pace. It is the lumbering pace that is referred to in the standard as "moving like a bear." It is normal for the breed.

As the Neapolitan Mastiff increases his speed again from the pace or amble, he usually breaks into a trot. Some rings in which Neapolitan Mastiffs are shown are not large enough for the dog to get up enough speed to trot. As stated before, a Neapolitan Mastiff's trot is a very forceful, propelling gait, and he moves forward resolutely, not easily turned or swayed off course. For all these reasons, movement in a Neapolitan Mastiff should be used as a means of determining strength and soundness, but not in order to create an aesthetically pleasing picture which will aid in choosing the most pleasing dog in a show ring.

In the United States, people are very concerned with athletic prowess and physical fitness. Sports and body in motion are a part of every school curriculum, TV advertisement, recreational event, in short – the American way of life. We tend to look at beautiful motion as beauty, and in many instances it is. A skier jumping, a diver diving, a dancer soaring through the air in a leap, an Arabian

Neapolitan Mastiffs galloping. Photo: S. Allen.

Briarwood Mario, two-year-old male. Breeder and owner: C. Dedmon. Photo: S. Allen.

Caracalla at one year old. A good-moving dog can be detected as a puppy. This dog grew up to be an exceptional mover. He tends to be light-framed for a Neo, but he is still young. In this photo, he shows the typical head and tail carriage and the strides of a well-balanced, sound Neo. Photo: S. Allen.

horse racing along the beach, head up, nostrils flared, mane and tail streaming – these instances of motion are beautiful. An Irish Setter floating around a show ring with silken red hair flowing is beautiful. The moving image adds to the judge's impression of beauty in picking the most beautiful dog in the ring.

However, the criteria of beauty in motion should not be applied to the Neapolitan Mastiff. The beauty of a Neo is in his statuesque stillness and massiveness. To look at a Mastino is like looking at the train station in Milan, or the Roman Coliseum and being in awe of the mightiness and solidity of these immense stone structures. The aesthetics of a Greyhound or an Azawakh are in its ability to run with the wind. The speed and elasticity of their bodies in motion elicits awe from us slow mortals rooted to the ground in comparison to them. The aesthetics of the Neapolitan Mastiff is in its awesome stationary physical appearance. Its movement need not be part of the picture. We admire Michelangelo's David on a pedestal. We do not want to see him move. A swan gliding on a lake is elegant and beautiful. A swan waddling on the ground is ludicrous.

So it is with Neapolitan Mastiffs. Movement should be used to assess soundness, not beauty. When it is used to assess beauty, the judge will invariably pick the lighter-bone, less typey Mastino. For a dog to move elegantly, it must, by the definition of elegant, be lighter in body type. A massive, heavy-boned Mastino can move with strength and force, but he will shake the ground with his movement rather than glide elegantly over it.

The standard says the Mastino rarely gallops.

Above: **Gray (blue) male. Ch. Cartouche des Arénes di César, six-year-old male. Breeder: M. Drahé. Owner: D. Guilloux. Photo: S. Allen.** *Below:* **The thick, loose skin is evident on the dog in this photo. Note the double dewlap. Ch. Debora de la Font de Nîmes, four-and-a-half-year-old female. Owner: H. Weber. Breeder: A. Aiello. Photo: K. Zimmerman.**

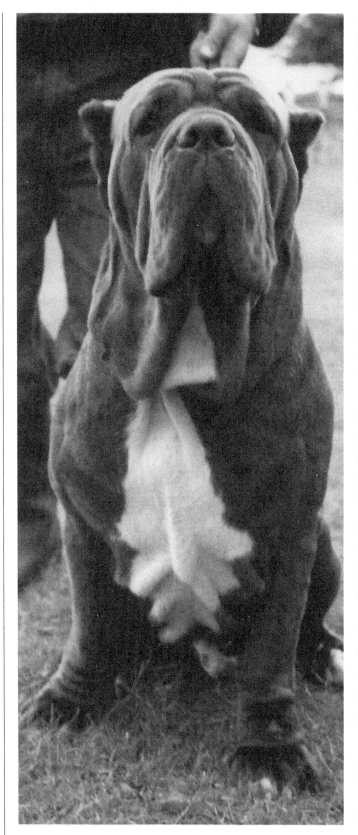

Above left: **Ch. Lumeloris. Breeder: Pouwels. Owner: P. Van Melis. Photo: Schumacher. This multiple champion has very evident amounts of white, which does not detract at all from his overall excellent quality.** *Above right:* **Mahogany male. Carpe Diem puppy, eight weeks old. Breeder: E. Schiavo. Owner: M. Freeman. Photo: S. Allen.**

Tawny male. Fido de la Fouinerie, three-year-old male. Breeder: M. et Mme. Dupuis. Owner: M. Pini. Photo: S. Allen.

Concave bridge of the nose. Photo: S. Allen.

Ch. Frazier della Grotta Azzurra, four-year-old male. Breeder: G. Siano. Owner: G. Mira. Photo: Schumacher.

Dog with an absence of wrinkles and folds.

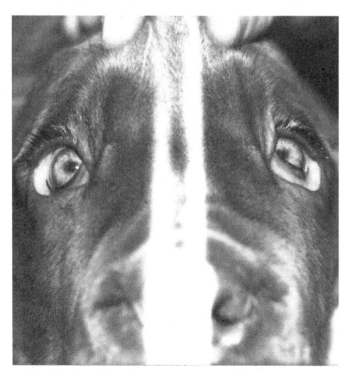

Bilateral strabismus (cross eyed). Photo: S. Allen.

All Mastino owners in the U.S. as well as in Europe will probably disagree with this statement. The Mastino can gallop very fast. The problem is, he cannot stop his mass once he has broken its inertia. So take warning, and never stand in the path of an oncoming, galloping Neapolitan Mastiff!

Skin:
Thick, abundant and loose over all the body, particularly on the head, where it forms many wrinkles and folds, and on the lower border of the neck, where it makes a double dewlap.

Hair/Coat:

NATURE OF THE HAIR
Short, stiff, hard and dense, of uniform length and smoothness all over the body, it is fine, and measures 1.5 cm (one inch) maximum in length. There must not be any trace of fringe anywhere.

COLOR OF THE HAIR
The preferred colors are: gray, lead gray and black; but also mahogany, tawny and dark tawny (stag), with, sometimes, small white patches on the chest and on the tips of the toes. All the colors may be brindled. Also tolerated are light brown, turtle-dove gray, and isabelle.

The question of the amount of white allowed on a good dog is purposely vague. Judging from current European champion Neapolitan Mastiffs, almost any reasonable size of a white patch on the chest, ventral neck under the dewlap, throat, feet, backs of the pasterns, and penis sheath and abdomen is acceptable.

Above: **Black male. Ironstone Authority, two-year-old male. Breeder and owner: S. Allen. Photo: S. Allen.** *Below:* **Ch. Ombrone di Ponzano, five-year-old male. Breeder: M. Querci. Owner: E. Crepaldi. Photo: M. Rogen.**

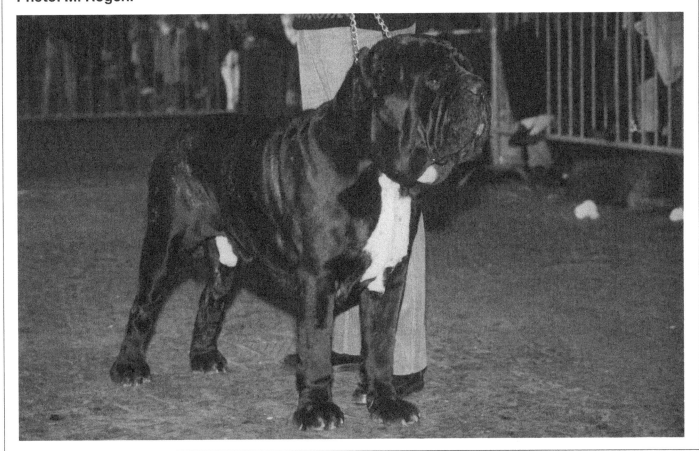

White is not acceptable on the face, as it detracts totally from the dog's expression. Neither is white allowed on noticeably visible parts of the upper body

In general, if white enhances the dog's appearance it is accepted. If white does not detract from the dog's appearance, it is accepted. If white is so excessive that it makes the observer wonder how so much white got on the dog, it may be too much. The term in the standard "excessive white" is therefore actually left to the discretion of the judge.

Height And Weight:

HEIGHT AT THE WITHERS:
Males, 65-75 cm.   (26-30 inches)

Females, 60-68 cm.   (24-27 inches)
A tolerance of 2 cm (1 inch) plus or minus is allowed.

WEIGHT: Males, 60 kg. and greater (135 pounds and greater). Females, 50 kg and greater   (110 pounds and greater)

These heights and weights were set 50 years ago, when the first standard was written. The dogs tend to be a lot heavier now. Females in show condition average 125 pounds, and males average 155 pounds. The stated heights still hold true, and the Italians do not believe a Neapolitan should exceed the 31-inch maximum height or it will tend to lose the harmony of its proportions.

White stripe down dog's face Photo: S. Allen.

Sky-blue eye. S. Allen.

Faults:

Any deviation from the characteristics indicated in the description constitutes a fault which must be penalized according to its severity and its amount.

Severe Faults:

Pronounced prognathism (undershot lower jaw); tail held curved over the back; heights more than or less than the tolerated limits.

Faults Which Result In Elimination:

Enognathism (overshot upper jaw); marked convergence or divergence of the cranio-facial axes; bridge of the nose concave or convex, or very aquiline; total depigmentation of the nose; total depigmentation of the borders of the eyelids; sky-blue eye; strabismus (cross-eyed); absence of wrinkles, folds, or dewlap; short tail whether congenital or artificial; extensive white patches; white marks on the head.

NB: Males must have two testicles of normal appearance, completely descended into the scrotum.

Sansone II, adult male. Breeder: M. Querci. Owner: E. Di Tomasso. Photo: courtesy of Vandoni.

Neapolitan Mastiffs in Europe

The Neapolitan Mastiff that we know today is a product of Europe, and specifically Italy. The European breeders have been working on the development of the Mastino much longer than we in the United States have been. In respect for the efforts of the Italian Mastinari and their cohorts in neighboring countries, I feel it is appropriate to take a look at their dogs before discussing the Neapolitan Mastiff in the United States. We can learn a lot from them and their hard work, so that, hopefully, we can continue in the right direction in our attempts to influence and propagate the breed.

Fazia della Dea Partenopea, two-year-old female. Breeder: O. Le Méhauté. Owner: P. Salomon. Photo: Salomon.

Neapolitan Mastiffs in Italy

Since Italy is the mother country of the Mastino, it is Italy that determines the breed type of the dog that we in the United States seek to emulate. Because of the much smaller size of Italy in comparison to the United States, the Mastino breeders there have formed a more tightly knit circle of fanciers of the breed. Everyone knows each other and what the other person has accomplished with his or her dogs. Whether the breeders are friends or enemies, there is still a brotherhood among them that is hard for a foreigner to penetrate. The best way to learn the essence of the Mastino is to go to the Mastino shows in Italy and study the dogs and the people. In lieu of that, you just have to persist in looking at pictures of their dogs, reading about the dogs, and incorporating

Ch. Hatrim della Grotta Azzurra, four-year-old male. Breeder: G. Siano. Owner: S. Di Micco. Photo: S. Allen.

the essence of them into your mind.

The Italians are so successful in producing awesome-looking Mastini because they are concerned with creating a dog that evokes an emotion. Dog breeders and owners in many other countries are often more concerned

Ch. Mosé, four-year-old male. Breeder: P. Turci. Owner: A. Dionizi. Photo: K. Rossé.

Chemais della Dea Partenopea, two-year-old male. Breeder: O. Le Méhauté. Photo: Méhauté.

Ch. Caligola di Ponzano. Breeder: M. Querci. Owner: A. Pegoli. Photo: Schumacher.

Ch. Euphemia di Ponzano, seven-year-old female. Breeder: M. Querci. Owner: G. Mira. Photo: S. Allen.

Italian *Mastinari*: Salvatore Di Micco, Gian Pietro Arrigoni, Giovanni Maja.

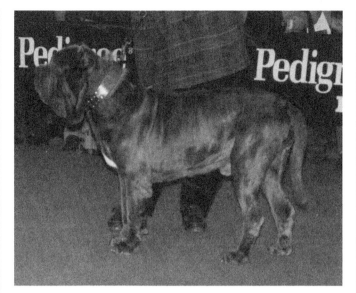

Rugantino dell'Altafiumara, three-year-old male. Breeder and owner: A. Di Lorenzo. Photo: S. Allen.

Ch. Barone del Nolano, three-year-old male. Breeder and owner: M. De Falco Jovane. Photo: M. De Falco.

Young male. Breeder and owner: Panico. Photo: G. Travers.

Regina, adult female. Breeder and owner: U. Miranda. Photo: G. Travers.

Carina di Ponzano, four-year-old female. Breeder: M. Querci. Owner: G. Mira. Photo: Schumacher.

Ch. El Gavilan dell'Altafiumara, four-year-old male. Breeder: A. Di Lorenzo. Owner: G. Beta. Photo: A. Di Lorenzo.

Ch. Bruno, four-year-old male. Breeder and owner: P. Paduano. Photo: Paduano.

Ch. Berry, male born in 1961. Breeder and owner: Tina di Gandolfo. Photo: courtesy of G. Travers.

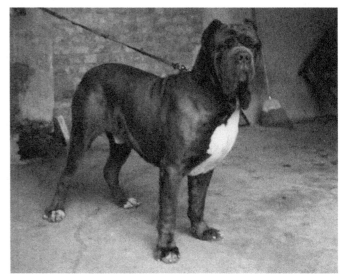

Argo del Bonrampino, four-year-old male. Breeder and owner: G. Maja. Photo: G. Maja.

with producing dogs with purely structural soundness, for which they can attach lifetime guarantees against congenital defects. Rather than breeding Neos purely for the purpose of selling them, the Italian breeders breed to create the most aesthetic-looking dog so that someone will want to buy their dogs. Those people in Italy who buy Mastini are usually knowledgeable as to what the breed is about, so they are not looking for a puppy that comes from OFA-certified parents who will grow up to be good with the children, be free from all congenital defects and be easily housebroken.

Since they have a limited market made up of connoisseurs who are looking for that supreme art form, the Italian breeders can concentrate on creating aesthetics and emotions rather than a living being that will be guaranteed to be maintenance free. For this reason, the Italian Mastini are consistently more impressive and awe inspiring than those Neapolitan Mastiffs produced in other countries where society exerts stronger controls on the breeders. Unless those people who buy Neos in other countries become more educated as to what a Mastino really is, the Italian dogs will continue to maintain the supremacy they have as far as breed type and looks are concerned.

To experience the Mastino is to succumb to your emotions as you look at the dogs. Then you understand what words can't explain when attempting to define the essence of this living relic.

The Neapolitan Mastiff Club of Italy is SAMN (Società Amatori Mastino Napoletano), www.samn.it.

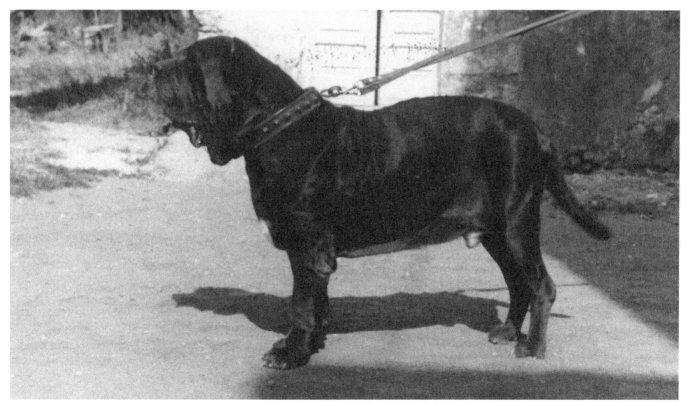

Oro della Nuova Futtoria. Breeder: Allocca. Photo: courtesy of G. Travers.

Minerva del Bonrampino, five-month-old female. Breeder and owner: G. Maja. Photo: G. Maja.

Andria del Bengasche, young female. Breeder: Uberto Gasche. Photo: G. De Nisi

Ch. Califf della Dea Partenopea, four-year-old male. Breeder: O. Le Méhauté. Owner: G. Oliviero. Photo: courtesy S. Freeman.

Gemma, 18-month-old female. Breeder and owner: U. Miranda. Photo: P. Morisco.

Ch. Gik when young; Luca and Antonio Sorbo (with cane) in background. Breeder and owner: Antonio Sorbo. Photo: courtesy G. Travers.

Neapolitan Mastiffs in France

The French Mastino fanciers have, in the past decade, worked with obvious care and love for the breed to produce some fine examples of Neapolitan Mastiffs. Perhaps because of their Mediterranean nature, they have the inborn feel for the essence of the Mastino. Their dogs retain the Mastino type while exhibiting a harmony of body that I attribute to the French flair for creating elegance and style. In addition, the French Mastino breeders have a rapport with their dogs as companions, not just objects for show. They give their dogs great care and love.

The Club du Mâtin Napoletain is made up of enthusiastic and creative Mastino lovers. The club news magazine is very well constructed, always containing wonderful photos. www.clubdumatindenaples.com.

Neapolitan Mastiffs in Germany

The Neapolitan Mastiffs in Germany reflect the emphasis placed on physical soundness and precision of physical construction. The German Mastino breeders have been compelled to produce only dogs with the proper physical structure of each separate body part. Hips must be rated for hip dysplasia on all breeding dogs. In Germany, there are five classifications of hip dysplasia: HD free, transitional HD, mild HD, middle HD, severe HD. A dog may be bred if it is rated according to one of the first three classifications. All the teeth must be present, and emphasis is placed on a scissors bite.

Ch. Cartouche des Arènes de César, six-year-old male. Breeder: M. Drahé. Owner: Didier Guilloux. Photo: S. Allen.

Bitches are only allowed to be bred between certain ages, and can be bred only once a year depending on the number of puppies in a litter for a certain number of litters. Certain club-imposed rules for the dogs and the breeding practices have resulted in the production in Germany of sound and healthy dogs that differ somewhat in type from the Italian Mastino.

Ch. Tazio di Ponzano, four-year-old son of Toscano and Boumpie di Ponzano. Breeder: M. Querci. Owner: G. Mira. Photo: S. Allen.

Frasier des Molosses d'Or, three-year-old male. Breeder and owner: Mme. Galiment. Photo: S. Allen.

Faustina de Néropolis, four-month-old female. Owner and breeder: J. Beck. Photo: J. Beck.

Erwood des Molosses de Lugdunum, four-year-old male. Breeders: M. Guilloux et Mme. Rouvarel. Owner: M. Descamps. Photo: S. Allen.

Fantos de San Basile, three-year-old male. Breeder: A. Aiello. Owner: M. et Mme. Sicre. Photo: S. Allen.

Fabrizzio des Mines du Roi, three-year-old male. Breeder: Mme. Salomon. Owner: Mme. Joëlle Pfaff. Photo: S. Allen.

Mme. Salomon and M. et Mme. Dardenne at the Club du Mâtin Napolitain National Show, September 5, 1993.

Dzarko de la Fouinerie, 19-month-old male. Breeder and owner: J.M. Dupuis. Photo: J.M. Dupuis.

Fabrizzio des Mines du Roi, six-month-old male. Breeder and owner: M. et Mme. Salomon. Photo: Salomon.

Ch. India di Ponzano, seven-year-old female. Breeder: M. Querci. Owners: M. et Mme. Dupuis. Photo: Dupuis.

Don Juan Lavarenne de Bois Dins, male. Breeder and owner: M. Tuel. Photo: Dupuis.

Ch. Désiderio de Néropolis, three-year-old male. Breeder and owner: J.P. Beck. Photo: Beck.

Ch. Dolli de Néropolis, three-year-old female. Breeder and owner: J.P. Beck. Photo: Beck.

Elio de la Fouinerie, nine-month-old male. Breeder and owner: M. et Mme. J.P. Dupuis. Photo: Dupuis.

Gringo de San Basile, two-year-old male and Albin Aiello. Breeder and owner: A. Aiello. Photo: Aiello.

Erius des Mines du Roi, two-month-old male. Breeder and owner: M. et Mme. Salomon. Photo: Salomon.

Deborah de la Fonte de Nimes. A six-year-old female bred by A. Aiello. Owner: E. Küttler. Photo: E. Schiano.

Christofer Habig with two of Ms. Denger's beautiful dogs, Rumina and Ragna di Colosseo Avallu. Mr. Habig is a renowned Molosser judge and former editor of the marvelous *Molosser Magazin*. This semi-annual international publication devoted to all the Molosser breeds was treasured by all Molosser dog enthusiasts until cessation of its publication in 1988.

Neptune de la Grande Vanousch. Breeder: C. Wingel. Owners: Klein and Weber. Photo: K. Zimmerman.

Agira di Palazzo, two-year-old female and K. Zimmerman. Breeder and owner: K. Zimmerman. Photo: R. Schmalzbauer.

The challenge of Mastino breeding is for the breeder to have the intuitive feeling of which dog to breed to which dog to create the Mediterranean impression of massive elegance. Massive and elegant are possibly contradicting ideas, but the Italians succeed in combining the two to make the Mastino. Massive body parts that may be individually measured as perfect will make a Mastiff. But a Mastino has a special look about it which stamps it as a Mastino. Many of the Italian Mastini do not have perfection of each individual body part, but as a whole, they have their own characteristic harmony.

Each country will stamp its societal characteristics on the Mastino. It appears that the German breeders have been constrained by over-regulation from a technically oriented bureaucracy. A good Mastino must exude romanticism. Sometimes perfection produces a product that is too sterile in appearance. A harmonious joining of perhaps incongruous parts can often result in the utterly unusual. Unusual, which is for some reason pleasing –that is the Mastino. One well-known, long-time German breeder, Liliana Denger, who understood that concept, has since moved from Germany to Italy in order to continue with her Mastino breeding program.

After a decade-long hiatus or slowdown of interest in breeding the Neapolitan Mastiff in Germany, the breed is once again becoming important and sought after. Today's breeders are eager to produce that "true" Mastino. Their job will be difficult, in view of the regulations with which they must comply. But where there is a will, there is a way,

Nathan v. Vagantenhof, three-year-old male. Breeder: W. Weisse. Owner: R. Stahlke. Photo: M. Rogen.

Ambrosius. Photo: K. Zimmerman.

Artos v. Sternbergzee. Photo: Schumacher.

Astarte von Epirus, five-year-old female. Owner: K. Zimmerman. Photo: R. Schmalzbauer.

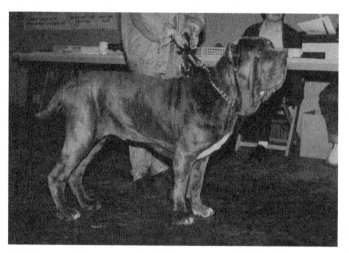

Kalif vom Vagantenhof. Breeder: W. Weisse. Owner: M. Frank. Photo: M. Rogen.

O'Lady van Worikben, female. Breeder: P. van Melis. Owner: K. Zimmerman. Photo: R. Schmalzbauer.

Jade v. Vagantanhof, six-year-old female. Breeder: W. Weisse. Owner: I. Christmann. Photo: M. Rogen.

V. Weinberg dog, name unknown. Photo: Schumacher.

O'Cora van Worikben, three-year-old female. Breeder: P. van Melis. Owner: Not identified. Photo: Zimmerman.

Antonio van Tanneneck, male. Breeder: U. Nowak. Owner: S. Fack. Photo: Zimmerman.

Amanda del Castello. Owner: D. and U. Süss. Photo: Süss.

Ciatone del Gheno. Breeder: A. Gheno Tessarolo. Owner: D. and U. Süss. Photo: Süss.

Don and Darius di Palazzo, 10-week-old puppies. Breeder: H.K. Zimmerman. Photo: Zimmerman.

Turco, young male. Owner: Gerlinde De Nisi. Photo: De Nisi.

Nathan v. Vagantenhof, two-year-old male. Breeder: W. Weisse. Owner: R. Stahlke. Photo: M. Rogen.

Above: **Brigante del Nolano. Breeder: M. De Falco. Owner: Dieter and Ursula Süss. Photo: Süss.**
Below: **Don Corleone van Bennato, two-year-old male. Breeder: Mme. Bleijenberg. Owner: A. Van Doremalen. Photo: S. Allen.**

Masaniello of the Thatch Roof, four-year-old male. Breeder: A. Van Doremalen. Owner: U. and D. Süss. Photo: M. Rogen.

and the German Mastino breeders are very determined to set a name for themselves and their dogs.

The website of the German Molosser Club, which encompasses the Mastino, is www.molosser-club-germany.de.

Neapolitan Mastiffs in Belgium and the Netherlands

In recent years, some serious Mastino breeders in Belgium and the Netherlands have begun to produce excellent quality dogs. Like the Germans, with whom they have a lot of reciprocity in the dog fancy, the breeders in these northern countries have made an effort in the past to create dogs with substance and soundness. By the introduction of some excellent Italian- and Spanish-bred dogs in recent times, these Dutch and Belgian breeders are striving for

Califf II della Dea Partenopea, two-year-old male. Breeder: O. Le Méhauté. Owner: M and Mme. Dardenne.

Natasja van Worikben, four-year-old female and Piet Van Melis. Breeder and owner: P. Van Melis. Photo: M. Rogen.

Ch. Lumeloris. Breeder: Pouwels. Owner: P. Van Melis. Photo: courtesy Van Melis.

Pacha, two-year-old male, son of Lumeloris. Breeder: A. Roggeman. Owner: M. Welscher. Photo: Welscher.

Xanthos of the Thatch Roof and a young dog from the Worikben kennel. Photo: Zimmerman.

Aida, four-year-old female. Breeder: Van der Hulst. Owner: M. Bloemendaal. Photo: M. Rogen.

O'Moon van Worikben, male. Breeder and owner: P. Van Melis. Photo: Zimmerman.

Intoccabile del Nolano, three-year-old male. Breeder: M. De Falco. Owner: A. Van Doremalen.
Photo: M. Rogen.

the all-around Mastino.

Americans and Germans alike are turning to some of the well-known Belgian and Dutch breeders for purchase of breeding stock. The breeders are reported to be very conscientious and fair in their business dealings. Some of their dogs are becoming well recognized in Mastino circles.

The website of the Mastino Napoletano Club Nederland is www.mncn.nl.

Neapolitan Mastiffs in Hungary

A relative newcomer to the Mastino world, Hungary is just opening up to show the rest of the world what it can produce. The breeding program of one Mastino breeder in Hungary whom I visited is very impressive indeed. They have blended some of the most beautiful Italian stock in a successful effort to breed quality Mastini. Like the country

Emir della Grotta Azzurra, two-year-old male. Breeder: G. Siano. Owners: A. and A. Spiriev. Photo: S. Allen.

Fruit d'Amour Dandolo, seven-week-old male. Breeder: Andrea Spiriev. Owner: S. Allen. Photo: A. Spiriev.

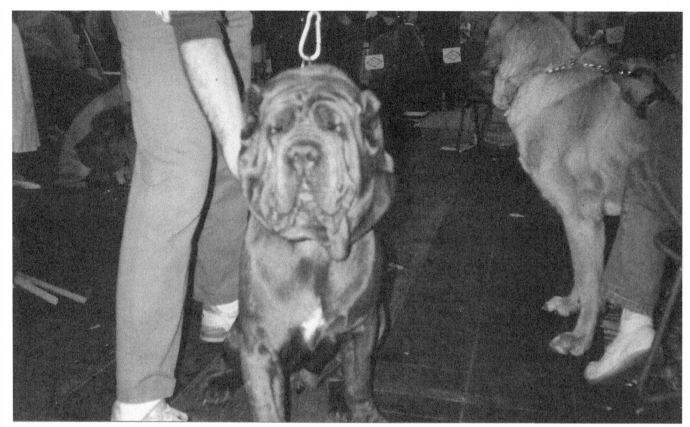

Fruit d'Amour Bellissima, one-and-a-half-year-old female. Breeder and owner: A. Spiriev. Photo: A. Spiriev.

Female puppy from Spain's Roy Fonte Kennel. Breeder: José M. Roy Anglada. Photo: J. M. Roy.

Fruit d'Amour Baronessa, one-and-a-half-year-old female. Breeder and owner: A. Spiriev. Photo: A. Spiriev.

Nero, three-year-old male, son of Perecles of the Thatch Roof. Owner: Bent Quist. Photo: Quist.

and the people themselves, the Hungarian Mastini have a fiery and spirited beauty.

Neapolitan Mastiffs in Spain

We in the United States do not often see Neapolitan Mastiffs from Spain, but there are some devoted breeders there who produce very excellent Mastini. It seems as though marketing their dogs is not important to the Spanish breeders. When you do find the breeders, you will find good dogs.

The Club Español de los Molosos de Arena: www.clubmolosos.com.

Neapolitan Mastiffs in the Scandanavian Countries

As my contact with Mastino owners in these countries has been limited, I don't have many photos of the dogs there. I do know that the popularity of the Neapolitan is increasing dramatically there as it is all over the rest of the world. Above is a photograph of a dog in Denmark that I know was born in July 1985, and is from one of the first Mastino litters to born in Denmark. As I mentioned previously, in the last decade interest in the Neapolitan Mastiff has burgeoned worldwide.

Ch. B and V's Tank, mature tawny male, U.S. Breeders and owners: Bob and Virginia Gagnon. Photo: Gagnon.

Neapolitan Mastiffs in the Western World

Italian-Americans will tell you the stories of the mastiff dogs their grandpa0rents brought to the United States in the 1950s and earlier. Even so, with such few dogs hidden away in Italian neighborhoods, it took until the 1970s for the breed to become an organized entity here.

In the United States, the American Kennel Club is the main all-breed registering body and central organization for the regulation of dog events. The AKC, however, recognizes only about 140 breeds of dogs. There are many more breeds of dogs in the world. Some other national kennel clubs, such as the United Kennel Club and the States Kennel Club, are also large dog-event-regulating organizations. They recognize that some of the breeds that the AKC does not recognize, but they do not recognize all the other breeds, and they do not recognize Neos. Any of these other breeds that are brought into the United States, therefore, have no recognized organization with which they can be registered.

(Editor's note: The American Kennel Club has since recognized the Neapolitan Mastiff, in 2004.)

On a global scale, most of the rest of the world's national kennel clubs are under the aegis of the FCI, or Fédération Cynologique Internationale. The FCI recognizes about 342 breeds of dogs. Some countries such as England, are not FCI associated, and have their own kennel clubs. In general, the FCI and the AKC offer reciprocal arrangements

Ch. Ironstone Evening, one-and-a-half-year-old black female, U.S. Breeder: S. Allen. Owner: C. Kemp. Photo: S. Allen.

Vanguard's Arielle, mature gray female, U.S. Breeder: G. Schaffer. Owner: K. Nixon. Photo: Nixon.

Cara Mia, 13-month-old female, U.S. Breeder: P. Bailey. Owner: D. and B. Welty. Photo: B. Welty.

Ch. Rasputin dell'Altafiumara, two-year-old black male, Italy. Breeder: A. Di Lorenzo. Owner: S. Allen. Photo: S. Allen.

Igri of Ironstone, three-year-old gray male, U.S. Breeder: S. Allen. Owner: G. Santos. Photo: Santos.

Vanguard's Masero, one-year-old gray male, U.S. Breeder and owner: G. Schaffer. Photo: S. Allen.

Julie di Alaric, three-year-old gray female, U.S. Breeder: M. Sottile. Owner: Max Soliman. Photo: S. Allen.

Ironstone Sophia, one-year-old gray female, U.S. Breeder: S. Allen. Owner: L. Valentine. Photo: L. Valentine.

Crisna della Dea Partenopea, one-and-a-half-year-old gray female, Italy. Breeder: O. Le Méhauté. Owner: Z. Najdovsky. Photo: S. Allen.

Carpe Diem Saba, eight-week-old female, U.S. Breeder: E. Schiavo. Owner: H. Arya. Photo: Schiavo.

Alaric's Legendary Santana, two-year-old black female, U.S. Breeder: M. Sottile. Owner: L. Sannino. Photo: S. Allen.

Vito di Prisco, one-year-old gray male, U.S.
Breeder and owner: N. Prisco. Photo: S. Allen.

Poseidon of the Thatch Roof, two-year-old
male, Belgium. Breeder: A. Van Doremalen.
Owner: C. Dedmon. Photo: S. Allen.

Torione, one-year-old gray male, U.S. Breeder and owner: J. Hospodar. Photo: Hospodar.

for registering and showing dogs bred in the United States, only if they are registered under the aegis of the FCI or the AKC. As a result, as more and more breeds of dogs that are not recognized by the AKC have been introduced into this country, more and more organizations have been created in order to accommodate the need for breed clubs and dog shows where these so-designated "rare" breeds can be shown.

In 1973, Jane and Carmine Pampalone and Michael Sottile established a Neapolitan Mastiff club in the United States and called it the Neapolitan Mastiff Club of America. It became a registering body for the Neapolitan in the United States, and the club organized several large rare-breed shows in the following years. Since then, as more people in the U.S. began to acquire and breed this dog, they organized more and more Neapolitan Mastiff breed clubs as well as all-around rare-breed dog clubs. In recent years, it has become common for each individual "rare" breed to be represented by not only one but several different American clubs.

One of the larger democratically run clubs for Neapolitan Mastiff fanciers is the USNMC, or United States Neapolitan Mastiff Club. This club was incorporated in 1991. It has its own computerized registry and holds several shows and specialties at other rare-breed shows each year. It is dedicated to preserving the Neapolitan Mastiff true to its Italian type as set forth in the Italian standard adopted by the FCI.

There was a Neapolitan Mastiff club in California that was called the USA-NMA.

Queenie di Prisco, two-year-old gray female, U.S. Breeder and owner: N. Prisco. Photo: S. Allen.

Carla, three-year-old gray female, U.S. Breeder and owner: B. Sell. Photo: S. Allen.

Stonehenge Alexandra, 10-month-old black female, U.S. Breeder: R. Evans. Owner: W. Groening. Photo: S. Allen.

Atena del Nolano, one-and-a-half-year-old black female, Italy. Breeder: M. De Falco Jovane. Owner: C. Kemp. Photo: S. Allen.

Ironstone Ebony Oxide, one-year-old black male, U.S. Breeder and owner: S. Allen. Photo: S. Allen.

BBK Bodacious Altobello, two-year-old tawny male, U.S. Breeder and owner: J. Aldret. Photo: Aldret.

Ironstone Hippolyta, two-year-old gray female, U.S. Breeder: S. Allen. Owner: M. Soliman. Photo: S. Allen.

Paloma de Aldan, one-and-a-half-year-old black female, U.S. Breeder: M. Soliman. Owner: J. Lemos. Photo: S. Allen.

Sameas, two-year-old black male, U.S. Breeder: C. Kemp. Owner: D. Ayitoro. Photo: Ayitoro.

Above: **Ch. Arturo El Maestro di Baritone, two-year-old black male, U.S. Breeder: J. Lemos. Owners: M & D. Estell. Photo: Harold.** *Below:* **Rea della Correzzana, one-and-a-half-year-old gray female, Italy. Breeder: G. Vandoni. Owner: L Mantes, Photo: S. Allen.**

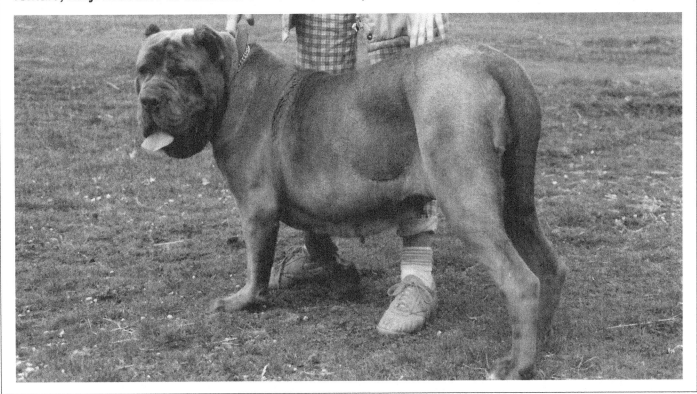

Ironstone Belinda, one-and-a-half-year-old black female, U.S. Breeder: S. Allen. Owner: S. Allen & G. Schaffer. Photo: S. Allen.

Wind Song's Winston, two-year-old gray male, U.S. Breeder and owner: R. and C. Tussing. Photo: Tussing.

Ironstone Machiavelli, five-month-old gray male, U.S. Breeder: S. Allen. Owner: J. Spilman. Photo: J. Spilman.

Carlotta del Gheno, three-year-old gray female, Italy. Breeder: Gheno Tessarolo. Owner: Dogstar Kennels. Photo: S. Bennett.

Ch. Argo del Nolano, one-year-old gray male, Italy. Breeder: M. de Falco Jovane. Owner: B. Yarnall. Photo: S. Allen.

Ironstone Islero, 10-month-old gray male, U.S. Breeder: S. Allen. Owner: H. Booker. Photo: S. Allen.

Marko, four-month-old black male, U.S. Breeder: C. Kemp. Owner: V. Marino.

Wind Song's Pitra, six-month-old gray female, U.S. Breeders: C. and R. Tussing. Owner: C. Johnson. Photo: Tussing.

Bear, one-year-old gray male, U.S. Breeder: M. Zinni. Owner: J. Clark. Photo: Clark.

Ironstone Atlas, one-year-old black male, U.S. Breeder: S. Allen. Owner: A. Rivera. Photo: S. Allen.

Ironstone Mikela, one-and-a-half-year-old gray female, U.S. Breeder: S. Allen. Owner: M. Connor. Photo: S. Allen.

Ironstone Palatia, two-year-old gray female, U.S. Breeder: S. Allen. Owner: P. Schreier. Photo: S. Allen.

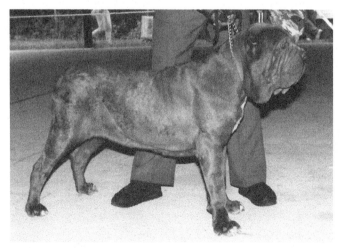

Ironstone Diva, nine-month-old gray female, U.S. Breeder: S. Allen. Owner: R. Evans. Photo: S. Allen.

Ironstone Aurora, one-year-old mahogany female, U.S. Breeder: S. Allen. Owner: J. Spilman. Photo: J. Spilman.

Di Nobilita Optimus Maximus, one-year-old gray male, U.S. Breeders: C. Austin and S. Allen. Owners: A. Bryant and J. Slack. Photo: S. Allen.

Aronne, one-and-a-half-year-old gray male, Italy. Breeder: M. Blam. Owner: S. Allen. Photo: S. Allen.

Eight-week-old gray male puppy, U.S. Breeder: J. Hospodar. Photo: J. Hospodar.

Ironstone Epimetheus, six-month-old black male, U.S. Breeder: S. Allen. Owner: C. Arts. Photo: S. Allen.

Carpe Diem Pan, nine-week-old tawny male, U.S. Breeder: E. Schiavo. Owner: M. Kass. Photo: S. Allen.

Hannibal di Alaric, two-year-old gray male, U.S. Breeder: M. Sottile. Owner: R. Monaco. Photo: S. Allen.

Cipriano, one-year-old male while still in Italy, now brought to the U.S. Breeder: R. Sconamiglio. Owner: G. Travers. Photo: De Nisi.

It has since been absorbed into an all-breed club and registry called the International All Breed Kennel Club of America (IABKCA). This organization has a registry and holds shows according to the German and FCI protocols.

An additional club and registry for Neapolitan Mastiffs is based in Texas. It is called the American Neapolitan Mastiff Association, or ANMA. This club also hosts shows and is dedicated to establishing their breed in the United States.

NMCA president for 20 years, Michael Sottile died in 1994. He is greatly missed. His son, Michael, has assumed leadership of the club.

Another all-breed organization that was

Ironstone Thor, one-year-old gray male, U.S. Breeder: S. Allen. Owner: C. Kemp. Photo: S. Allen.

created for the promotion of the "rare" breeds in the United States is ARBA, the American Rare Breed Association. It has been in existence since 1990, and already has made major inroads into conducting large-scale, prestigious shows all over the United States. ARBA has undertaken as one of its missions the education of the public and prospective judges on the various "rare" breeds such as the Neapolitan Mastiff.

ARBA has given much publicity to breeds heretofore unrecognized in the U.S., and has provided a needed cohesive force uniting American rare-breed dogs and dog owners.

Fortunately for the Mastino, enthusiastic interest in the breed sweeps across the U.S. The registration numbers are impressive: 10,000 registrations from one club; 200 litters from another; more than 2,000 in two other registries. Not impressive enough for the AKC, which still has not recognized the breed, despite the efforts of the USNMC.

Ironstone Rebecca, one-year-old black female, U.S. Breeder: S. Allen. Owner: S. Allen. Photo: S. Allen.

Development of the Breed in the United States

Since the beginning of the rise of popularity of the Neapolitan Mastiff in the 1970s, quite a few people have undertaken the challenge of breeding and raising Neos. A number of people have imported stock for potential breeding, and there are a few people who are well-informed brokers for others who are seeking dogs from Italy. Jane Pampalone was kind enough to give me some letters and correspondence between some of the early American Mastino fanciers in 1973

Ironstone Eros, one-and-a-half-year-old black male, U.S. Breeder: S. Allen. Owner: E. Schiavo. Photo: S. Allen.

Monaciello, two-year-old gray male, Italy. Owner: G. Travers. Photo: S. Allen.

Ironstone Diogenes, two-year-old gray male, U.S. Breeder: S. Allen. Owner: C. Costello. Photo: S. Allen.

Ironstone Rosa, two-year-old gray female, U.S. Breeder: S. Allen. Owner: R. Kaplan. Photo: K. Drager.

Sarena, 10-week-old female, Italy. Breeder: Scognamiglio Owner: A. Sullivan. Photo: S. Allen.

Ch. Brutus del Querceto, two-year-old gray male, U.S. Breeder: F. Maritote. Owner: M. Sottile. Photo: S. Allen.

Ironstone Attila, one-and-a-half-year-old gray male, U.S. Breeder: S. Allen. Owner: R. Evans. Photo: S. Allen.

BBK puppies, eight weeks old, all colors, U.S. Breeder and owner: J. Aldret. Photo: Aldret.

Turillo, one-and-a-half-year-old gray male, Italy. Breeder: Panico. Owner: G. Travers. Photo: S. Allen.

Fruit d'Amour Contessa, four-month-old female, Hungary. Breeder: A. Spiriev. Owner: S. Allen. Photo: S. Allen.

Vanguard's Alana, two-year-old gray female, U.S. Breeders: S. Allen and G. Schaffer. Owner: G. Schaffer. Photo: S. Allen.

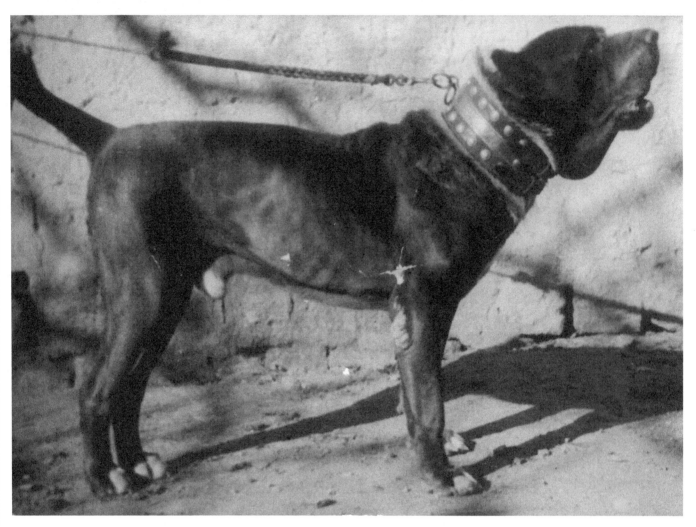

Neapolitan Mastiff in the 1950s. He is black. Note the white on the feet and penis sheath. Contrary to disseminated misinformation in the U.S., white markings have always been part of the Mastino heritage and were most likely more extensive in the earlier Molosser dogs. Those Mastiff dogs shown in paintings made during the Renaissance times had quite extensive white markings. As long as our present-day Mastini retain the primary genotype of their direct ancestors, the genes for white will always be present. Photo courtesy of Jane Pampalone.

and 1974. Interestingly, these letters between the Pampalones and John Di Prinzio allude to dogs imported at that time from Nicola Imbimbo and Paolo Testa. They were black Mastini and mahogany Mastini. These two colors then fell into obscurity in the ensuing 13 years. Only recently, as breeders have begun to seek out the more dominant traits that would tend to be found in dogs carrying other dominant genes recognizable by coat color, have these two dominant coat colors

again become popular.

Along with the rising interest in the breed in the United States, some people have begun to breed Neos in an attempt to make money. On the other hand, there are also dedicated individuals who have been trying for a number of years to make a contribution to Neapolitan Mastiffs in America by breeding quality dogs true to the Italian type.

The breeding of Neos is so time consuming,

frustrating and more often than not fraught with disappointment that only the hardy (or perhaps foolhardy) will stick with it. According to the AKC statistics, the average time span for a breeder to be involved with one breed of dog is five years. With Neos, this time span seems to be shorter. Those people hoping to make money by breeding will usually give up before five years. Those people hoping to make a contribution to the breed often give up around five years just because of burnout.

So far, there are a few individuals who have made a real difference to the development of the breed in America. There are currently a number of enthusiastic fanciers who are trying to breed excellent dogs. More and more Neapolitan Mastiffs are being shown at the rare-breed dog shows put on by ARBA, the USNMC, and other rare-breed and Neapolitan Mastiffs clubs. The future of the Mastino in America is ever promising.

To list the people and the dogs that have made an impact on the development of Neapolitan Mastiffs in the United States would be to leave out many. Many of the early promoters of the dogs are not active in the Neo organizations today. The people active today may not be so tomorrow. For lack of one main publicly accessible record-keeping organization, it is difficult to trace pedigrees and bloodlines of the Neapolitan Mastiffs prevalent in the U.S. today.

It is safe to say that the dogs in the United States today are descendants of dogs obtained from nearly all of the most renowned breeders in Italy. Those Americans

serious about breeding then went on to develop their own kennel names, which should appear on the progeny of dogs originating from a successful American breeding kennel. Because the easiest way to identify the origins of a dog is from the breeding kennel prefix or suffix on the dog's name, it is proper etiquette for all owners of purchased puppies to refer to their dog by its official name plus its kennel name when advertising or otherwise publicly acknowledging the dog.

Recently, several Americans have imported dogs from other European countries such as France, Germany, Holland, Belgium and Hungary. The dogs in these countries are usually direct descendants from the Italian dogs. Following the Italian pedigrees is sometimes impossible, since the Italian Mastino breeders prefer to keep accurate records of their dogs' lineage in their heads, rather than on paper.

Also, because of the leeway in naming dogs given by the several different registering bodies in the U.S., Italian dogs' names were often changed when they arrived here. Tracing an American dog's pedigree is therefore more often impossible than not. In this book, rather than attempting to trace the progeny of foundation lines, I prefer to show as many photos of dogs as possible to give an idea of what kennel names and dogs are prevalent in this country. Perhaps, in years to come, when the organization of Neapolitan Mastiffs becomes unified under a single publicly accessible entity, tracing foundation stock and progeny will be possible.

Neapolitan Mastiffs in South America

Dog enthusiasts in South America are physically and spiritually attuned to ownership of the Mastino. A dramatic surge of interest in the breed has occurred in all of the South American countries during past decade. Many of the South American fanciers have bought dogs from stock in the United States, since we are the closest large source of Mastini to them. At present, those fanciers seriously interested in the correct Mastino type are looking to improve their stock with dogs from current champion Italian lines.

Neapolitan Mastiffs in Mexico

Neapolitan Mastiffs thrive in Mexico. In spite of the heat, the altitude and dryness of Mexico City must somehow enhance reproduction in Neos. Litters are frequently reported to be quite large.

The Mexicans like a lot of flash and pizazz in their dogs as they gait around the ring. The qualities of flashy, swift movement and high spirit are found more frequently in the tighter-skinned, more muscular, but less massive dogs. In general, Neos in Mexico are of a more lean, muscular type, more reminiscent of some of the Italian Mastini

Ch. Brutus. Photo: courtesy E. Dada.

Ironstone Modigliani, nine-month-old mahogany male.
Breeder: S. Allen. Owner: E. Dada. Photo: E. Dada.

Above and below: **Four stud dogs from the La Montaña Kennel in Merida, Venezuela, 1988. Photos courtesy Pablo Celis.**

Above left: **Ch. Brutus. Photo: courtesy of Dada.** *Above right:* **Ch. Ivaan, three-year-old male. Breeder and owner: G. Zamudio. Photo: S. Allen.**

of the 1960s. In recent years, however, a demand has increased in Mexico for the more massive, wrinkled dogs as seen in Italy today.

The Mexican breeders are very aware of type in the Mastino, and a number of enthusiastic breeders have been avidly seeking the more typey Neos. In view of their energy and fascination with the breed, the Mexican breeders will soon be a major source of excellent Mastini.

Kaos, 14-month-old male. Breeders/owners: Rod and Sharri Jacobs. Photo: R. Jacobs.

Living with Neapolitan Mastiffs

In the United States today, people tend to want dogs more for companionship than for their working ability. Because of society and the increased crime rate, many people want dogs for personal protection also. The Neapolitan Mastiff provides all these functions in one – albeit humonous – package.

The Neapolitan Mastiff as a Companion

The Neo's world revolves around his owner. He forms an intensely strong attachment to his owner and his home. He is not a wanderer from the property because his reason for living is the property. He does not want to associate with strangers, and for this reason, transferring ownership of an adult dog is often very traumatic for him. He will not eat well for weeks or months because he misses his original owner so much. If you acquire an older dog, you may eventually get him to bond to you, but it is best to acquire a puppy if you want the dog for companionship.

As a quiet, steady, loyal companion, the Neo is second to none. He goes where his master goes, and when his master stops, he lies down at his feet until the master moves again. The Neo waits for his master to tell him what to do. His master is everything, and he would rather be with him than eat.

One caveat is that the Neapolitan Mastiff needs a master. The Neapolitan has by nature a dominant personality. If he does not learn his proper place in the family hierarchy early as a puppy, he will try to be the leader of the pack. To understand what a dominant Neapolitan Mastiff would be like in a family situation, you have to know a little bit about canine language. So here are a few quick lessons.

When a dominant pack leader establishes his territory, he does not want anyone else intruding in his spot. His language to say "stop" is by growling first, biting next, and then attacking if the lesser being persists in his approach. Any being is considered a lesser being to the pack leader. This means the baby crawling toward the rawhide chewy the dog is chewing on, or the child pulling on his dewlap when he is not in the mood, even though he would let him pull on it for hours at a time previously. A lesser being may even mean you trying to get into what you consider to be your bed while the Neo is sleeping on it.

Female Neos have never read Dr. Spock. They believe in corporal punishment with their children. A female Neo may mother your child just as she does her own puppies. But when she is trying to teach them manners such as not to eat until the adults have finished, or not to chew on her dewlap, she simply and swiftly snaps at them. Sometimes she does not make contact, and sometimes she does. Puppies quickly learn what makes their mother irate, and they sometimes lose their lives in the process. Neapolitan Mastiffs do not make good baby sitters for little children.

I had a female Neapolitan Mastiff that was very devoted to me. She had had several litters of puppies, and she was an excellent mother as far as Neapolitan Mastiffs go. She also was very good with my two young preschool children. One day, my one little boy figured out how to use a hand saw, and cut down a little tree I had just planted as a potential shade maker for the dogs.

When I saw the cut-down little tree, I became wildly furious. I picked up the cut-off top, which was the size of a switch and ran around the yard chasing my little son in an attempt to swat him with it. (I don't put much faith in Dr. Spock either.) My Neapolitan Mastiff saw this scene, and decided that I was trying to attack the lesser being, my child. If I was going to "kill" him, then she was going to kill him, and in a flash, she took off after him, hackles up and roaring. I immediately had to stop trying to catch my son, and grab the dog instead. After that incident, the dog never could be trusted with my children again. In her mind, if I, the pack leader, was attacking them, then they should not be around. If they tried to come near her, and she did not want to be bothered, she would snap at them. She was so devoted to me that she thought it was her duty to help me in my attempts to "bring them down" as she saw it.

Because the Neapolitan is by nature a dominant animal, it can only live in an American family situation if it is capable of being dominated by every member of the family. It is hard for a human baby to dominate a 150-pound adult dog. For this reason, a requirement for successful keeping of a Neapolitan Mastiff is a chew-proof place both inside and outside the house where you can put him when you cannot monitor him with people or children to whom he is not subservient. Some dogs, such as Beagles are subservient, make wonderful children's dogs because they are subservient to most anyone or anything except a rabbit. Neapolitans are very subservient as puppies. (If you had a mother like theirs, you would be, too.) But just as your sweet little child turns into that teenager who tests you at every opportunity because he or she thinks they are now vastly superior to you, so does the Neapolitan go through that stage. If you do not let him know that he is not the boss of the family, he will soon be bossing you.

I have a friend who had a male Neapolitan Mastiff that slept in the bedroom with her and her husband. Things went along fine until the dog became a mature male. He became very devoted to and protective of his mistress. One night the woman's husband woke up and wanted to play in bed. The jealous dog soon made it evident who was going to play with his mistress and who was not. The husband had no recourse but to escape into the bathroom. He could not come out until the wife was able to calm down the dog enough to put him into a kennel in the garage.

I do not recommend that Neos sleep in the bedroom. They snore too loudly anyway. A Neo's place to sleep is someplace he thinks

Ironstone Dinero, one-year-old male. Breeder: S. Allen. Owner: R. Evans. Photo: S. Allen.

is his own, where he can guard the property as is born in him to do. He must never be allowed to be put in a position to guard one family member from another. Remember, you cannot separate out of a Neo the companion dog from the working dog. He is always working while being your companion.

As a jogging companion, long-distance runner or tireless flying-disc catcher, the average Neapolitan Mastiff does not do well. We have said before, the proper Neapolitan is very heavy for his size, and therefore, he is not built for athletic endurance tests. Also, too much forced exercise while he is a puppy will destroy his joints and ligaments

and cause permanent structural damage to the growing dog. This is not to say that he cannot engage in athletic endeavors. He can, in moderation. In the winter, the Neapolitan becomes full of energy, and an adult can be harnessed to a sled and pull you or the kids around in the snow. In the summer, they can go swimming at a lake or the ocean. Many Neos love to swim, and it is a good form of exercise for them.

Another friend of mine, Mark Baldassare, has two Neapolitan Mastiffs whom he has trained to perform feats unbelievable for Neos. His three-year-old jumps over six-foot fences on command. He weight-pulls. He

Romolo della Nuova Fattoria, one-and-a-half-year-old male. Breeder: V. Allocca. Owner: S. Allen, then M. Zinni. Photo: J. Yarmush. This is the easy way to pull your children around in the snow.

pulls his owner around on a skateboard in the summer and a sled in the winter. He runs 20 miles a week. It is breathtaking to watch his dogs in action.

The dog is in wonderful shape, but there is only so much shock that the shock absorbers of the front end of 140 pounds coming down from over a six-foot-high fence can take. The heavy and constant exertion has taken a toll on the big dog. He is beginning to get some arthritis in his neck from an old neck fracture (but his hips are great – no arthritis there!). Neos will try to do anything you ask them to do for you. I simply believe that you should never ask them to do more than they are physically built for doing.

Like the dog I just mentioned, there are always exceptions to what I tell you Neos can or can't do. There are even some Neos that are not dominant dogs and that have never been seen by their owners to behave aggressively. But remember, I am telling you about the average Neapolitan Mastiff, because it is the average one that you will be most likely to come into contact with.

In formalized obedience work, Neos are adequate, but they do not work with the quick gusto of, say, a Sheltie or a German Shepherd. The Neo is a loner or leader rather than a follower. They do not get excited about following a person around heeling, sitting and staying on command. Also, they are very sensitive to punishment in spite of their enormous size, and they become sullen if jerked around by their collar. They react to being jerked around by the neck much in the same way as you would. Whereas many

breeds of dogs will freeze in submission when their neck area is threatened by someone grabbing it or by correction from a collar, Neos seem to react just the opposite. Somehow remembering their instincts for self-preservation when they were bred as fighting dogs, they react instinctively with rage to pressure or attack at their neck. A week-old Neo baby will snarl and open its mouth toward your fingers if you grab it around the neck. I have had eight- to 12-month-old puppies turn themselves inside out trying to attack a collar and leash put around their neck when it was first put on them. I have seen Neos totally flip out with a pinch collar. I recommend a chain choke collar for a Neo because you need the control. Stay away from a pinch collar. Pinch collars only agitate Neos more.

Playing with a Neapolitan Mastiff must be done in a very controlled way. Play behavior in dogs is a subdued modification of the actions that the dog's instincts drive it to do in order to catch food, eat, protect itself and reproduce. Neapolitans are easily excited by the chase and the pouncing on and finishing off prey. Play behavior can also too easily become the real thing with these dogs, who were made by man 3,000 years ago to fight gladiators, bears, lions and even elephants. Neos play very roughly, and human skin is very soft and easily penetrable. For these reasons, I never allow a Neapolitan, even when it is a puppy, to be on top of a person. They are never allowed to chew on fingers as puppies, and you must never play "sic 'em!" games with them. Wrestling, as people are so wont to do with other breeds of dogs, is never allowed. When that animal attains

150 or 175 pounds and has pinned you or a child to the ground wrestling with it, you will know the meaning of panic.

I had a male Neo that I made the mistake of training to Schutzhund. At one of the training classes, we started teaching the dogs in the class to jump. After the dog jumped the jump, we were supposed to exuberantly praise the dog, which I did. The dog got very excited with my praising, just as he had been accustomed to do when I would praise him for latching onto the sleeve of the Schutzhund agitator. Only this time, the only person for him to latch onto in his excitement was me. All I can say is that it is good it was wintertime and I had on a coat, and that I could react quickly enough to yell at him to stop it. When he realized that I was not happy, he stopped. My point is, when a Neapolitan Mastiff is aroused to intense excitement, whatever the situation, his primitive instincts can take over. The release for a dog's pent-up energy is biting, grabbing, shaking, tugging and gnawing. If a dog has been encouraged from puppyhood on to grab and tug (as in tug-of-war games), he will instinctively do those things when he is aroused.

The gentlest dog I have is one of those exceptions to all I have said. He is an eight-year-old male by the name of Islero del Bonrampino. When my children start running around the yard screaming and yelling, and riding bikes that clatter on the

Lalla dell'Altafiumara, one-and-a-half-year-old female bred by A. Di Lorenzo, and Romolo della Nuova Fattoria. Owner: S. Allen. Photo: S. Allen.

Antonio o'Milanese di Samarcanda, one-and-a-half-year-old male. Breeder: L. Samamé. Owner: S. Allen. Photo: S. Allen.

macadam, or bouncing a ball, the Neos all become very excited. Any that are loose want to join in the play. Their idea of play happens to be to chase and try to grab the ball, the bike and the kids. Can you guess how long it takes a Neo to totally destroy a first-rate basketball? Islero, on the other hand, runs over and grabs a plastic detergent bottle and starts barking at it and ripping it to shreds. Islero is the kind of Mastino you can have around children, so, as I said, there are some Neos that are the exception to the rules.

This behavior I described is normal for working dogs that were bred as fighters, hunters and protectors. The behaviors are necessary for the dog's survival as well as for him to be good at his job. They are behaviors that most civilized people are not familiar with, and will not understand if they happen. My recommendation is that only those people familiar with powerful, dominant dogs should acquire them as companions.

The Neapolitan Mastiff as a Working Dog

"Working" for the Neapolitan Mastiff is defined as protecting his master and his property. His massive build and gargoyle-like head are meant to scare away intruders. He doesn't even have to move to scare them away. Neos really do not do a lot of moving anyway, especially in the summertime; but when they do move, they are surprisingly quick. Part of the reason they are able to move so quickly in spite of their heavy size is because they are not excessively tall. The English Mastiff is taller than the Neapolitan. The Neapolitan's maximum height is 31 inches, and the English Mastiff's minimum height is 30 inches. If the Neapolitan were as large as the English Mastiff, it would be slower moving because of the greater weight and body size.

Neos are very good in police work for crowd control. They also have good noses and can track very well. Actually, it is interesting to me to see the number of traits Neapolitan Mastiffs and Bloodhounds have in common. Bloodhounds also have a lot of loose skin that hangs in wrinkles all over their face. They have a marked dewlap, and they have a strong musky odor about them, which some people complain of also in Neos. The Neapolitan Mastiff's best-developed sense seems to be its olfactory sense, and they are always sniffing the ground. One reason it is difficult to show Neos in the show ring is they pull their heads to the ground constantly, more preoccupied with sniffing than with observing their owner or gaiting around the ring. Some of the more narrow-headed, more excessively wrinkled Neos even have the same noble and tragic expression of the Bloodhound.

As an historical aside, it is interesting to speculate whether these similarities are a result of the Bloodhound's ancestry being an expression of the ancient mastiff dogs from which they were derived, or whether some

crossing of these breeds occurred in ancient times.

The Bloodhound descends from the St. Hubert Hound, developed by the St. Hubert monks in Belgium. These hounds were more wrinkled and heavy boned, with longer lips and dewlaps than today's Bloodhound. Also, the St. Hubert Hound descended from heavy black Scenthounds used by the Celts during the times of the Romans, but in the regions of what is now France. Since the main groups of dogs at that time 2,000 years ago were the mastiff hunting dogs and the sighthounds, it is logical to believe that the ancestors of the Neapolitan Mastiff and the St. Hubert Hounds were closely related. Now, 2,000 years later, these two totally different breeds retain so many of the same physical characteristics. It would appear that the Bloodhound retains its Mastiff heritage more than the other Scenthounds in today's world, and that the Neapolitan Mastiff retains the original traits of the ancient mastiff dogs more than the other breeds of mastiffs of today.

This diversion was to shed a little more light on why the Neo still behaves more primitively than other modern breeds of dogs. I believe it remains closer in type to its original ancestors. Also, it explains why the Neo, a guard dog, has such a good nose and does so well in tracking exercises. Because of its excellent nose, another potential job for Neos in today's world is for search and rescue if the climate is not too hot, since they do fatigue easily in the heat. Also, certain of the higher-spirited, more active Neos would be good as drug-sniffing dogs.

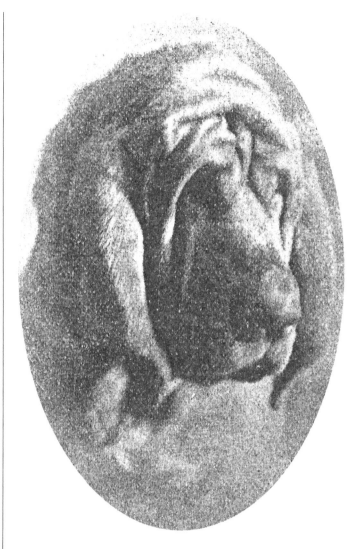

over their own feet as they run around with lips and excess skin flapping in the breeze will make you want to take one home instantly. But I say, Stop! You are not buying a cute, wrinkly, clumsy, cuddly puppy. You are buying a 150-pound slobbering companion who will expect you to clean up after him for at least the next eight years. For better or for worse, for richer and for poorer, in sickness and in health. They will eat more than you do per day, and dog food is not cheap. They drink a lot of water, an extraordinary amount of water, and invariably afterward, they need to lay their

These two photos, taken from H.A. Graaf van Bylandt's *Hondenrassen*, show the Bloodhound (St. Hubert Hound) as it was in the late 1800s and early 1900s. The wrinkling and expression are very similar to some of the longer-muzzled Neapolitan Mastiffs of today.

Above all else, the Neo's best "work" entails being there for his master, whenever he wants, and for whatever he wants. All you have to do is touch him on his big head now and again, and he will be faithful to you forever.

Acquiring a Neapolitan Mastiff

If you have read this book up to this point, you should now have a good idea of what a Neapolitan Mastiff is. Then when you find someone who has puppies for sale, and you see them for real, you will fall instantly in love. Those fat little wrinkly things tripping

Ch. Ironstone Attila, six-month-old male. Breeder: S. Allen. Owner: R. Evans. Photo: R. Evans.

Pia, one-year-old female. Breeders: M. Bardsley and L. Johnson.

soaking chin and dewlap on your lap. What goes in, must come out, but with puppies you will swear that more comes out than goes in. Remember, however, that constantly bending over, paper towels in hand, is good for the waistline, and you can't go wrong buying stock in paper products.

If you saw the movie *Turner and Hooch*, and the slobbering of another large mastiff type, the Dogue de Bordeaux, it was not an exaggeration. The only consolation is that Neo slobber flakes off the walls and ceiling easily when it dries. It is hard to get off cars, however, if you thought you could keep the dog in the garage. Also, I remember one friend who tried to keep his Neo in the garage, and came back home to find what he thought had been a bomb explosion. A rule to remember is this: Neos and antiques do not co-exist in the same house. If you try to break this rule, you will find your antiques modified with so many distress marks they may be unrecognizable.

Neo puppies grow at such a fast rate that they need to drink a lot of water to maintain their hydration. Consequently, they seem to urinate every time you turn around. When you are trying to housebreak them, and you see them squatting on the floor, your instinct is to run over, scoop them in your arms, and quickly carry them outside. To pick up a Neo puppy is to become a weight lifter, for the babies will weigh 25 pounds at two months of age and 50 pounds at three months. They cannot hold their urine well at all until they are four months of age, and by then you had better be Mr. Atlas.

They can't do flights of stairs because they are too clumsy and they fall all the time. This then leads to damaged hips, elbows and shoulders. So you can't get a Neo puppy if you live in a walk-up apartment. If you have a nice yard to let the Neo run in, it won't have trees or plants in it for long. It will have nice holes in it, sort of like World War II foxholes. Remember, what you think is just an adorable puppy is a baby lumberjack in disguise.

After listening to all this, you then say, "Well, I live in a one-floor rancher in the desert. I won a five-year supply of dog food in a lottery. The home is decorated in 1950s-style molded steel and vinyl furniture, and the floors are linoleum. I'm all set for a Neapolitan Mastiff."

I reply, "Then what do you want, a show dog or just a pet, male or female?"

"What are the differences?" you ask. "And how would I know?"

No one can really tell what an eight-week-old puppy will become at three years of age when it is mature. The closest idea you will be able to get on what it will become is to look at the parents. One thing I have learned from breeding Neos is how absolutely predictable genetics are. Everything is hereditary: body type, head type, size, temperament, personality, intelligence – everything. Assets as well as defects will be passed on. It is important that you look at the parents, and ask questions about the parents. If you live far away from the breeder from whom you want to buy a puppy, then ask for photos

Ironstone Thalia and Ironstone Agamemnon, six weeks old. Photo: S. Allen.

They look adorable, don't they? The owner of these innocent-looking little puppies has (had) a magnificent house in the Capitol district of Washington, D.C. The puppies just did not think antique furnishings, mahogany stair railings and wainscoting belonged in the house. So they removed them all. Jove and Max Jr. Owners: John Slack and Anita Bryant. Photo: A. Bryant.

Fido Bravo Belli van Hadimassa. Breeder and owner: Martens. Photo: Schumacher.

of the parents, not the puppy. All seven- to eight-week puppies are cute. Neither you nor an experienced breeder will be able to tell from looking at a seven-week-old puppy what it is going to develop into. But a breeder who knows his or her stock can tell pretty well what a puppy from two particular parents will look like – not from the appearance of the puppy, but from that of the parents.

You must ask the breeders questions about

the parents, pertaining to body type, temperament, assets and faults. As I have said before, Mastinos are very difficult to breed. To get a good puppy is harder than it is to get a poor-quality one. The better quality ones, or those closer to show type with all the attributes mentioned in the standard, will be more expensive than those poorer in type or with some defect that makes them unfit for the show ring. The breeder should be willing to try to work with you and your pocketbook. But do not expect to get a show dog for the price of a pet dog. And do not try to buy a pet dog because that is the price you want to pay, and then expect it to be a perfect specimen. The breeder should tell you about the faults or problems with the puppy, and let you decide if that is what you want for the money you have to spend.

Another realization you must have when purchasing a dog is that it is not an inanimate object that comes with a lifetime guarantee. I have said that I believe everything that makes up a living organism is genetic. However, the expression of certain traits or defects is definitely affected by the environment and the stresses imposed on that living organism. A breeder can never tell you exactly which genes were inherited from which parent, and what they in combination can do. A breeder can only sell you a dog that is healthy and sound at the time you get it. If the puppy has been properly inoculated, dewormed, nourished and socialized, and if the puppy has no apparent problems and comes from healthy stock, then the breeder is acting in good faith.

Some breeders stipulate that you must take your new puppy to a veterinarian within a certain period of time post-purchase, and get it certified as healthy by your own veterinarian. This protects both the buyer and the seller. The buyer is assured by an unbiased professional that he is getting an apparently healthy dog, and the seller can be assured that the buyer does not just keep the dog for a period of time, perhaps unknowingly or knowingly mistreat it, and then try to blame a problem with the puppy as a hereditary defect or illness.

In today's litigious society, where the American consumer expects guarantees on everything purchased, selling a puppy can sometimes be fraught with more problems than it is worth. As a purchaser, you must specify to the seller exactly what you want, and the seller must tell you exactly what you are getting, to the best of both your knowledge. You should also put any stipulations or guarantees in writing, and then assume the responsibility for an animal and breed about which you should be well informed before your purchase. Just as you do not know when you are going to get the flu, or a heart attack, or a cataract or breast cancer – hopefully you will never get any of these – neither does the Mastino breeder know when your puppy is going to get these things, if ever. The breeder cannot be responsible for the dog forever. You have to accept the risk in purchasing a living thing that the possibility for misfortune exists. By the same token, you have to be satisfied that what you are getting from the start is as

A batch of eight-week-old puppies. Which one will you choose? Photo: S. Allen.

Six-week-old puppies. Which one do you think will grow up to be the best? Photo: S. Allen.

healthy a dog as can be had from the breed in its current state of development.

Many conscientious breeders will stand behind their stock to the degree to which they represent it. They feel that as part of protecting their reputation, they will stand behind a dog that they represent as a certain type. You should get such a "guarantee" in writing.

If you want to purchase an excellent quality puppy, one that will possibly develop into a show dog, you should ask the breeder why he/she thinks this particular puppy will develop into an excellent dog. Conversely, if you want only a pet dog, and you do not care that it has certain faults, ask the breeder to explain to you why the dog is not a show-dog prospect. Two things you yourself can tell about a puppy are personality and physical appearance, which is aesthetically pleasing or not pleasing to you.

If the breeder brings in two eight-week-old puppies, and one has legs and paws that look too big for its body, which is draped by loose skin hanging in folds all over its head and neck and elbows; and the other puppy is wiry, and has thinner legs, and tight skin and a not-so-smushed-in muzzle, then you can be sure that the first puppy is closer in appearance to a show specimen than the second one.

Personality is easy to tell in Neos: They are either friendly and unafraid as puppies, or they are scared and shy. Those that run up to you, tail wagging, and jump on you or start chewing on your shoe laces or skirt

are outgoing and unafraid. Those that take one look at you and run to the back of the cage, cringing, urinating and sometimes defecating, are problems. In my experience, it is these latter type Neo puppies that grow up to be so wary of people that they become fear biters. Strangely enough, you can get such a dog to be faithful and unafraid of you, and you will be able to handle it fine. But no one else will ever be able to go near it, and that means the veterinarian, whom you will want to be able to handle it when and if it needs medical attention. Many overly inbred or irresponsibly bred Neos have this personality trait. I believe it can be such a problem that most dogs with this fear-biting attitude should be put down. If you are the type who believes you can "tame the feral beast," then it is your responsibility to keep it from hurting anyone. Such a Neo should be neutered. It should never be bred.

Ironstone Amanda, six weeks old. Photo: S. Allen.

The decision of whether to get a male or female is usually decided by the purpose for which you intend to use the dog. There is no question that in general, the males grow up to be more impressive-looking than the females. They are larger, and their heads become much more massive and important-looking than the heads of females. However, as I stated before, a healthy, sound male Neapolitan Mastiff can only be owned by a dominant person who can teach it its place in society.

Neapolitans are puppies until they are one and a half years old. They retain their puppy personality until then. Before this age, both males and females are usually friendly, submissive, obedient and easily manageable. After puberty kicks in, and the hormones take over at one and a half years, the male Neo becomes very protective of his property and very dominant with other animals and people. The male Neo wants to be king of his jungle, and he wants to rule. If you can handle and control this temperament on a better than 150-pound dog, and you want to show the dog in dog shows, and the dog is the quality for breeding, then you need an intact male. For other than these reasons, there is no reason for a person in a family situation to maintain an intact male.

I have devoted many pages to describing the innate nature of the Neapolitan Mastiff, and I will repeat it again here. With a few exceptions, an adult male Neo is a powerful, aggressive animal, with a strength and dominant personality the likes of which most people in today's Western civilization cannot imagine.

This seven-week-old puppy has oversized legs and paws and much loose skin, promising correct breed type. Photo: S. Allen.

If you want a male Neo for a pet and companion, then neuter him. I realize men cringe at the thought, but, believe me, the dog and the family will be better off for it. Yes, it will affect the dog's looks. No, the head of a neutered male will not develop to be as big and wrinkled as the head of an intact male. Yes, he will grow taller and lankier than the muscular, intact male so developed because of his male steroids. But a good-looking puppy from good-looking stock will still be good looking. And more importantly, you will be able to keep him until he attains old age, instead of coming back desperate that you have to get rid of him.

Females make excellent companions and guard dogs. They do not get as large as the males in general, but I have some 165-pound

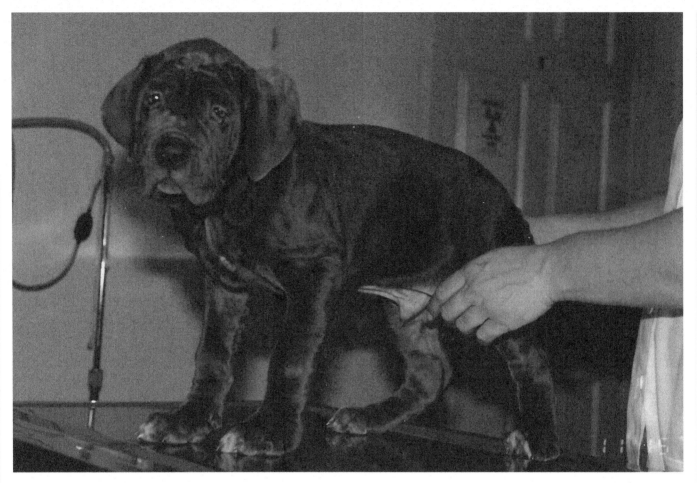

Ten-week-old puppy with thinner legs, tight skin and a longer muzzle – a less-promising show prospect. Photo: S. Allen.

females that are larger than the males. They can also be very beautiful, and in the past year, I have seen more females winning Best of Breed at shows all over the world than males. After one and a half years of age, they naturally also become excellent guard dogs, but they usually are more apt to remain subservient to the rest of the family – subservient being defined as controllable.

When housed with a male Neo, the female Neo, (like female humans) usually becomes quite the boss. It is sometimes comical to watch a female Neo figuratively "tear a male to pieces" while the poor big hunk just takes it. As I have said, a male Neo can be controlled by those who are more aggressive than he is. You just have to jump all over him, snarl viciously, and bite hard! One of the best methods I have found for putting a young teenage male who is feeling his oats in his place is to house him with an older, experienced female. He very quickly learns some manners. This newly found etiquette usually transfers over in his dealings with humans.

How do you find the Neapolitan Mastiff you are searching for? There are actually quite a few sources. Word of mouth from other people you know who have Neapolitans is a good start.

Dog-fancier magazines have listings and advertisements of breeders. The breed clubs can usually refer you to members who have litters of puppies or people who know of individuals who import dogs from Italy or other countries. In any case, you must personally speak with the person you have found to help you, make it clear to him or her what quality of dog that you want, then listen to the advantages and disadvantages of buying a dog in this country versus importing one from another country.

Feeding

Every breeder of Neapolitan Mastiffs and every book on Mastiffs that you read will

differ on what to feed the dogs. The goal in feeding giant-breed dogs is to allow them to grow to their maximum genetic potential without making them grow too heavy too fast. This is tricky, since every dog is an individual and has different nutritional requirements, if only slightly different. There are several metabolic bone diseases that are prevalent in giant-breed dogs. The predisposition to these conditions in the dogs is genetic. How much effect diet and other environmental factors have on the clinical expression of these orthopedic conditions is questionable, but many studies have proven that oversupplementation and overfeeding of a puppy during its growing stages does cause these orthopedic problems to be expressed. Some of these conditions are

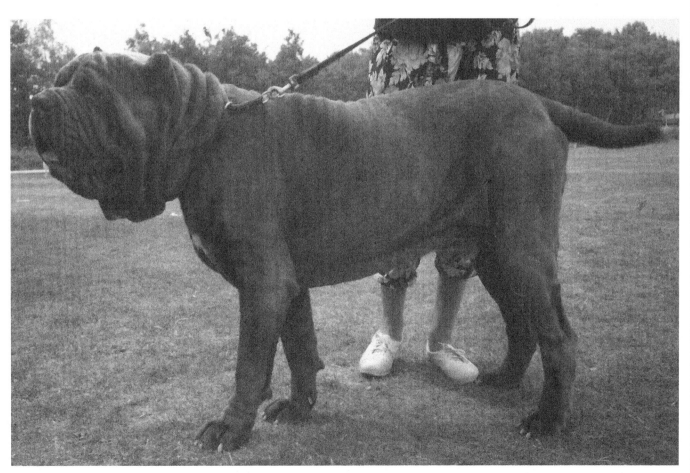

Corleone de Can Rayo, male. Owner: P. Van Melis. Photo: Zimmerman.

accelerated by overzealous feeding, which may force the dog to carry around too much weight at too early an age when its joints and bones are still rather fragile. Such conditions include osteochondrosis dissecans of all the joints, hypertrophic osteodystrophy, hip dysplasia and elbow dysplasia.

A puppy that is forced to become too fat too early will also go down in its front pasterns. The damage caused to the growth plates in the bones in the carpus (wrist) will cause the front feet to turn outward too much because of changes in how the damaged bone grows. Neapolitans have lax connective tissue all over their bodies. This is why their skin is so loose and lies in so many wrinkles and folds. This laxity also accounts for inherently loose joints and stretchy ligaments. The Neapolitan puppy is, therefore, not held together very well until after it begins to mature at a year of age. By then, it finally has developed enough muscle to carry its heavy, loosely connected bones in a more stable manner. At this time the ligaments and tendons seem to strengthen and grow tighter.

This development is analogous to that of the child who is double jointed. When young, he can bend over and touch elbows to the ground, or put his foot behind his head, or do the splits. Then by age 35 or so, those tendons have tightened up, and he is lucky if he can even touch fingers to the floor when he bends over.

This loose-jointed, overly heavy puppy can also hurt himself in roughhousing with other dogs or people. If he turns and twists too abruptly, he can rupture cruciate ligaments in the stifle joint (knee). Excessive feeding at an early age can contribute to an increased chance of him injuring his joints. The goal in feeding is to feed the right amount of protein, carbohydrates, fat, vitamins and minerals, but to not let the puppy get too fat or too large too fast.

Of course, everyone wants their mastiff to be the "biggest" and the best. Neo owners tend to want to feed a lot so that their dog will grow big. The dog's final size does depend on it getting the proper nutrition, but as long as it is not starved, it should reach the size and height for which it has been genetically programmed. If the genes for massiveness and height are not there, all the feeding you can do will not make it grow big. It is important not to confuse substance and heavy bone structure with obesity. The Neo's massiveness comes from huge, thick bone and body structure that is covered by heavy muscle and thick, abundant skin. A light-boned, thin-skinned, wrinkle-less Neo can be made to look bulky and fat with overfeeding, but that is not the physical type that we are looking for in the Mastino.

Knowing how the Neo matures then enables us to feed it in a rational manner. We have to keep in mind that it takes a human being about 20 years to grow from a seven-pound baby to a 165-pound adult. A Neapolitan Mastiff goes from two pounds to 165 pounds in two years. Some dogs weigh 90 pounds at five months of age, and you are desperately trying not to feed them so they don't grow too fast. That is a lot of weight for a little baby to carry around.

Fruit d'Amour Baronessa, one-year-old female. Breeder and owner: A. Spiriev. Photo: A. Spiriev. You couldn't ask for a better head, no matter what the sex.

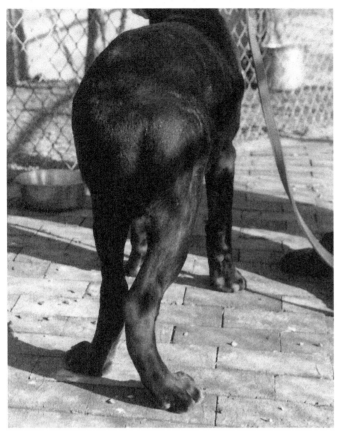

Hind-leg stance typical of a dog with osteochondrosis of the stifle joint. The damage is to the cartilage in the knees, so the bone grows in such a way as to make the dog cow hocked. (The hocks knock together and the back feet turn out laterally.) Photo: S. Allen.

The plan is, then, to feed the puppy the proper amount of vitamins, minerals and protein for proper bone and muscle development, and give it enough calories in the form of carbohydrates and fat so that it will grow. The question is, what foods will provide these requirements the best?

Nowadays, in the United States, there are a myriad of dog foods available that are made supposedly complete and balanced for any stage of the dog's life or health condition that you want. These complete foods come in cans or in dry extruded or pelletized form. The dry extruded foods are usually the

cheapest, so these forms of food are the most convenient and economical for owners of giant-breed dogs.

Suffice it to say that over the past 10 years I have experimented with practically all of the name-brand premium dog foods. I have supplemented the dry foods with canned meats of all varieties, or with fresh cooked meats. I have tried, on the other hand, only non-processed foods, buying food fit for human consumption and cooking it all to make a stew. I have tried using a lot of vitamin supplements versus only a little supplements or none. I have observed other dogs from other kennels in the US. that were on particular feeding programs, to see if their dogs turned out differently from mine. I have placed sibling dogs with the same genetic backgrounds in different kennels

Female Neapolitan Mastiff that is not fat; the backbone is even evident. She is massive in her bone structure (look at the front legs) and in the amount of heavy muscle and skin that she has. Minerva, female. Photo: Schumacher.

in the U.S. and in Italy to see if different feeding programs made any difference in the development of the dogs and an increased or decreased incidence of orthopedic problems. I have come to a number of conclusions – all anecdotal, since no truly accurate experiments were carried out. I will state what I have observed for what it is worth.

The Neapolitan Mastiff in Italy looks as it does because of its genetic makeup, the food and exercise it receives, and the climate that influences it. The same genetic stock brought to the United States grows slightly differently than it does in Italy, and these differences are accentuated even more according to the different regions and climates in the U.S. in which they grow up.

The dogs in Italy are stockier, have more massive bone, and have heavier, thicker skin in general than the dogs in the United States. By comparison, littermates of dogs in Italy that have been brought to the U.S. are in general taller, lighter boned, with tighter skin. Dogs of the same genetic stock which are sent to the southern United States grow by comparison even taller, but with much less weight and subsequently thinner, tighter skin. The reason I attribute to these differences are as follows:

The skin becomes thicker and heavier according to the fat intake of the dog. Those dogs that are allowed to get heavy as puppies, but are kept tightly penned up so that they get very little exercise, tend to be stockier

Thin, light-boned, non-typey Neapolitan Mastiff that is carrying a lot of body fat to make it look larger.

Ironstone Authority, four-month-old male. Breeder: S. Allen. Owner: C. Kemp. Photo: S. Allen.

and develop thick bones to support their heavy weight. Because they get practically no exercise, they do not do damage to themselves as they are growing.

Those dogs that live in dry climates, even though the summers may be hot, eat more than Neos that live in hot, humid climates. Neos do not eat in hot, humid weather. They drink a lot, but they do not eat. Those dogs that are fed less fat and are allowed a lot of exercise grow taller and leaner and tighter muscled than the Italian ideal Mastino. The result of all these different environmental factors is that we end up with dogs of the same genetic makeup all looking different from one another.

Their ultimate orthopedic soundness is also

affected by their environment. Neapolitan Mastiffs in Italy are for the most part kept in very small enclosures or courtyards. They get very little exercise in comparison to American standards. They are fed raw or parboiled chickens and meat scraps – bones, organ meat and all. These raw meats contain a lot of fat, and the bones are calcium and other minerals. The organ meats not only have high amounts of fat-soluble vitamins, but also hormones such as thyroid and adrenal and even the sex steroids. Because the meat is raw or parboiled, all these vitamins are not destroyed, and are in a more natural and possibly metabolically usable form for the dog. The dogs are also fed a lot of bread and pasta, i.e. a lot of carbohydrates, which are plentiful in Italy and form the staple of the people's diet as well.

Since the mastiff dogs in Italy were raised on this diet for thousands of years, it is the diet that has most contributed to creating their breed type, or otherwise stated, "you are what you eat." Now the dogs are transferred over to a different culture. The genetics are the same, but the food is not. Our diet-conscious society wants lean, athletic dogs. In an effort to make a food that will help create this body type, dog-food manufacturers have created for the most part foods high in protein, low in carbohydrates and lower in fat. These premium extruded dry foods are just the opposite of what the Neo requires – i.e., high carbohydrate and fat, and a lot of minerals (bones) with comparatively less protein.

The commercially produced dry foods are little brown balls or cubes that we really don't know the makeup of. The bag containing the pressed food lists all the ingredients that are supposed to be in these brown cubes, but how do we really know what is in them? We do not know the state of the scrap animal that was used as the source of poultry or meat meal before it was ground up and cooked to death and compressed into balls with added vitamins and minerals to replace all those that were lost in the cooking process.

We do not know the state of the grains and forage products that were put into the recipe – i.e., the fungal, pesticidal and preservative contents. The foods are supposed to be properly balanced, but as I said before, balanced for the average American lean and active sporting dog. Besides, dog-food companies usually use

Beagles or hounds for their feeding trials, since these breeds are good laboratory dogs. There have been no studies, to my knowledge, of whether a Mastino can get the proper amount of vitamins and minerals it requires in a quantity of dry food that it can safely eat without bloating. Dry extruded dog foods consist of a lot of grains that are roughage, and not totally digestible by dogs. Consequently, Neos on dry food have voluminous stools.

The bags of dry food are easy for us busy Americans, so it is inevitable that we use them. As I said, I use the dry food to one degree or another, and this is what I have remarked at my kennel: Neos on a dry food diet grow to be lean and muscular. They also grow taller and have less wrinkled skin than their littermates that I send back to Italy.

The Neos at my kennel also get a lot of exercise. They have large areas to run in, and because of the constant commotion associated with my place and business, they are in constant motion. I keep them separate from each other while they are growing up, so they do not hurt each other in their wild melees. Consequently, my lean, muscular Neos also grow up to be quite sound. The problem is, they do not look like the massive, weighty statue of antiquity that is desirable. After all my experimenting with a dry foods, I ended up preferring a dry-food brand that had the highest fat content coupled with the highest carbohydrate content that I could find, and with a protein content of not more than 27 percent. I give this to the puppies from weaning time at four weeks right on through to one year of age. I feed the puppies three times a day up to 10 weeks of age, and then cut back to twice daily for the rest of their lives. Feeding the dry food keeps the puppies from getting too fat while they are young, and since they are lean, they do not have too many orthopedic problems during their growth.

If I feel the puppy is not eating enough, or is too thin, then I will add other foods to the dry food. It may be canned meats, leftover table scraps, or frozen beef or chicken obtained from the butcher and cooked. Many Neo puppies will start eating stones or dirt. Since this practice can ultimately kill them, I had to find a way to stop it. I found that puppies given more red meat with their dry food stopped eating the stones. I speculate that the red meat gives them needed iron or some other nutrient not found in the extruded food but which they think exists in the red shale dirt in their pens.

Every dog from four weeks of age gets a vitamin and mineral supplement daily. I use regular human, name-brand vitamin and mineral supplements that contain all the vitamins and minerals and at least 600 mg calcium phosphate. When puppies start sinking down on their pasterns, I give them 1,000 units of vitamin C per day, and sometimes cut back on the amount of food.

Some people add yogurt and cottage cheese to the weaning formula of puppies. I have done this, and recently I have not. I see no difference in my puppies with or without cottage cheese.

Basically, as the puppies are growing, I juggle dry food alone or with added meat or pasta,

according to the eating habits and body condition of the dogs. I try not to even look at them for a year, because looking at the lanky, skinny things that are supposed to be substantial and massive makes me cringe. But now that I have learned I can trust in their genetic expression, I simply sit back and wait for them to get to a year of age safely and soundly. Then I can start adding more pasta, bread, potatoes and meat to pack on the proper amount of weight. At this time I put them on a regular exercise routine to build up their muscle while I am building up their weight. I never overstress them. From a four wheeler, I jog them around for a few minutes each day. I stop before they look like they are beginning to tire.

Recently I was introduced to a marvelous system of feeding by Neo breeder friends of mine, Denise Rappaport and Eveanne Schiavo. I was always fussing at Denise for having her dogs too fat, but they were in excellent shape, and every one of them grew up to be very sound. (I reiterate, she started with dogs of good genetic potential.) Her secret, which I have been using now and think is wonderful, is to pressure-cook whole chickens.

Now we are back to the Italian system a little bit, and the natural diet of the Mastino. We are perhaps overcooking the meat and killing the vitamins, but the pressure-cooking cooks six quarts of chicken, making the bones like mush, in one hour. Now the dogs are getting those wonderful bones and bone marrow without possibility of intestinal laceration or obstruction from sharp, hard chicken bones. There is a lot of fat on the chicken, and the fatty broth can be poured over the dry food for the second meal of the day. One has to be careful with pressure cookers, but the results are wonderful. The dogs do not need much of the chicken mixture to keep their condition up. It can be added to a dry food, or mixed with pasta or some other form of carbohydrate and some frozen vegetables. Depending on the number of dogs you have to feed, you can make up your own recipes with the chicken, dry food or whatever.

That is part of the art of feeding, and you can tailor it to your own dogs' particular needs.

Water

Neapolitan Mastiffs require a lot of water. Clean water must be available to them at all times. When they drink, they also seem to wash their mouth out in the bowl. As soon as the water becomes slightly slimy, they do not want it anymore. During the summer months, each of my dogs has three huge bowls of water from which to choose. The water in these bowls is changed without fail twice daily. Neos suffer excessively in hot, humid weather, and drinking or dunking their heads in the bowl is one way they can

Caracalla del Bonrampino, nine-month-old male. Breeder: G. Maja. Owner: S. Allen. Photo: S. Allen. This puppy is a son of Frazier della Grotta Azzurra and a mahogany daughter of Vanguard's Alana and Rasputin dell'Altafiumara. His brothers, still in Italy, are shorter and heavier boned than he is at this stage of development. This is only one example of the influence of exercise, diet and climate on body structure.

cool off.

Any fancier who has been involved in the breed for a number of years can recount a tragedy that has occurred in the hot summer months, when a Neo became overheated and had no access to water. Put plainly, Neos die in the heat.

They sometimes die when they are being shipped in those crates that are never large enough for them on an airline in the hot summer. They die at dog shows in any weather above 60 degrees Fahrenheit, where they are stressed out first of all, and then have to stand out in the sun as judges are examining other dogs. They die if you leave them out in the backyard for the day where

there is no shade or water. The only way to prevent their dying of heat exhaustion in the hot, humid summers is to keep them cool. Hosing them off with water several times a day is good to do when it is really hot out. At dog shows, where they get overheated really fast, they must be hosed down and kept wet the whole time they are in the heat. I cannot stress this enough.

Unless you really like mopping floors, you might want to give your Neapolitan Mastiff its food and water outside. I have on several occasions, with several different dogs, tried to feed them inside. Watching them eat is disgusting for the meticulously fastidious such as I. One soon learns that Neos cannot eat without first pulling their food out of the

Ironstone Hermes, four-month-old male. Breeder: S. Allen. Owner: M. Wolf. Photo: S. Allen.

dish and laying it on the floor. Then they try to eat it off the floor and end up smearing the food all around. Next they take a drink and pull their heavy lips out of the bowl, dripping water in a puddle all over the food crumbs on the floor. Soon, a very large area of your floor becomes a gooey, slimy mess.

You get the point – so I feed and water all my dogs outside. When they are finished and want to come in, I greet them at the door, towel in hand to wipe their mouth and dewlap before they are allowed inside.

Housing

Generally Neos prefer to follow their master around, lying down to sleep next to where he has stopped for a while. This is fine during the day, but as I mentioned before, it is best to provide them with their own place to stay for the night. In keeping with their nature as guard dogs, they seem content to sleep outside at night, next to the front door where they can be assured they are watching the place. In warm climates or during the summer months they need only an overhang shelter to protect them from rain or sun. In cold winter months, they need a good insulated dog house with bedding to curl up in.

Whereas Neos do not tolerate heat and humidity, they do quite well in the cold. They also generate so much body heat that they can keep quite warm in a proper-sized dog house, even in temperatures down into the teens. I would bring them in if it got below 10 degrees Fahrenheit, just because it seems

awfully cold to me.

If you do not have a suitable property situation for them to sleep outside, you will have to bring them inside to sleep. In this case, a proper-sized crate is a must. First you use the crate to prevent the puppy from soiling all over the house. The puppy will eventually begin to think of the crate as his domain. As he gets older, he will actually want to go in the crate whenever he wants to rest or chew on something that is his. The crate becomes the natural sleeping spot for the Neo.

If you want the dog to be able to roam free in the house as a guard at night, then at least confine him to an area outside of the family's bedrooms. It has been my experience to observe that, as soon as people allow the Neo to become part of the family pack, he wants to elevate himself too high in the pecking order. Again, I say that those people who are used to dealing with animals and understand their ways may have different experiences with Mastini. I am speaking of what tends to happen with the novice Neo owner, which is more often the situation than not.

No matter where you have laid out the primary domains for your Neo, he will need a soft, cushioned bedding to prevent his getting pressure calluses and sores on his elbows and hocks. In these areas the bones are very prominent, being poorly protected by muscle and thick skin. They are also areas that are constantly being traumatized as the heavy dog plunks down to rest. Not only does the continual trauma cause the calluses, which then develop into infected decubitus sores, but constant banging of these areas on hard surfaces does damage to the growth plates in the elbows and hocks of growing puppies. This constant trauma possibly contributes to the development of arthritis and osteochondrosis of these areas.

Cedar shavings are a good bedding for use inside doghouses. Straw and hay are not desirable as the sharp ends of the dried grasses poke the dog's skin, leading to skin abrasions and subsequent infection. Also, straw and hay, especially if made in damp weather, often harbor a lot of fungi, which irritate the dogs' skin, leading to contact allergies or dermatomycosis. Chiggers, which often inhabit hay, are another cause of skin irritation.

What to use as flooring inside dog pens is a dilemma. Dirt is the best because it is the softest, but it soon becomes mud in areas where it rains. Wood is next best because it is softer than other materials, but it is slippery.

Growing puppies fall a lot on slippery surfaces, thereby damaging their joints. Also, the toes slide out on the slippery wood also, causing the puppies to grow with splayed toes instead of nice tight feet. Concrete makes for properly shaped feet, as its roughened surface keeps the toes tight and the pads toughened, but it is so hard and rough that dogs do enormous damage to their elbows and hocks. Small stones would seemingly be a good flooring, but they irritate the skin between the toes of the Neos' feet. The dogs then lick their feet and they acquire intractably sore feet. Sand is good for the feet, but gets all caught up in

the lips and nose and drooping eyelids of the dog. In summer, especially, the dogs get conjunctivitis and gastric problems from ingesting all that sand sticking to the saliva which is dripping all over.

Grass is perfect, but put a Neo on grass, and the grass will not be there long. Indoor outdoor carpeting is a great floor for outside if you can figure out a way to keep the dog from ripping it up. Rubber mats are no good, as the urine lies in puddles on the rubber, the dog lies in the urine, and eventually ends up with dermatitis.

Inside the home, Neos need a rug to lie on as opposed to bare floors. Fake sheepskins make good bedding for inside their crates. They are easily washable and Neos do not tend to chew them up if they have other chew toys in the crate with them. For true pampering, those giant-sized dog beds advertised in mail catalogs are very nice. They are also great for preventing calluses. My old man Mastino, Islero, has earned the right to have full run of the house, but as soon as he comes inside at night to go to bed, he trundles over to the room with his bed and plops down, snoring contentedly the whole night long.

Grooming

One nice thing about Neapolitan Mastiffs is their short coat, which requires very little care. They do not shed very much. Nature had to bless the Neo with some good points to compensate for the slime. They do, however, go through a major shedding period in the spring and again in

Nerone del Nolano, puppy male. Breeder: M. de Falco Jovane. Owner: W. Weisse. Photo: M. Rogen.

Ironstone Casey in her own nice soft bed with her own toys, four months old. Breeder: S. Allen. Owner: J. Stroup. Photo: Stroup.

the autumn. New Neo owners are always shocked in the spring following the first winter of their puppy's life. The puppy hair turns a lighter, dead color and starts falling out amid the new, darker incoming hair. The owners routinely call up panic stricken that their dogs have some weird mange or have been eaten by moths. It is just the puppy coat shedding out. Using a horse curry comb or shedding blade on the hair coat will speed up the process, and the new coat will be beautiful.

Neos do have a strong, musky odor that some people find objectionable, and other people cannot even smell. One remedy for this is frequent bathing. All my dogs get a bath at least once a week, all year round. The frequent bathing also reduces the incidence

of skin problems. It keeps them parasite free and also removes the bacteria that can invade the skin, causing such problems as staph infections. The popular notion that frequent bathing will dry out the coat is an old wives' tale. Frequent shampooing with good-quality shampoos doesn't dry out your hair. Neos have very oily skin anyway, and the oils attract dirt, which dulls the coat. Bathing them often removes the oily film as well as the musky smell.

Puppies at my kennel start getting baths at seven weeks of age. They soon get used to it and learn quickly that they must stand nicely without moving much for their bath. It is important to train them to be hosed down at an early age, because it is often necessary to hose them down during the summer months. At dog shows, which are normally held during the summer months, hosing down your Neo to keep him cool might just be the most important part of the show.

I cannot mention too often that Neos literally die in the heat. Their internal heat-regulating system does not work well for some reason. I remember one dog show several years ago where it was about 90 degrees and sunny, and there wasn't a source of water available for easily wetting down the dogs. I had tried as best I could to wet down my large male by panning water over him. It was not sufficient. It was my turn to go into the ring. I proudly walked my dog up to the judge to be examined. He stopped, looked up at her and fell over on his side, stiff! He was being held tightly with the choker collar. It was hot. He was hot. The pressure of the choker on the carotid arteries in his neck caused reflex increase of vagal tone, which slowed the heart so much he fainted. He became unconscious for several seconds. It was quite a shock to the judge, as well as to me!

Luckily, he recovered, but you can bet that my priority of the day was to make the show officials provide hoses and water for the dogs. Unfortunately, one Neo did die that day of heat exhaustion. The owner just did not know how hot he was. He didn't hose him off. He just did not know. But now you do.

Socializing

The socialization you give your puppy is absolutely the main determination of his future behavior as an adult. Neos are by nature wary of strangers. They are homebodies and do not like change. One could say that they are introverts.

For Neapolitans to get along with other people successfully in our modern society, you must teach them not to be so introverted. You must have them interact with people, and be constantly subjected to noise, and change from very early on. You must teach them that other people will not hurt them. If you do not do this when the puppies are young, they will grow up to be fearful of new situations and people. As they mature, this wariness, which is in essence fear, will be manifested as viciousness. Unsocialized females will urinate in submission when approached by a person. Unsocialized males will stand their ground,

Nice wooden platform made of roughened but not splintery wood so it is not slippery. D'Annunzio de Néropolis, 13 months old. Breeders and owners: M. and Mme. J.P. Beck. Photo: J.P. Beck.

Neos must be taught to like people, especially children. Their protective natures must be properly challenged. Photo: S. Allen.

sometimes urinate, but more often than not, bite when someone tries to touch them.

It is as if our attempts to breed the abject aggression out of the Mastino has resulted in a large population of Neos who now retain the original wariness, minus the aggressiveness to equal a fearful personality. It is the Mastino breeder's job to try to correct this personality problem. It is up to the owner to modify it. It can be done.

The way to socialize a Neo is to simply take him and put him in scary situations daily until he gets used to them. One such horrifying situation for a Neo is the ride in a car. They start out hating cars, defecating all over the automobile every time you take them for a ride. This becomes very

inconvenient, not to mention disgusting, for the owner. To remedy the problem, you persist in taking them in the car, starting with short trips. As long as they do not defecate in the car, make the trips a little longer each succeeding time. Give them food treats in the car. Put them in a crate in a van or station wagon and make them sleep in the car. (Never lock them in a car on a day whenever the temperature is over 50 degrees Fahrenheit. They will die of heat exhaustion in a closed vehicle.)

Start the car rides as soon as you get the puppy. If you keep up the bribes in the car, eventually the puppy will learn to like autos. It can be done. Be persistent.

To teach your Neo to like people, take him into crowded areas from the time he is a puppy. Tell people to pet him and touch him. Jolly him up and praise him when people pet him and he is happy. Never allow him to bark or growl at anyone. If your puppy or dog ever barks or growls at anyone when you are with him, you must severely reprimand him.

"But I want my Neo to be a guard dog and protect me and my property," you say. Don't worry; no matter how much you teach your Neo to like people, as soon as he reaches puberty, he will automatically try to protect your property whenever a stranger comes and you are not there. No matter how much you have told your Neo not to growl or bark at a person, he will when you are not around. It is bred in them.

If you allow your little puppy to ever bark or

Dog starting to shed out. Note mottled appearance. Photo: S. Allen.

growl at a person for whatever reason, you will eventually be sorry. A puppy who learns that it can exert its authority over others by growling will be uncontrollable as an adult. A puppy who is taught that you want him to like everyone he meets when he is with you will be a good citizen as an adult.

One very important thing to teach your puppy right away is to go into and like a crate. If you keep Neos in a crate whenever you are away from home, they will automatically think the crate is a safe place where they belong. Then whenever you need to transport the dog, be it by automobile or by airplane or train, he will stay put and travel happily in his crate. Neos are that way.

If, on the other hand, you do not start the crate training as a puppy, it will be very hard to crate train a 150-pound adult who has never seen a gauge wire in a cage that he did not think he could break out of. The cages, kennels and crates on the market today are not built to hold a Neapolitan Mastiff who wants to get out. If you habituate him to the crate while he is young, he will never even try to get out of those flimsy containers when he is big.

Do not ever let a puppy growl at you when he is eating or chewing on a toy. If he ever does, you must severely reprimand him. Severely reprimanding does not mean physically

Dog after shedding out. Photo: S. Allen.

hurting him severely. It means that you have to make him think his world is coming to an end. Grabbing him by his scruff, shaking him, and yelling at him all at the same time will let him know you will not tolerate his being possessive of his food. It will work, and he will learn. You just have to want to make your reprimands work.

In closing, let me repeat that your Neapolitan Mastiff will develop the personality that you guide him to develop. You must never allow him to behave in an aggressive manner to anyone. You must teach him to love and trust all people. You must get him off your property to go see the big world. All these things will make him a self-confident and

fearless dog. Believe me, once you have done this, you will have the guard dog and personal protection dog that you wanted. While you are at home or off your property with him, he should greet anyone who comes toward you with tail wagging. You think this is a contradiction of purposes? I can assure you it is not. Your properly socialized Neo will stand by you wagging, but carefully watching anyone that you willingly allow to be near you. Should you indicate to your dog in any way that you are in trouble from that person, that happy, wagging Neo will turn into a raging beast for you. It is bred into them to protect you. You will never change that in them.

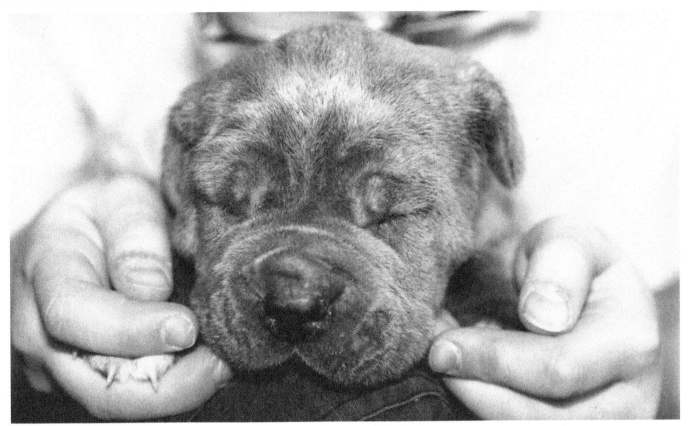

Ironstone Revellie, three-week-old female. Breeder: S. Allen. Owner: K. Dorsey. Photo: S. Allen. Happy to be asleep on a lap. This is a future guard dog.

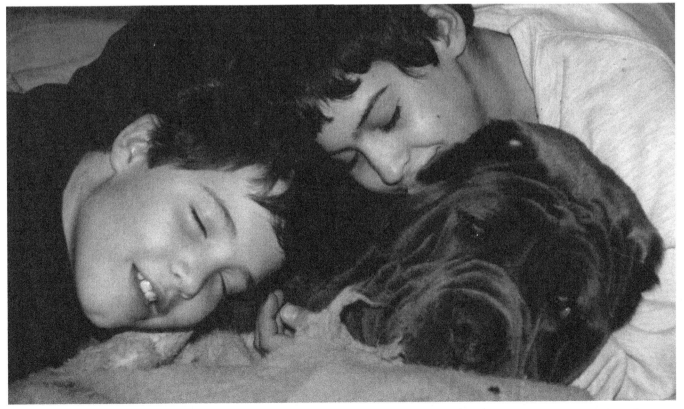

One favorite Neo passtime is napping ... Another favorite is napping with friends. Photo: S. Allen.

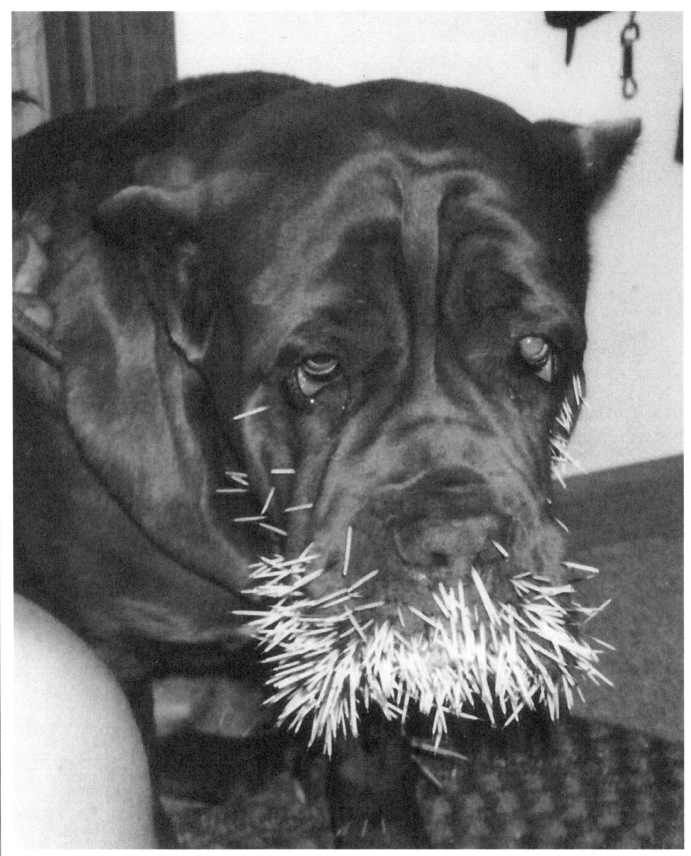

One recommendation on the subject of health care is not to let Neos let near porcupines! That is what happened to Elbe, this 10-month-old male. Breeder: P. Baily. Owner: R. Schmidt. Photo: R. Schmidt.

Health Care

The following is based solely on the knowledge and advice of the author – always consult your veterinarian first.

Because Neapolitan Mastiffs are not a common breed in the United States, many veterinarians are not familiar with them and their idiosyncrasies. There are certain medical conditions common to the breed, certain cultural practices peculiar to the breed, and certain behaviors characteristic of the breed. In this chapter, I will list these conditions and peculiarities and discuss them each briefly.

The physical appearance of the Neapolitan Mastiff is created by a purposeful blending of recessive traits that are usually considered undesirable in the more common breeds of dogs that we in the 20th Century are familiar with. Some of these traits are considered unsoundnesses in other breeds, but if we breed them out of the Neo to create a more sound dog, we breed out the appearance of the dog we are seeking to maintain. It is this contradiction of goals that makes breeding Neapolitan Mastiffs so difficult.

The Neapolitan Mastiff is a romantic and idealistic concept of an animal that would be more powerful than any other animal of equal and possibly greater size; an animal that arouses trepidation and awe in whoever beholds it. Because that which we are used to seeing becomes normal in our eyes, no matter what the true appearance, the only way to create shock value is to create something which has never before been seen. The art in breeding Neapolitan Mastiffs is to materialize a concept of an awe-inspiring primordial guard dog that is so frightful that we will be shocked.

Since that which is most familiar becomes beautiful in our eyes, that which is unfamiliar is viewed as grotesque. But to the Neo fancier, who is used to seeing the grotesque, that which is more grotesque becomes the most beautiful. To purposefully select for the grotesque is to select for the recessive genetic traits that most breeders try to eliminate in their breeds. The recessive

Mosé II, six-year-old male. Breeder: G. Siano. Owner: G. Mira. Photo: M. Rogen.

traits are sometimes linked to what might be considered by some to be genetic weaknesses. The Neapolitan Mastiff has been continued by man in its present day form by bringing together a cluster of unusual traits that fanciers of other breeds often want to eliminate. To accept ownership of a Neapolitan Mastiff is to accept the realization that it has practically the opposite traits of what people consider to be conformational attributes in a dog. To seek a Neo with only the dominant traits considered to be soundnesses is to end up with a dog that is healthy, perhaps, but not that primitive concept of the dog who is a living gargoyle; a dog whose very presence make him a deterrent against all evil.

Having studied this breed from a medical standpoint for the past 10 years, I have come to some conclusions as to why the Neapolitan Mastiff looks and behaves the way he does. Based on the results of clinical laboratory testing performed over the years on hundreds of these dogs, I believe that many of the Neapolitan Mastiff's attributes as well as his problems, in part, are a result of lower than normal thyroid-hormone levels.

The entire physical appearance of the Neo is characteristic of hypothyroid individuals. Typically, in the Neo, the lower the thyroid hormone levels, the more "typey" the dog becomes. The thickened skin, which is pushed into wrinkles and folds, the heavy hanging lips and eyelids, and the tragic expression, are due to infiltration of the subcutaneous tissues with glycosaminoglycans, which are gelatinous sugar-protein substances. The shortened face, short neck, and thick, rather shortened legs are due to retarded bone growth because of low thyroid. The Zacchero-type Mastini, which are actually disproportionate dwarfs, have the most grotesque type resulting from the lowest amount of thyroid hormone. Cranial and medial to lateral bowing of the radius in the front leg is a characteristic sequel.

Virginio del Vittoriale, two-year-old male. Breeder and owner: G. Mira. Photo: Zimmerman.

Understanding why the Mastino looks the way he does enables us to explain why he often develops certain conditions as he is growing, and why special care needs to be taken of Neos as they are developing. Luckily, as the dog matures, he usually grows out of these conditions. It is as if the end of such a fast growth rate in the puppy allows the dog's normal levels of thyroid hormone to return to adequate performance levels.

Thyroid hormone affects the dog's system in many ways. Low thyroid-hormone levels are common in many breeds of dogs today, but they usually go unnoticed. It is my opinion that breeders of many of the large breeds of dogs unconsciously select for animals with lower thyroid levels, because they are the calmer, larger, heavier dogs. Some of these large breed dogs that have normal thyroids are such a handful that owners cannot deal with their boundless energy. They are so full of energy that when bored (as dogs often are in today's society, where owners are gone for eight hours of the day working), the dog channels this energy into destructive

Excellent-quality Neapolitan Mastiff showing typical breed type and conformation. Ragna di Colosseo Avallu. Breeder and owner: L. Denger. Photo: Schumacher.

chewing, digging or barking behavior. The dog with low thyroid levels is "better behaved," sleeping all day until the owner comes home.

For the sake of education, it is important to recognize some of the more undesirable effects of low thyroid-hormone levels. Some of the symptoms of dogs with too low thyroid-hormone levels are inflammation of the muscles can lead to muscle weakness, stiffness, and reluctance to move, manifested by limping in puppies, and a shuffling gait in adults. Lethargy and mental dullness can occur. The cardiac muscle can be affected, leading to cardiomyopathies. Retarded growth of the bone-growth centers can lead to premature closure of the ulna, resulting in incongruent growth of the two bones in the forearm. Multiple rather than single centers of ossification can occur at these epiphyseal growth centers with resulting problems in the development of the joints. Incongruent bones and improper changing of cartilage to calcium leads to dysplasias, commonly called elbow dysplasia, hip dysplasia and

The movement of this dog is extraordinary. It is very rare to see a Neo that moves like this. As a puppy of four months of age, his front pasterns sunk down and he was reluctant to exercise. With proper diet and allowing him to exercise on his own, he grew into this beautifully conformed and sound-moving dog. Of special note is that he would not pass OFA because he has loose hips, which OFA would define as a degree of dysplasia. He does not have arthritis of the hips. The author believes that the term hip dysplasia may need to be redefined. Likewise, the value of loose hips in Neapolitan Mastiffs may need to be reassessed.

Normo-thyroid Neapolitan Mastiff showing less breed type but constitutional soundness. Photo: S. Allen.

osteochondrosis of the joints. Eventually these dysplasias can result in arthritis.

Other effects of the hypothyroidism are poor, dry hair coat and impaired immune system, which leads to increased susceptibility to infections, especially recurrent skin infections. There is also a decrease in gastric and intestinal motility, which can be a predisposing factor to bloat. Reproductive problems are common as the dog grows older. Testicular atrophy, lack of sperm production and reduced libido are manifested in the male. Females show infertility, early abortion if they do get pregnant, sporadic heat periods and frequent false pregnancies. In many cases, as the dog

grows older, the thyroid-hormone levels again become too low.

Thyroid replacement therapy, in the form of pills given daily for the life of the dog, corrects these problems in the adult dog and prevents them from happening in the growing puppy. Of course, when the dog becomes normo-thyroid, it then grows taller and leaner, develops longer, thinner appendages and a longer muzzle, and loses its wrinkles and heavy lips. In short, it begins to look less and less like the ideal Mastino. As a prospective Neapolitan Mastiff owner you must make a decision to get involved with a romantic vision that may have physical problems of varying degrees, or to go for a more constitutionally healthy dog that has no "originality" to its appearance.

I note the striking differences in the physical appearance of two known littermate sisters, one of which is normothyroid and the other, hypothyroid. This is clear-cut evidence in support of the theory that low thyroid hormone is a major determinant of the manifestation of the physical traits so desirable in the Neapolitan Mastiff.

The black female is tall and thin, with relatively tight skin and very little wrinkling. She is 27 inches tall and weighs 122 pounds at one year of age. Her skin is not puffy or thickened. The leg bones are straight, long and thin. Her muzzle is long. Because of the long muzzle, she is able to have full dentition and a scissors bite. Her topline is quite straight for a Neapolitan Mastiff. Her joints are tight, possibly because of tight ligaments and tendons. On radiograph, her hips are quite tight in the sockets for a Neo. She is very active, racing around outside and barking all day. She jumps four-foot fences easily and could probably jump higher ones. She has no skin problems. She is very healthy, very active, and such a handful that her owners could not stand her. She looks more like a Great Dane than a Neapolitan Mastiff. Her blood-thyroid levels are normal, because her thyroid functions normally.

The gray female is shorter and stockier than her sister. Her skin is loose and quite

Black female, one year old. Normal thyroid. Photo: S. Allen.

wrinkled. She is 25½ inches tall and weighs 130 pounds at one year of age. Her face is quite heavily wrinkled, her skin is thickened and puffy. Her legs are full and puffy. The leg bones are shorter and thicker than her sister's, and her front feet turn out slightly, in typical Neo fashion. Her muzzle is short and correct, and covered with wrinkles. Because of the shorter muzzle, there is not enough room for all her teeth, and so, in normal Neo fashion, she is missing some lower premolars. Her bite is level at present, but will become prognathic as she continues to grow. Her topline sags more than that of her sister. Her front pasterns and rear legs are more angulated, indicating weaker, or more stretchable, tendons. On radiograph, her hips are loose in the sockets. She is active in short bursts, but tires easily, preferring to sleep a lot. Her hair coat is coarser and wavier, like that of older horses and dogs as they become hypothyroid. Her movement, while sound, is more stilted and awkward, like that of a Neo and unlike that of her sister or other working-breed dogs. She is a beautiful and typical specimen of a Neapolitan Mastiff. Her blood-thyroid levels are low.

Since these two dogs are sisters, their bloodlines are exactly the same. Their genetics are essentially similar. Their appearances should be similar, but one happened to receive in the genetic roulette game a normally functioning thyroid. She became one of those undesirable Neapolitan Mastiffs, lacking type, but functionally superior to her sister. The gray sister is the more beautiful specimen, but will need thyroid-hormone supplementation in order to live a more disease-free life. The

development and continuation of the breed is in the hands of the breeders and the breed clubs that determine the standard of the breed. Whether or not health should be sacrificed to looks (as has been done in many of the other manmade breeds) is a subject for debate among Mastino fanciers. It is my belief, however, that the knowledge and the reasons behind the looks and also the problems of a breed will enable the prospective owner of a Mastino to better decide whether this is a breed with which he or she wants to become involved.

Another interesting consideration of the Neapolitan Mastiff and its physical appearance is the similarity of its features to those of people affected with a condition called Ehlers-Danlos syndrome. This syndrome is recognized in people and some other animals, but has never been officially studied in Neos, to my knowledge. The syndrome encompasses a group of disorders of connective tissue that result in hyperextensible skin and joints. People who have this condition often become contortionists. The loose connective tissue is a result of a biochemical abnormality in collagen synthesis, possibly the result of an inherited lack of a certain enzyme needed for the synthesis of the collagen. The clinical manifestation of Ehlers-Danlos syndrome is soft, loose-hanging, easily stretchable skin. With age, the skin sags markedly over the elbows and hands and feet.

The joints are very hyperextensible, such that motor control is difficult in early life. As the individual gets older, the connective-tissue strength improves, and together

Gray female, one year old. Low thyroid. Head study, *opposite page*. **Photos: S. Allen**

with increased muscle development, motor skills become adequate, and in many cases, normal.

Like people with Ehler-Danlos syndrome, some Neapolitan puppies often have a tough time getting around for the first year of their life. Everything on them is loose – their skin, their tendons, their joints. They grow so fast and become so heavy that their lax tendons and ligaments barely hold their bones together. The instability of the loose joints is further reason for the joints to become traumatized easily. Inflammation

results from trauma, and arthritis can be a sequential development.

Invariably, the Neo puppy begins to limp at four to six months of age. It often sags down on its front pasterns, and the toes start to splay. The collagen in the tendons just does not seem strong enough to support the weight of the dog. Then it limps behind, and the first diagnosis everyone wants to make is hip dysplasia. The veterinarian immediately radiographs the puppy and invariably sees loose hip joints. Sometimes the heads of the femurs can be pulled way out of the sockets.

Already programmed to look for the dreaded hip dysplasia, that now-household word thanks to effective advertising and scare tactics employed by certain organizations to assure financial gain, veterinarians and owners alike immediately jump to the diagnosis of doom.

Owners are often immediately given only two choices as to what to do for their dog. They are told that they can have the dog undergo very expensive orthopedic surgery to correct the problem, or they will have to have the dog put down because it will suffer intractable pain. Next begins the entire unhappy saga of distraught and irate owners finding someone to blame and from whom they can extract recompense.

Let's hold on, back track and look at the real story. We just finished saying how most all Neo puppies have loose connective tissue and joints, or they would not be Neos. They will inevitably do damage to their joints, especially if they are allowed to roughhouse uncontrollably while they are in this growing period.

Because they have loose connective tissue, they will always radiograph with some degree of joint laxity. This joint laxity includes the hips. But hip dysplasia is not just joint laxity. True, joint laxity can predispose a dog to develop hip dysplasia, but the term hip dysplasia is by definition the arthritis that develops from excessive wear on incongruent joints. Not all dogs with loose joints go on to develop arthritis or hip dysplasia. Of the hundreds of Neos I have radiographed over the years, all of them had loose hips – even the ones that passed OFA certification. I have seen only five with arthritis of the hips, or hip dysplasia, and of these five, all were extraordinarily sound to the degree that all of them had won championships in the show ring.

On the other hand, I am not saying that all Neos with severe forms of hip dysplasia are not lame. Some may indeed be lame because of hips. Some may have multiple orthopedic problems, and bad hips may be contributing to the overall unsoundness. I believe that severely unsound animals, no matter how beautiful they are, should not be bred.

I am stating that I have reason to believe that loose hips do not cause as severe clinical problems in this breed as they might in other breeds. I believe that more research needs to be done on the effects of loose hips and hip dysplasia in the breed, Judging a dog by the results of a radiograph on an anesthetized animal, which has no reflex muscular tone to hold his joints tight and which is placed in a totally abnormal position simply because that's the easiest way for us humans to get standard pictures of the pelvic area, is, to me, an example of tunnel vision. It causes amateurs to judge the Neo only by a picture of its hips. It causes neophyte breeders to forget about everything but a Neo's hips so that they can cater to a hip-fixated public. I suggest that people interested in Neapolitan Mastiffs look at many other characteristics of the breed in addition to hips.

That limping four- to six-month-old puppy is more likely limping from myopathies or generalized pain in all the joints associated with low thyroid hormone and abnormal collagen synthesis. You know that if you go out and do aerobics when you are not physically in shape, or ride a horse, how sore you will be the following couple of days. Stretching muscles and tendons causes soreness. Crushing and tearing immature cartilage causes pain. So what do you do for this dearly beloved prize on which you have spent a lot of money and who now can barely walk?

You wait. You avoid watching him while he his limping so that you do not get ulcers. You give him aspirin. You let him grow up. You can also give vitamin C, 1 to 2 grams per day, in addition to the proper food and multi-vitamin-mineral tablet. Some people also swear by beta carotene with vitamin E, for the anti-oxidant anti-inflammatory properties. I have also fund shark cartilage and/or Perna canaliculus mussel products to be very effective in preventing these developmental joint disorders and allowing the joints to develop in a healthy fashion. You keep the puppy light in weight to make it easier for him to move around – remember, he is already too heavy for his age just because he is a Neo. You may have to start thyroid-hormone-replacement therapy. And you wait.

Then, as the puppy grows, and you are feeding him properly, and giving him the vitamins and other supplements mentioned, and not letting him stress his joints with too much exercise or stair-climbing or roughhousing with other dogs, you will begin to see him coming up on his pasterns. By 10 or 11 months of age, his toes will start to come together again. The limping will be more intermittent. The muscles will begin to develop. By a year of age, things should all be back to functioning again. The growing pains will stop, and the dog will be able to get around quite well.

Of course there are always some puppies that do actually have more serious orthopedic problems than do the average limping Neo puppies. There are always individuals in any breed that can have all sorts of defects, and some of these dogs may not be able to lead pain-free, productive lives.

If the puppy is really hurting, you must go to

a veterinarian and get a proper, not a knee-jerk, diagnosis. There are some conditions that may absolutely require surgical intervention. However, I am amazed daily by dogs that I see as puppies and would swear that they will grow up to be crippled wrecks. These puppies usually have osteochondrosis of every joint and totally deformed legs. They are dogs that even I would think would have to be put down. But surprisingly, or not so surprisingly, as I am learning where Neos are concerned, these dogs grow up to be just fine. They may not become so sound that they are going to be show winners, but they walk and run around fine. I always reserve judgment on limping Neos, even if I know the diagnosis, until they are 12 to 18 months of age. They just seem to get better with age.

While we are on orthopedic conditions, I would like to mention several disease conditions that are prevalent in all giant-breed dogs, the Neapolitan Mastiff included. Some conditions are indeed best treated by surgical intervention, and some could be treated surgically, but in my opinion, are best treated medically.

Osteochondrosis dissecans of the shoulder joint

This disease entity occurs as a result of incorrect conversion of cartilage to bone in the growing dog, with resultant tearing of a flap of cartilage off the end of the bone. The cartilage piece floats around in the joint or remains attached at one end, and acts like a foreign body between the surfaces

Black female, one year old, head shot. Normal thyroid. Photo: S. Allen.

of the two bones that form the joint. Causes of osteochondrosis dissecans are multiple and not precisely known. Contributing factors are things that cause inflammation in the joint. These factors could be trauma, such a jolt to the joint when a puppy jumps off the deck and lands clumsily on immature, unstable joints; bacteria or viral infection, which sets up inflammation; simply too much weight in an obese puppy, or autoimmune phenomena perhaps associated with hormone imbalances, stress or vaccines or other chemicals. The hereditary disposition to the condition is certainly present. It is a matter of whether the environmental conditions to which the dog is subjected will result in the development of the disease.

Treatment of this condition is to surgically remove the torn cartilage flap. It is a relatively easy procedure and when performed by a competent surgeon, is 100 percent effective.

Ruptured anterior cruciate ligament

This is the old "football injury" that occurs when the dog (or person) gets rammed in the stifle (knee). It can also happen when the overly heavy dog with immature or poor muscle development is barreling across the yard, then plants one back leg and tries to turn. The result is a rip of the ligament that holds the knee together. The meniscus in the knee is often torn at the same time. Repair of this injury is tricky in such giant-breed dogs, but if performed by a competent orthopedic surgeon, and with proper compliance by owners and dog during the healing stages, it is totally successful.

Elbow dysplasia

This is a complicated but common condition in giant-breed dogs resulting from multiple factors. Earlier, we discussed the incongruent bone growth of the two bones which form part of this three-boned joint. This incongruent growth of the bones that form part of this three-boned joint can be caused by premature closure of one of the growth plates, usually the ulna, due to trauma or hormonal or nutritional imbalances. It is possible that bacterial or viral infections play a role in the inflammation and destruction of the joint. It is possible that autoimmune reactions contribute to the inflammation.

At any rate, the syndrome can be composed of multiple defects. In some cases, the anconeal process of the ulna fractures off. In some cases, the coronoid processes of the ulna fracture off. In some cases, all of these things are fractured. Then the cartilage of the joint is gouged out and eroded away. The whole joint is filled with excess fluid called effusion. In short, it is a mess. When an affected elbow is radiographed, you often see nothing on the film, and if you do see anything, it is not half of what is really going on inside that joint.

Some people advocate certain surgical procedures for correcting one of the problems once the condition has been diagnosed. The elbow joint is a very difficult joint to access, and if you are able to reach one side, you can't reach the other side of the joint without taking the whole joint apart so much that it would be more destroyed after surgery than before it. In addition, the amount of destruction that exists in some of these joints is so enormous that I can't see any way to repair it.

Some newly proposed surgeries involve cutting both bones of the forearm in half and realigning them and pinning them and readjusting the pins weekly or so until the dog stops growing so as to make the bones grow congruently. This procedure would have to be started before the dog showed any clinical signs of the disease, however, or the damage to the joint that the procedure is trying to prevent would already be done.

So what do you use for elbow dysplasia in Neos? Tincture of time. In addition, I give amoxicillin for three to four weeks when I first notice limping. Have the thyroid checked, and perhaps put the puppy on replacement thyroid-hormone therapy. Give vitamin C, 2 gms daily, and beta carotene and shark cartilage or Perna canaliculus mussel. Do this until the dog has stopped growing at one and a half years of age. By then healing mechanisms have usually taken place, and the dogs are usually fine.

Splay toes and down in the pasterns

This condition can result from severe nutritional deprivation, obesity in otherwise genetically sound individuals, or simply excessively weak genetics. In the first case, change to proper diet with proper vitamin and mineral content can be corrective if caught before severe damage to the joints has occurred. In the case of simply allowing the puppy to get too fat, feeding less and supplementing with vitamin C and beta carotene, coupled with waiting for the puppy to grow up, should correct the problem. If the puppy is simply a result of breeding parents that have too many crippling traits, nothing will make it totally correct. As with all Neos, its tendons and ligaments will strengthen as it matures, but they may never be strong enough to support the dog's body properly.

Cherry eye

A prolapse of the gland of the third eyelid of some dogs, or cherry eye as it is more commonly called, is unfortunately another nuisance factor that crops up in the breed. Cherry eye is not unique to Neapolitan Mastiffs. It is common in other breeds of dogs, such as Beagles, Cocker Spaniels, Basset Hounds and Bloodhounds, all of which also have an increased incidence of hypothyroidism. Whereas some veterinarians have good success with other breeds in sewing the prolapsed gland back down under the third eyelid where it belongs, this technique does not routinely work in the Neapolitan Mastiff.

As we said before, the Neapolitan has very loose and stretchy connective tissue. If you try to tack the gland down, the tissue just stretches and rolls over the other subcutaneous layers, and the gland pops out again. The only way to take care of this red, swollen and ulcerated gland is to snip it out. The operation takes about five seconds in the anesthetized dog. If it is done properly, there are no adverse effects that result from removal of the gland, and the eye will not become a "dry eye." The third eyelid itself must never be removed, however (unless it has been destroyed previously by someone else's misguided surgery).

A canine ophthalmologist once told me that he feels it is unethical to perpetuate a breed that routinely has this defect that needs to be attended to. I replied by asking him if he thought it was also unethical to perpetuate human children whose tonsils routinely

This page and opposite: **Neapolitan Mastiff moving, showing the long, ground-covering strides as well as his ability to turn on the forehand (opposite page). He is three years old. He does not limp at all. He developed elbow dysplasia as a puppy.**

become infected and need to be removed.

Unfortunately, I believe that if we try to breed a dog that will not develop cherry eye, we will have to breed tighter-skinned dogs. A dog without loose skin, wrinkles and loose connective tissue will no longer be a Neapolitan Mastiff. A Neapolitan Mastiff is a Neapolitan Mastiff because of the traits that are opposite to what is desirable in the more common breeds. As we said before, what is a defect in one breed is a source of beauty in another. Remove the reasons for why the Neo looks like he does – loose connective tissue – and you will no longer have a Neo.

One of my original early goals as a breeder of Neos was to breed out the cherry eye, just because it is a nuisance. After many generations I succeeded, and I ended up with

dogs that looked like large Pitbulls or Cane Corsos. They certainly did not look like the Neapolitan Mastiff anymore. I had bred out their loose connective tissue and their low thyroid levels.

Another rather frequently occurring defect in some lines of Neapolitans is called a dermoid, and it is actually skin and hair that grows over the cornea of the eyeball itself. There is also usually a defect in the eyelid rim. This is not a minor defect, and is not a result of those factors that make a Neo look like a Neo. It is rather one of those defects that crops up from excessive breeding within a particular line in the effort to maintain certain type. One should think twice about breeding a dog that was born with this defect, which must be surgically removed lest the dog go blind.

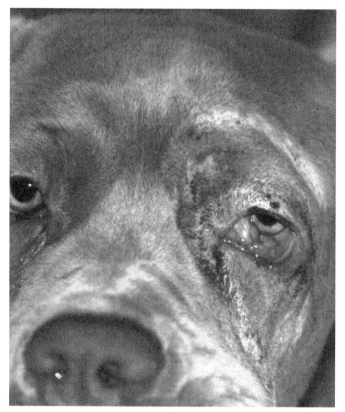

End result of someone's attempt to tack the cherry eye down. The operation was performed two times. The eye is weeping and infected, and the gland was so hypertrophied and scarred down to the third eyelid that it completely destroyed the third eyelid. In this case, there was no choice but to remove the third eyelid as well. This would not have had to be done if the gland had simply been removed in the first place.

Skin

If Neapolitan Mastiffs are kept clean and parasite free by frequent bathing, they do not really have severe problems with their skin. The potential for skin problems does exist, though, because Neapolitans in general do not have very strong immune systems. This means that bacteria and parasites can gain a foothold easily into the skin, where they can then wreak havoc. Parasites and bacterial and fungal infections make the dog itch. He scratches and licks himself, which makes the infection worse. A manifestation of the infection and irritated skin is hair loss and pustules.

Stress causes the immune system to function poorly. A Neo stresses out very easily. Things that cause stress in Neos include excessive heat, moving to a strange place, teething in puppies, estrus in bitches, whelping and lactation, and any type of change in their routine. Neos who spend a lot of time outside get dirty very quickly. Their paws, dewlaps and chins are usually always moist and warm

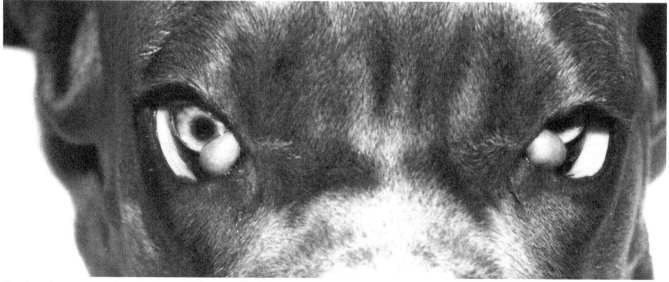

Early cherry eye in a puppy. Photo: S. Allen.

More advanced case of cherry eye in a puppy. The gland pops up and becomes infected and swollen, and covers over the entire eyeball. Photo: S. Allen.

from perspiration or drool and food that clings to their dewlaps. The perfect media for bacteria and fungi are warm, moist places. The perfect medium for demodex mange mites is irritated, inflamed skin.

A happy, unstressed, dirty Neo will be more resistant to infection than a stressed-out, dirty Neo. No Neo tolerates fleas well. If you let your Neo get dirty, stressed out, and attacked by fleas, as will happen nearly everywhere in the United States during the hot summer months, and especially in the hot humid areas of the Southeast, he will get a skin infection. Before you notice this, demodex mites may get a foothold on the dog. By the time you notice the bald patches and the pustules all over the belly and dewlap, you have an expensive mess to treat.

You can prevent all this by frequent bathing

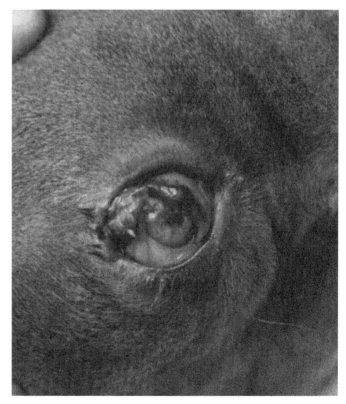

Dermoid on the eye of a Neo puppy. This is another defect that occurs rather frequently in some lines of Neapolitan Mastiffs. Photo: S. Allen.

and occasional dipping in a mitacide called Amitraz. If the dog begins to get pustules on the ventral parts of the body, it may need to be given antibiotics. Keep fleas away by environmental control and by treating the dog if necessary with systemic or external flea products.

Demodicosis

Demodex mites are microscopic mites that inhabit the skin of dogs. There is a variety of this mite that inhabits the eyelashes and eyebrows of people also. The two species of demodex mites are not contagious from animals to humans or vice versa. When the mites are able to multiply so extensively on the dog that they then exist in very high numbers, they cause the hair to fall out and allow more infection to set in. They then create the disease syndrome known as demodectic mange.

It is well known that some breeds of dogs are more susceptible to infection from demodex mites than other breeds. The Molosser and bull breeds fall into this category. Demodicosis is a complicated disease that takes on different form in different animals. Some Neos come down with localized areas of demodex mites when they are puppies. Dipping them with Amitraz cures the problem. Some females get the disease every time they come into heat. In between heat periods they are OK. Spaying them often cures the problem. Some males get localized demodex and pustules on their chins and dewlap area as they reach puberty. Then with Amitraz dipping and antibiotics, as

they mature, the pustules go away. I have seen some puppies with persistent demodex that just would not go away. Then, by the time they reached two years of age, it just disappeared for good.

Interestingly enough, a close look at the dewlaps and lips of some of the most beautiful Neos in the world will reveal the pustules and puffy lips characteristic of demodex in the dewlap. In actuality, the demodicosis sets up inflammation, which makes the lips heavier, thicker and more impressive looking. When it infects the feet, it makes them bigger and more impressive looking.

However, there are magnificent Neos who have long, thick lips and dewlap but are not infected with demodex. There are Neos who have large feet and thick skin on their legs, but are not infected with demodex. Though the appearance of some Mastini is created because of the demodex, there are very typical and grotesque-looking dogs which do not have demodex. Since this mite is such a problem to deal with, I suggest that those Mastini that have incurable or recurring demodex not be part of a breeding program. Yet you will see many Mastini winning in the show ring that have demodex on their lips. I believe that to try to breed out the susceptibility to generalized demodicosis is a worthwhile goal for breeders of Neapolitan Mastiffs.

The emotional and economic toll demodex takes on owners of Neos, not to mention the irritation it causes the dog, are reasons to try to eliminate it from the breed. Unfortunately, many of the best-looking dogs have it.

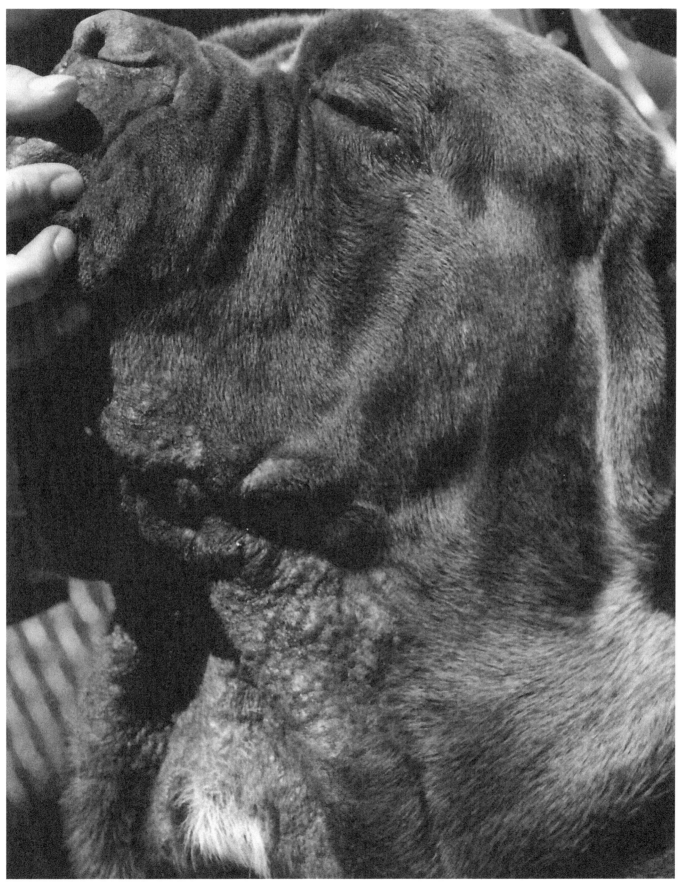

Demodicosis and secondary staph infection of the dewlap of a Neo. Photo: S. Allen.

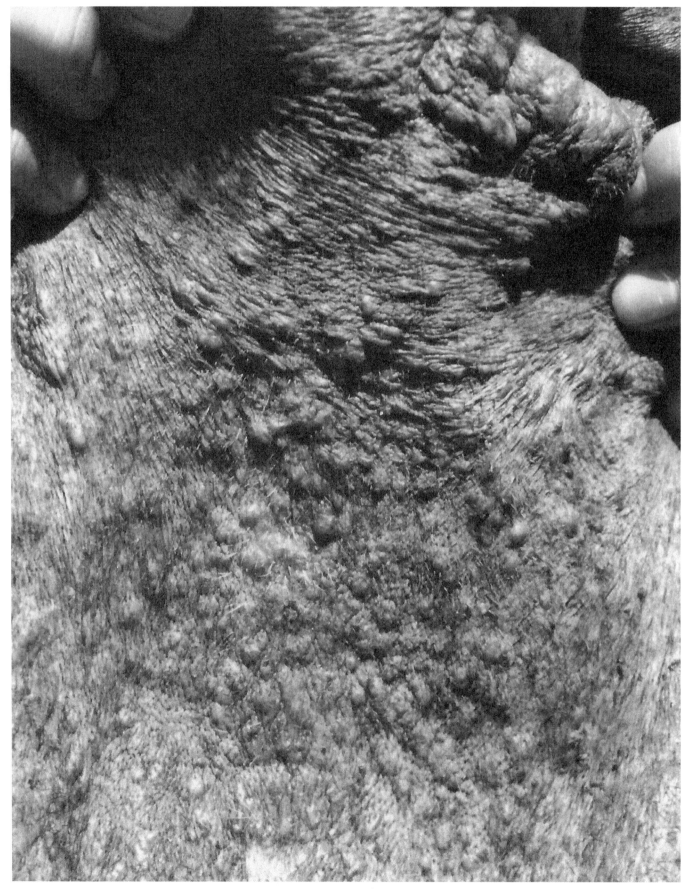

Close-up view of the pustules and infected skin. Photo: S. Allen.

Sore feet

This syndrome seems to occur in dogs in the United States who live outside in humid or rainy areas where the ground is often wet. It is not the same as pododemodicosis. It seems to be a result of bacterial or fungal infections that invade the bottom of the feet between the toes and make them itch. The dog then licks the bottoms of the feet. The licking causes a hot-spot-type reaction, and the whole process is self-perpetuating. Because stereotypic licking is considered by many behaviorists to be a type of obsessive-compulsive behavior in dogs, this licking is practically impossible to stop. Systemic antibiotics and various antifungal sprays on the feet will clear up the sores for a while. Then when the dog starts licking again, the whole process starts all over. I have no answers as to how to eliminate this. Neos that live inside most of the time or those that live in dry climates do not get the problem.

EARS

Since antiquity, as depicted in the artwork of thousands of years ago, the ears of the Molossian dogs were cropped. Cropping was most likely done to remove the impediment caused by a hanging ear, which was easily grabbed and torn by the Molossian's opponent, whatever it was. Today, ear cropping is done as a matter of custom and style. It also serves a functional purpose in that cropped Neo ears rarely get infected. Pendulous ears, on the other hand, seal up the ear canal, allowing it to become a dark, warm, moist haven for bacteria and fungi.

As with all pendulous-eared dogs, Neos with intact ears are more susceptible to ear infections.

Ear Cropping

The ears of the Neapolitan Mastiff are cut to the shape of an almost equilateral triangle. In Italy, the custom in the Naples area is to cut them a little longer so that they often bend over the top of the head. The custom in the north of Italy is to cut them a little shorter so that they barely stick up above the top of the head.

The surgical procedure is performed on the anesthetized puppy, preferably at seven to eight weeks of age. Neo puppies grow very fast, and by 10 to 12 weeks of age, they are very large. The surgery is made more difficult by the ear, which is very large and heavy and difficult to cut through. Older puppies also scratch at their ears more, making the healing process slower.

The ears are cut with scissors freehand, according to landmarks on every dog's ears made by the tubercles on the pinna. Hemostasis is performed by electrocautery, and the cut edges are sutured. The ears are then sutured over the top of the head for four days to keep them straight while the initial healing takes place.

Though cropping the ears has always been customary for the Mastino, it is the owners' prerogative as to whether they want the ears on their dog cropped or not. The Mastino can be shown in dog shows with or without cropped ears. In some countries such as Great Britain and Germany, ear cropping has been outlawed. The style of the crop is slightly different on each dog. In some cases, the ear may be cropped to the same length on different dogs, but it looks different because of the ear set and texture of the pinna.

Routine Health Maintenance

In the United States, the most common threats to a dog's health are parasites and viruses, and now Rickettsiae. There are many treatments for these diseases on the market, and drug manufacturers are continuously coming up with new drugs or vaccines to attack these enemies.

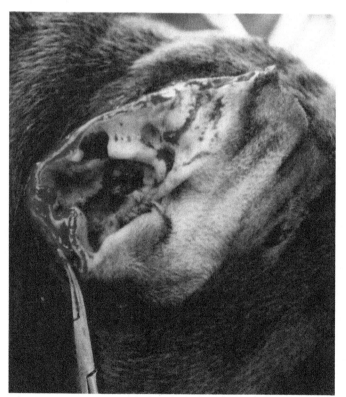

The cut of the ear in relationship to the landmark tubercles is clear in this photo. Photo: S. Allen.

The major worms that infest dogs are hookworms, roundworms, whipworms and tapeworms. The larva or eggs of these worms enter the dog's body through its skin or mouth. Roundworms get into puppies while they are still in the mother's uterus, and then are passed to them after they are born through the mother's milk. All these nematode worms end up in the intestines of the dog (after they have migrated through many other organs in the dog's body), where they set up shop eating from the intestines or sucking blood from the intestines and laying more eggs. A severe roundworm infestation can totally block a puppy's intestines. A severe hookworm infestation can make a puppy lethally anemic. There are certain vermifuges that take care of hookworms, roundworms, and whipworms all at the same time. A different product must be used to eliminate tapeworm, which is a cestode worm instead of a nematode like the first three.

The heartworm Dirofilaria immitis is another nematode that enters the dog's body via the bloodstream when the dog is bitten by a blood-sucking insect that is harboring the infective larvae in its body. Heartworm larvae migrate to the heart, where they lodge themselves, reproduce, and do damage to the heart and heart valves. There are presently two products on the market that can be given to the dog once a month to prevent the development of the heartworms if the larvae were injected into its body. Ivermectin is one of these products, which prevents heartworm infection, and in higher doses also deworms the dog for all worms except tapeworms. Ivermectin also kills insects on the dog

This picture shows the shape of the ear cut with respect to the landmarks. It shows the suturing of the edge and the buttons that are keeping the ears up over the head. Carpe Diem Balzac, eight-week-old male. Breeder and owner: E. Schiavo. Photo: S. Allen.

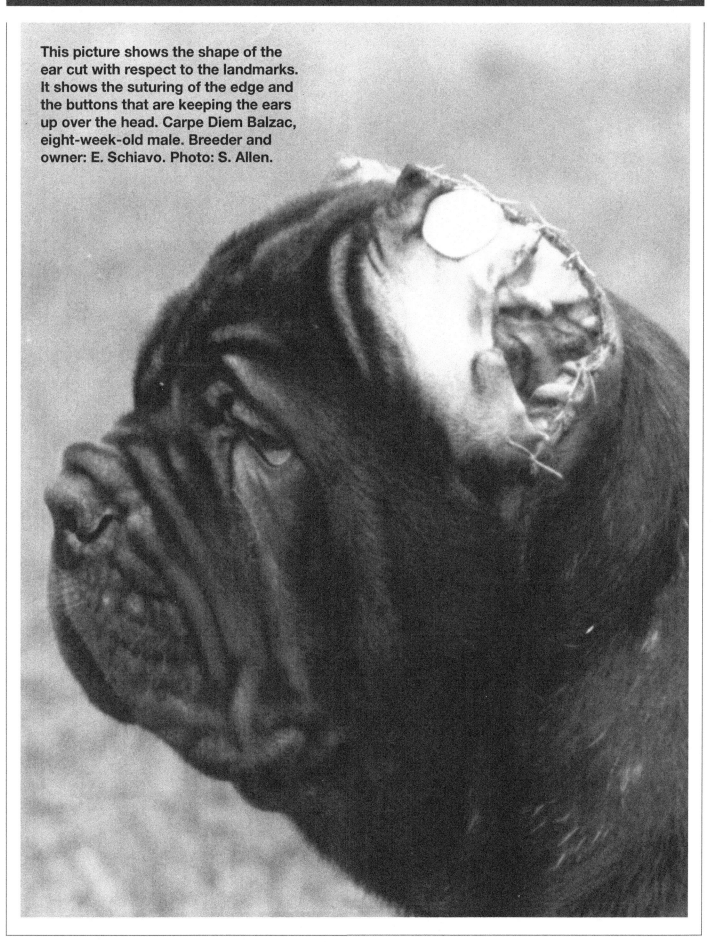

Puppy waking up from anesthesia after the ear cropping. Photo: S. Allen.

Longer-style ear crop, where the ears flop over the top of the head. In some dogs, the ear cartilage strengthens as the dog grows, and the ear eventually stands straight up. In other dogs, the ear cartilage remains soft, and they stay flopped over the head. Either style is acceptable. Axa, four-month-old female. Breeder: A. Dionizi. Photo: S. Allen.

Ear crop from the front view. Carpe Diem Balzac. Photo: S. Allen.

Ch. Caligola di Ponzano, four-year-old male. Breeder: M. Querci. Owner: A. Pegoli. Photo: Schumacher.

Inzio von Brabent, male. Photo: Schumacher.

Ironstone Thor, four-month-old male. Breeder: S. Allen. Owner: C. Kemp. Photo: S. Allen.

Faience de San Basile, three-year-old female. Breeder and owner: A. Aiello. Photo: S. Allen.

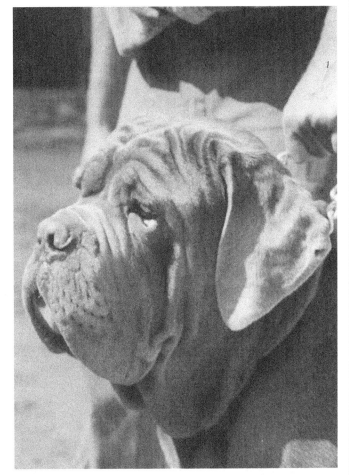

Dardo v.d. Reutemühle. Owner regretfully not identified. Photo: Schumacher.

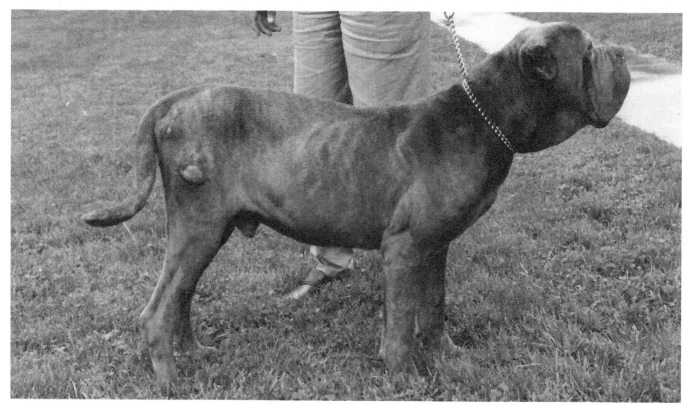

The photos on these two pages illustrate how much good common-sense care can do. This year-old male Neo was not fed by his owner, and was forced to lie on concrete. Note the sores caused by trauma to skin overlying non-fleshy areas. Photo: S. Allen.

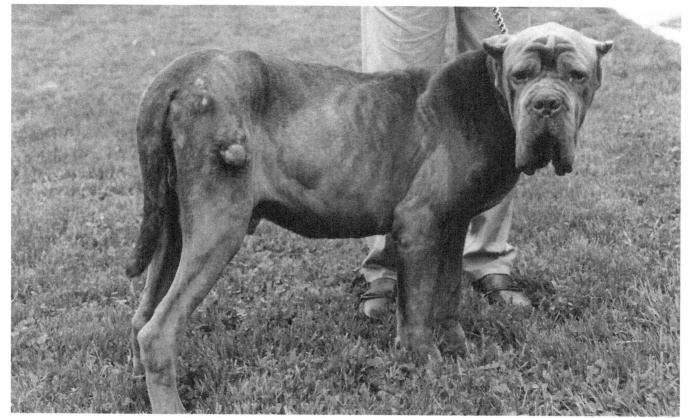

The conformation does not look good. Photo: S. Allen.

Two months later, after the dog had been fed and watered on a daily basis and been given wood to lie on instead of cement. Notice the sores are simply disappearing. No surgery was done. The coat is shedding out. The topline is now straight, and the conformation is lovely. Photo: S. Allen.

This photo was taken another month after the previous two. The dog now appears to have excellent conformation and head type. The sores disappeared. A scar remains. All the poor thing needed was a little care. Photo: S. Allen.

and reproductive disease. The market is loaded with products to kill and repel ticks and fleas. Amitraz-impregnated collars are excellent for repelling ticks. A vaccine is available to prevent the Lyme disease.

Neapolitan Mastiffs, along with Rottweilers, are highly susceptible to parvovirus. There are several strains of parvovirus in the field, and several different parvo vaccines available. It is imperative that any breeder of Neapolitan Mastiffs or new Neo owner establish a vaccination protocol for the puppies. The routine puppy vaccines usually comprise distemper virus, hepatitis virus, parainfluenza virus, parvovirus and leptospirosis bacterin. Some vaccines also include coronavirus. Each veterinarian will establish his or her own regimen, but most important for the Neapolitan puppy is the parvovirus vaccine.

Leone, 10-month-old mahogony male. Breeder: L. Del Prete. Owner: J. Hospodar. Photo: Hospodar.

such as ear mites, scabies mites and even Demodex. The other product, milbemycin, prevents heartworms and kills all the other nematodes at the same time with the regular heartworm dose. With such readily available and safe products, there is no excuse for any owner not to have a worm-free and heartworm-free dog.

Ticks and other arthropods are being recognized as more of a danger than they were once thought to be because they are also vectors for the rickettsia-caused Lyme disease. Lyme disease causes crippling arthritis and also liver, kidney, heart, ocular

Parvovirus kills Neos quickly. Sometimes all you see is that a puppy that was fine in the morning begins to vomit in the afternoon. By the next day it is totally dehydrated, and it may already be too late for treatment to work. The puppy may seizure and die before you even see any bloody or pure water diarrhea. Parvovirus is also a very hardy virus. It lives on open kennel surfaces for years. It even seems to survive disinfecting with bleach or parvovirus virucidal detergents. Parvovirus can wipe out an entire Neo kennel in days. It is so contagious that it can be transmitted by one person touching an object that has simply been touched by another person who has touched a parvovirus-infected dog. That person then goes home and touches his or

Lisandro, three-year-old male.
Owner: R. Barani. Photo: S. Allen.

her own puppy. The puppy comes down with parvovirus three days later. I have seen this happen. Anyone who owns Neos must take great pains to prevent parvo in their dog or dogs.

The only way to prevent parvovirus is by vaccinating. The parvo vaccine should be given to puppies at six and at eight weeks of age. Distemper, hepatitis, parainfluenza should be given at seven and at nine weeks of age. The distemper and parvo vaccines should not be given together to Neo puppies under 12 weeks of age. We keep reiterating that Neos have poor immune systems. Giving too many modified live virus vaccines at once stresses the immune system of Neo puppies too much. To be safe, give the vaccines separately. If parvo is a problem in your kennel, the parvo vaccine may be given to the puppies at five, six and eight weeks of age. Parvo vaccine can be given again at 12 and 16 weeks to make sure the puppy acquires proper immunity.

Exercise

Once a Neapolitan Mastiff has reached maturity at about one and a half years of age, he will be a pretty tough dog. He will most likely love to exercise with you any way you

Agira di Palazzo, two-year-old female. Breeder and owner: K. Zimmerman. Photo: S. Allen.

and he want to, whether it be hiking, trotting alongside a bicycle or horse, mountain trail climbing or swimming. The only warning I would give is to make sure he is not getting overheated. The amount of exercise he will be able to tolerate will depend upon climatic conditions and the amount of weight you have allowed him to put on. Unlike the sighthounds, which have a need to run every day, the Neapolitan actually bases the amount of exercise he does on you. He adapts his lifestyle to yours, so you will be the determiner of how much exercise he will need.

The story of how much exercise a Neo can do is a different story when he is young. As we mentioned before, the baby Neo is really too heavy for his immature bones, and he can damage his bones and joints very easily while he is growing. It is best to leave the puppy

Orso, five-month-old male. Breeder: R. Blasio. Owner: S. Allen. Photo: S. Allen.

to his own devices to exercise as much as he sees fit. If a puppy is tired or sore, he just won't move around much if he is left to do what he wants to do. If you make him go for a walk with you, he will keep going just to be with you, even though he may be exhausted or hurting. If you do take the puppy for a walk, and you notice that the walk has become too long, and the puppy is dragging, there is no way you will be able to pick him up and carry him back home. Neo babies are heavy! To force him to walk back home could do irreparable damage to his joints.

"Max." A six-year-old male. Breeder: S. Allen. Owner: M. Baldassare. Photo: S. Allen.

If you live in an apartment or do not have

"Do I look like a long distance runner?" Atena del Nolano, eight-week-old puppy. Breeder: M. De Falco Jovane. Photo: S. Allen.

access to a yard where you could leave him out for a good part of the day to exercise at will, then you will have to go on short walks with the puppy. As each puppy is different,

you will have to observe by his attitude how much exercise he can take, and stop before he gets tired.

Every purebred-dog breed has its own special problems. This section has been an attempt to explain some of the idiosyncrasies in a breed little understood by the general public and veterinarians alike. Other than these few idiosyncrasies mentioned above, the Neo does not require a great deal of specialized care. Once he is mature, the Mastino is actually hardier than many other breeds of dogs. He is easy to take care of because he is little inclined to wander. When he is with you, he is most content to stay by your side. When you are away, he is happy to just await your return.

Messicano, five-year-old male. Breeder and owner: R. Sconamiglio. Photo: K. Zimmerman.

Frazier della Grotta Azzurra. Breeder: P. Siano. Owner: G. Mira. Photo: Schumacher.

Three-week-old mahogany puppy. Photo: S. Allen.

Breeding and Whelping

Any chapter on breeding dogs must address the philosophical question of "Why breed?" and, if you do choose to breed, "Which dogs to breed?" There are many reasons why people decide to breed their dog, some more noble than others. In any case, those who decide to breed must be ready to accept a number of responsibilities.

The first responsibility is to the breed you have decided to perpetuate. You must feel that the dogs you mate together will produce offspring with attributes that you feel will contribute to the breed in accordance with the breed standard. You must be certain that the two individuals you decide to breed have most of the qualities or a particularly excellent quality called for by the breed standard. Breeders have a moral responsibility to try to improve the breed they are working with. There is no other really good reason to get involved with creating new specimens within a breed.

Secondly, you must be prepared for the financial responsibilities that accompany breeding, whelping and selling puppies. Neapolitan Mastiffs are not easy dogs to breed. In fact, they are one of the most difficult breeds from which to get excellent quality puppies. You must be prepared to pay a stud fee that is routinely equal to the cost of a puppy produced by the stud dog. In some instances, the stud fee is paid by giving the stud-dog owner one or two pick puppies instead of money. In any case, you must be prepared for the instance in which a stud fee is paid or promised, and only one puppy is born, or several are born but they all die.

You must be prepared to pay the veterinarian's costs in preparing the bitch for breeding and informing you of when to breed her. You must then be prepared to pay costs of doing an artificial insemination, which is more commonly performed than not with Neapolitan Mastiffs. There are many things that can go wrong during the pregnancy, for which you must be prepared to pay. Finally, there is the possibility your bitch will need a Cesarean section with the ensuing costs. If your bitch happens to reject the puppies, you must be prepared to be with them day and night for three weeks at least, feeding them every two to four hours and stimulating them to void.

Puppy, five weeks old. Photo: S. Allen.

Some bitches get pregnant easily, whelp easily, and are wonderful mothers. Many are not. Usually one experience of having to keep puppies alive for three weeks when a mother will not care for them is enough to dissuade sane people from ever breeding again. Of course, the experience will drive some people insane. They then undertake the nightmare over and over again for some unknown reason. They are the ones who become the Mastinari.

The third responsibility the breeder assumes is toward the animals whose lives he or she is affecting. Pregnancy is not easy for any female, especially big, heavy Mastini.

Complications can occur, and the breeder must be concerned with what can happen to the mother, and must be responsible for the lives of the puppies he or she has elected to bring into the world. It takes a lot of effort to find people suitable to own a Neapolitan Mastiff. A Neapolitan Mastiff breeder should know what he or she is going to do with potential puppies before bringing them into the world.

Lastly, the breeder has a responsibility to the buyers of the puppies. Buyer trust that breeders are the experts who are giving them the product they have bargained for. It is up to the seller to inform the buyer about

Theoduta del Vittoriale, four-year-old female. Breeder: G. Mira. Owner: R. Barani. Photo: S. Allen.

the breed and the particular puppy that the buyer would like to have. The breeder must be knowledgeable enough about what he or she has produced to be able to properly represent it to the buyer. Be aware that the buyer will call you for the life of the dog whenever any little problems occur. Buyers look to their breeders forever for help and solace. They will even call you to tell you when their pet dies.

How to Breed Neapolitan Mastiffs

The success achieved in breeding Neapolitan Mastiffs is directly proportional to the proper preparation of the two prospective parents. The first consideration is whether the two dogs are suitable according to breed type and temperament to even be bred. Once the choice of dogs for the mating is made, the sperm from the male has to be put into the female at the right time in her heat cycle. With Neapolitans, this is not so easy as one would think.

At this point, many readers will stop and say to themselves, "That is not true. I called so-and-so whose bitch just had a huge litter, and it was an accidental breeding. The dogs just got together when the owners weren't home and mated, like dogs usually do. The owners didn't even know it happened. What is so hard about that?" It is a fair question, so here is the long explanation:

First of all, true conscientious breeders of Neapolitan Mastiffs do not have pairs of dogs running around unobserved for long periods of time such that they could miss the bitch

being in heat. True breeders of Neapolitans usually have special dogs that they have shown or raised expressly for breeding. They are usually very aware of their animals' status at all times. Their dogs generally are, or should be, of the very epitome of breed type, being very massive and heavy. Heavy, massive Neos do not go cavorting around when a bitch is in heat with a cavalier Don

Salvatore, two-year-old male. Breeder: S. Allen. Owner: L. and I. Somogyi. Photo: Somogyi.

Giovanni attitude. The males are usually so big and heavy that the bitch cannot hold them up, and if she is able to, the males, who invariably can't find the right spot, get exhausted after five or 10 minutes of trying to breed. Not all Italians are great lovers, despite common rumors.

In contrast to the massive, weighty males whose genes a true breeder wants to perpetuate, the lighter, slimmer, less typey, and by definition, poorer quality males usually can breed a bitch by themselves. It is usually this latter type of male Neo that has accomplished the "accidental breeding." The scenario is usually a family that had acquired a male and female Neo as puppies so that "the two could have companionship when the owners were not home." Usually, the dogs are house dogs, and the owners just never knew the bitch went into heat. Now, you would have to be either blind or totally oblivious to your Neos not to know when a bitch is in heat. When Neos come into heat, they bleed for about 10 days. This period is called the proestrus. The color of blood is red, and very noticeable. In addition, the vulva of the bitch swells up to such an extent that her whole back end looks very puffy.

By day nine or 10 of the proestrus, the bitch usually ovulates. When she ovulates, she goes into estrus, or true heat, and this is the time that she is receptive to the male. If there is a male Neo anywhere within smelling distance of her, he turns into an impossible-to-tolerate maniac. Someone living in the same household with a male Neo and a female in heat would have to be a total stone not to know that something was up! If you leave them together, the male will start chasing the female wildly through the house. He will jump on her, crash on her and over her and into the furniture. He will be panting, slobbering and crazy with desire. If you separate him by putting him in another room of the house, he will simply break down the door and get out. If you put him outside in a pen, he will howl and bark and try to jump out. He may even chew through the chain-link fence to get out. He won't eat at all, and he will get very thin. Even if you missed the pools of blood on the floor for 10 days, it is practically impossible not to know when a

bitch is in heat while your male is acting like a lunatic.

After the bitch ovulates around day 10 from the start of bleeding, two to four more days are required for the ova to mature sufficiently to be fertilized by the sperm. The mature ova remain viable and ready for two to four more days after that, then begin to disintegrate.

The most fertile period for the bitch is, therefore, days two to six after ovulation. The dog has a total period of about six days to successfully impregnate the bitch. That is a long time for the owners to be out of the house and not know what was happening. A true breeder would be counting the days to know exactly when to breed the bitch.

This diversion has been an effort to explain why you will hear contradictions to what I am really going to talk about next, and that is, the preparation of the male and female for breeding.

The Male

Before trying to mate the male dog, the breeder should have the dog's semen analyzed to make sure he is reproductively sound. A veterinarian experienced in reproduction can collect the dog's semen and check it for proper numbers and quality of sperm. About 200 million sperm per insemination are needed to achieve pregnancy. If the male dog does not produce this amount of sperm in one ejaculation, pregnancy will not normally result. The sperm produced must have the proper structure and forward motility in order to successfully fertilize the ova. The semen can also be examined for evidence of infection of the reproductive tract, and, if necessary, cultured for bacterial growth. Dogs as well as bitches should have their blood tested for brucellosis. Brucellosis is a contagious venereal disease, though its incidence is rare in the United States. When dealing with expensive breeding dogs, it is better to do the test than be sorry later.

If the male checks out to have good semen and to be free from infection, he can be bred naturally depending on if he can do the mount, if he can penetrate the bitch, if the bitch will allow him to mount her, and if the bitch can hold him up. As I said before, with Neos, it is rare that these four criteria can be met.

If the male is found to have a reproductive problem – in other words, insufficient or poor-quality sperm – the only way to get the bitch pregnant may be by means of artificial insemination. Poor sperm quality is not uncommon in the giant-breed dogs, Neapolitan Mastiffs included. A reproductive specialist often needs to be enlisted to help with the breeding of such dogs. In these cases, it may be necessary to collect the dog several times to get numbers of sperm sufficient for a good insemination. Certain buffers can also be added to the semen to enhance its quality. I repeat, it is very common for the dog that has the breed characteristics you desperately want to reproduce to have poor-quality semen. A good reproduction specialist can do wonders.

In the United States, as canine reproduction is becoming more and more sophisticated, owners are more frequently demanding alternative methods of breeding their bitches. Artificial insemination is being employed more often because it is faster and easier, especially with Neos, than natural breeding. There is also less risk of introducing infection to either bitch or stud. Now that techniques for chilled semen and freezing dog semen have been perfected, the "stud dog" can be sent to the bitch, eliminating the stress and costs associated with shipping a prize bitch to a particular stud dog. In comparison to bovine and human semen, canine semen has been traditionally touted as being very difficult to freeze successfully. Thanks to the developments by such laboratories as CLONE labs in Chester Springs, Pennsylvania, owners can freeze the semen of their prized dogs forever. Puppies can be produced from exceptional sires long after they are dead. The ability to freeze a dog's semen allows the owners to breed that dog only when they really want to make puppies rather than being forced to breed litter after litter during the short reproductive life span of the dog when there may be no need to make more puppies.

The Female

Neo bitches normally come into heat every five to six months. The heat is usually very obvious because the whole vulva area swells up and becomes very floppy, and bleeding is usually copious and obvious. When the owner first notices the bitch coming into heat, she should be taken for a bacterial

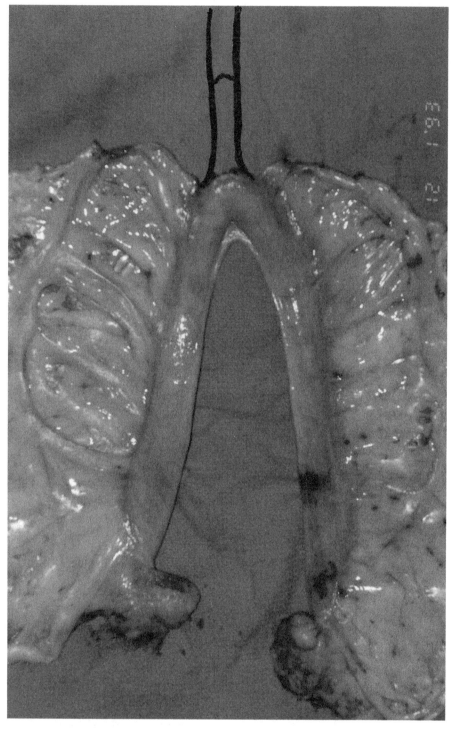

Uterus of Neapolitan Mastiff. The photo shows the two uterine horns, which in the case of this bitch were each 11 inches long. The body of the uterus is not included in the specimen, but is indicated by the black drawn lines at the top of the photo. The cervix is indicated by the drawn line representing the division between the uterus and the vagina. The vagina of the Neo can be about 10 inches long. The body of the uterus is another two to three inches. So the path from vulva to Fallopian tubes where the eggs are sitting can be about 23 inches long. That is a long way for easily fatigued Neo sperm to swim.

culture and cytology of the deep vagina to make sure there is no active infection going on. A brucellosis test should also be done on a blood sample, as most stud-dog owners will want proof of a negative canine brucellosis test.

The blood tests and cultures are the easy part. The tricky part is to pinpoint the day on which the bitch should be bred so as to assure pregnancy. The even trickier part with Neos is getting the bitch bred.

Ovulation timing

If male Neos are bred several times over a seven-day period, the numbers of sperm found in the later ejaculations is less than the numbers of sperm produced in the first one or two ejaculations. Neo sperm does not live as long as sperm of some other smaller-breed dogs, and, like the dogs themselves, the little swimmers are rather sluggish and slow moving. The uterus of female Neos is very long, so the sperm have a long way to swim. With all these factors taken into consideration, the chances

Two Neapolitan Mastiffs tied together after the male has penetrated the female. The female is still standing over the bar that supported her during the mount. Photo: S. Allen.

of getting a Neo bitch pregnant are greatly enhanced if large numbers of sperm can be deposited in the uterus during the two- to four-day time period after the eggs have ovulated and are ripe for fertilization.

In the past, dog breeders have come up with many formulas and devices for determining the optimum time for mating the bitch. Some breeders will always breed on day 13 of the heat cycle, whereas others will swear by day 11. Some breeders will advocate breeding the bitch as soon as she starts flagging, and continuing every other day until she no longer accepts the male. Since canine reproduction has become more of a science, we have learned that these methods are not reliable. Some bitches ovulate on day 10, but some may ovulate as early as day seven or as late as day 14 or longer. Simply relying on the

bitch's behavior or a fixed average number of days is not adequate for successful breeding of Neapolitan Mastiffs (or other breeds as well).

In the past few years, great inroads have been made in developing methods for predicting ovulation in bitches. The two methods that are reliable and easy if used together are vaginal cell cytology and progesterone testing. These tests should be performed on the bitch starting on day seven of the heat cycle, and continuing every two days until the tests indicate that the bitch is ovulating. Since the tests themselves are approximate indicators of when the bitch is ovulating, the success of the testing is also dependent upon the expertise and experience of the person doing the testing. There are several progesterone kits commercially available to veterinarians and breeders. The test requires a blood sample from the bitch, but is otherwise quickly run in the office.

Another method that also works quite well in the hands of experienced operators is the fiberoscopic exam of the vaginal tract of the bitch. The vaginal mucosa undergoes very characteristic changes with each stage of the heat cycle. An experienced operator can pinpoint with excellent accuracy the day of ovulation. The drawbacks to this method are finding someone experienced in the use of this expensive equipment, and the necessity for daily examinations of the bitch until the day of ovulation is detected.

Once the day of ovulation of the bitch is determined, half the battle of breeding is over. What remains is to get viable sperm into the uterus of the bitch. This can be done in two different ways. The first is for the male to naturally mount the bitch and form a tie with her. The .2 to 1 cc of Neo sperm is ejaculated into the bitch and then forced through the cervix into the uterus by the 30 to 100 or more cc of prostatic fluid that the dog pulsates into the bitch during the 15- to 30-minute tie.

As we said before, getting the male to tie with the bitch is not easy. Neapolitan Mastiff females are extraordinarily opinionated as to whom they want to breed with. They usually will not let a male breed them unless they know him very well. I have even had some bitches who want to breed with one male in the kennel, but not the one I have chosen to mate with them. A general maxim that you can take to the bank is that a Neapolitan

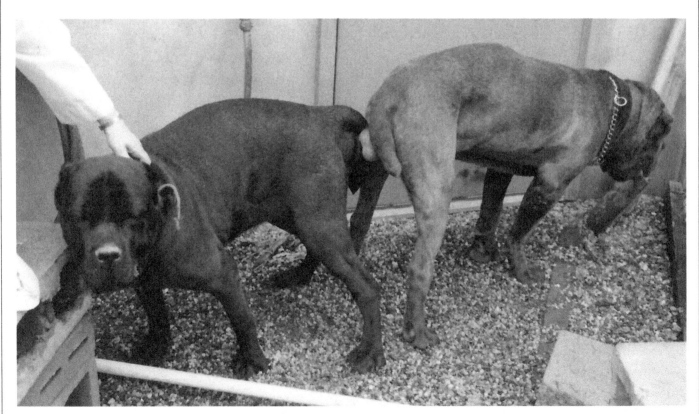

The tie. Notice that the male who was able to accomplish this mating is lean and muscular. Photo: S. Allen.

Mastiff who has been sent or brought to you to be bred by your stud dog will absolutely under no circumstances whatsoever allow herself to be bred by you dog. I can also guarantee that one Neo bitch is stronger and slipperier than three men and a male dog.

There are tricks to getting a female Neo bred naturally, and that is perhaps the secret of successful Mastinari. If you have taken up the challenge of breeding Mastini, you must take up the challenge of figuring out how to get the bitch bred. You will be proud of yourself when you do, though you may have to go to the hospital for back surgery afterward.

Easier and more convenient for the breeder than naturally breeding Neapolitans is to breed them by artificial insemination. This may be done with fresh semen deposited into the bitch's vagina or uterus immediately after collecting it from the male. For those owners who want to breed to a dog that is far away and do not want to ship their bitches, fresh chilled semen may be inseminated within 24 hours of collection. And for even longer distances, across country borders, or for male dogs who are no longer alive, frozen semen can be employed.

The trick to getting the bitch pregnant by artificial insemination is to get the sperm into the uterine horns. If the sperm are deposited into the cranial vagina only, they are never going to get to the eggs in the Fallopian tubes. To reiterate, the vaginal tract and uterus of the Neo can be 23 inches long. The vagina is also comprised of heavy mucosal folds that will trap the sperm and prevent them from getting into the uterus.

The semen must be deposited through the cervix directly. This can be done by one of two methods. The first is by using a special catheter developed by Jan Fougner in Norway. In the hands of a skilled technician, the catheter can be passed into the vagina and through the cervix of the dog. The sperm-rich fraction of the semen can then be deposited directly into the uterus.

The second method, which is becoming more and more popular with owners of giant-breed dogs, is by surgical implantation of sperm into the uterus. The method works very well, but must be done by an experienced veterinarian. It entails all the risks of a major surgery and anesthesia.

Artificially inseminating by any method other than the above mentioned two methods is a gamble as far as obtaining a successful pregnancy is concerned. I know of pregnancies in Neos that have resulted from haphazard deposition of semen into the vagina, but for as many that were successful, a lot more were not. If you are serious about breeding Mastini, my advice is to take the time and incur the expenses of preparing the bitch for breeding, pinpointing the day of ovulation, and having her bred at the right time by someone who is experienced with Neapolitan Mastiffs.

Pregnancy

Once the bitch has been bred, usually one or two times, depending upon each individual situation, she can be checked for pregnancy starting at about 18 days after the

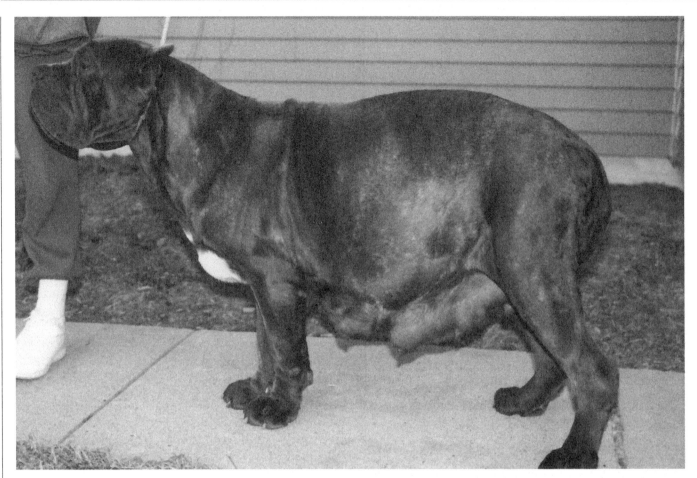

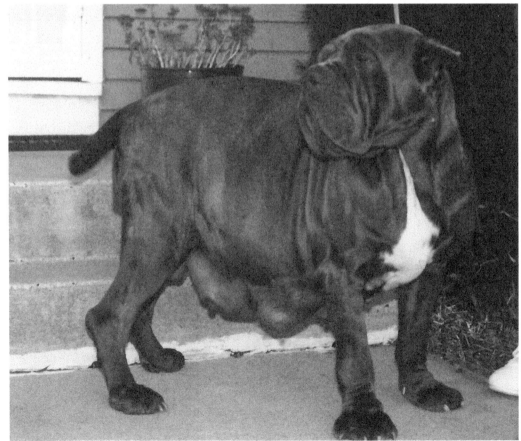

Pregnant Neo bitch. Many people think their bitches are pregnant just because they were bred. For those who are unsure whether your bitch is pregnant, these photos show you that there is no doubt when a female Neo is pregnant. If your bitch does not look like this at six weeks pregnant, she isn't. Vanguard's Adrianna, two-year-old female. Breeder and owner: G. Schaffer. Photo: G. Schaffer.

last breeding. To date, there are two reliable methods for determining pregnancy in the bitch. The fastest is by palpation of the fetuses by an experienced veterinarian or technician. The best time to do palpation is between 21 and 28 days after the last breeding. If the bitch is too heavy or tense or uncooperative, then ultrasound can be done. Ultrasound can be done reliably at 18 days after the last breeding. There is a blood test for pregnancy being currently marketed, but I have found it inaccurate. A new test is in the works that should be available soon and able to determine pregnancy within a week of breeding.

Other signs of pregnancy that the owner of the bitch can observe are the following: Right after breeding, the bitch will have a ravenous appetite. By three weeks of pregnancy, she will begin to slack off eating. She may even have morning sickness and vomit periodically. At six weeks pregnant, she will start to eat a lot again, as the puppies inside her are really beginning to grow. Then, during the last week, if she is very large, she will not eat as much again.

At three weeks post breeding, the pregnant bitch will not be noticeably larger in the belly. Her abdomen may be more tense or harder than usual. This is in contrast to the non-pregnant bitch who is in false pregnancy. Her abdomen will usually be markedly enlarged by three weeks, and the owner will believe she is pregnant. The bitch in false pregnancy will usually not have any mammary development at this stage. In contrast, the pregnant bitch will have swollen and firm mammary glands. The bitch should be put on

Whelping box. Photo: S. Allen.

a human prenatal vitamin-mineral pill at this time. She should be fed adequately, but not allowed to get too heavy, or parturition will be difficult.

The bitch should have steady exercise throughout her pregnancy to maintain good muscle tone. Neapolitan Mastiffs are poor whelpers. They tire easily during the whelping process, and many have uterine inertia. Keeping the bitch thin and physically fit will aid her during the whelping.

A necessity for the new mother and her puppies a whelping box. It is made of two-foot-by-six-inch boards, and is at least five feet by five feet. The sides are made by standing the boards on their side. The top is made by nailing the two-foot-by-six-inch boards on top so that they form an overhanging lip toward the inside of the box. The lip is important so that the puppies can crawl under it to escape being crushed by their mother when she lies up against the

Whelping box set down over blankets. There can be no holes in the blankets or space between the blanket edge and the whelping box. Puppies always crawl into holes and under blankets if there is a space. The mother then lies on them. Photo: S. Allen.

sides of the box. The box should be varnished to seal the wood and make it washable. There is no floor to the box. The wooden frame is simply set down over a blanket or sheet, underneath which are several layers of paper. When a Neo gives birth, there is fluid, blood and placental discharge all over the place. You will need something to soak up the fluid and can be easily cleaned. Papers alone are too messy. They get crumpled up, the babies crawl underneath them, and then the pups get squashed by the mother, who does not see them under the papers. Papers also do not make a good flooring for Neo puppies because they are too slippery. The Neo puppies need a surface that provides traction for them in their attempts to crawl around. It is best to lay a blanket over a lot of papers. The blanket should be changed twice daily, and the papers underneath as often as they

get soiled through the blanket.

Whelping

The pregnant Neo bitch routinely goes into labor 60 days after the breeding, which was done two days after ovulation. It is very important to keep track of the due date because some bitches do not go into labor properly. Normally, 12 to 24 hours before whelping, the bitch will not eat and will start to urinate and defecate to empty herself out. First she will shiver, and she will get a very pained and scared look on her face. Her teeth may chatter. She will want you to be with her. Then she will start to pant and dig. She will want to go outside and dig a hole. If she is in her whelping box, she will dig and rip the sheets and papers all up. For this reason

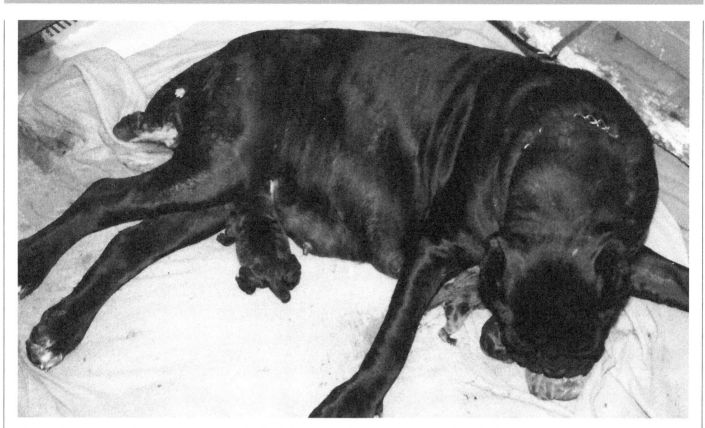

Neapolitan bitch in the process of whelping. She is so engrossed with licking one of her puppies that she does not know another is in the process of being born. This is one reason many puppies do not survive the birth if the owner is not present. Had this puppy been born enveloped by its sac, as is usual, it may have suffocated while its mother was paying attention to one of its siblings. Photo: S. Allen.

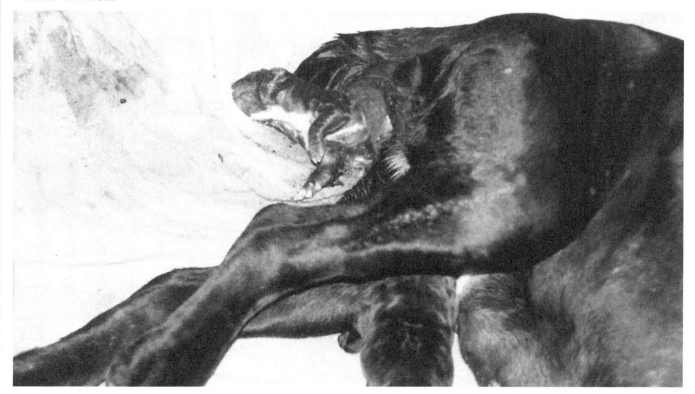

Close-up of puppy being born. Photo: S. Allen.

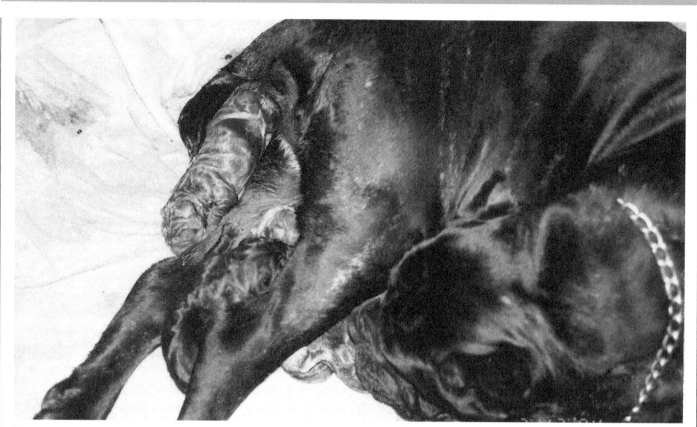

The mother finally realizes there is another puppy coming out. Bitches of other breeds would normally at this time be reaching back and cleaning the puppy. This mother, typical of Neos, is just staring at the puppy. Photo: S. Allen.

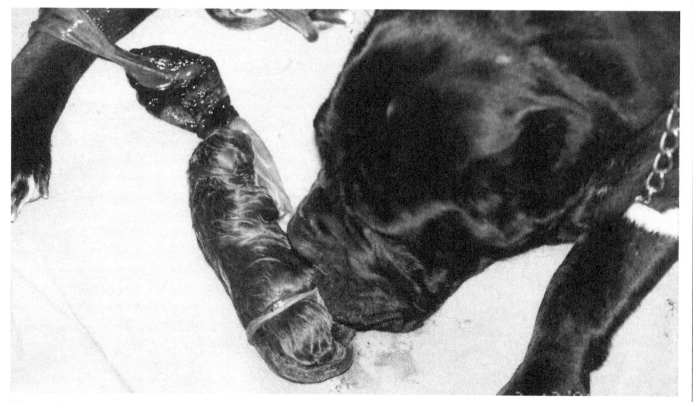

When the puppy and placenta were finally pulled out by the human attendant and placed in front of the bitch, she began to chew off the placenta, eat it and clean the puppy. Photo: S. Allen.

it is best to put raggedy sheets or blankets in the whelping box in the beginning of labor, then change to good ones without holes after the whelping is over. Finally, a bitch who is a good whelper will start to push out the puppies.

Some Neo bitches do not push. They just lie there, enduring the pain stoically, but not pushing. These are problem whelpers, and you may end up having to reach in and pull out each puppy as it comes into the birth canal.

Some Neos will go into labor, the water will break, they will push and dig violently for an hour, and nothing will come out. If they are pushing and digging violently, and nothing comes out, it usually means a dystocia, or stuck puppy. Usually in these cases, a Cesarean section must be performed.

Sometimes Mastino bitches will not even go into labor, or at least a labor recognizable by their owners. If 61 days from the last breeding go by, and your dog has not gone into labor, she will have to be checked by your veterinarian. Most likely a Cesarean section will have to be performed. Some bitches just have complete uterine inertia, and if they go over their due date, the puppies die. Nothing is sadder than to do a Cesarean section on an overdue bitch to find a whole uterus full of term puppies now in there dead and decomposing. You must watch your bitch like a hawk.

The commercial progesterone kits are a useful tool at whelping time because they can be used to predict when the bitch will whelp. When the blood progesterone levels fall to less than 2 ngml, the bitch will usually whelp within 12 to 24 hours. If your bitch is not going into labor and you think she is due, you can have a progesterone test run. If the test says the progesterone has dropped, and she is not in labor, you will know precisely that a Cesarean section must be done.

If the bitch does go on to whelp naturally, the process is still a nightmare for the owner. Neos whelp very slowly. Sometimes they go two or more hours in between puppies. Sometimes they forget to push when the puppy is in the birth canal, and you do not know it. So the puppy dies there. Sometimes you have to give oxytocin to induce uterine contractions that have stopped, and you will get one or two puppies to come out. If you give oxytocin too frequently, however, the uterus will become resistant to its effects. Then the uterus will not contract at all, and the rest of the puppies inside the bitch will die.

Whelping a Neo bitch is an art in itself. The owner has to have the right "feel" for when a puppy should be coming and isn't, or if the bitch is just resting. The owner may have to pull out every puppy, or the bitch may have them herself. The bitch may clean them properly, or the owner may have to end up doing it all. The owner has to make the decision as to whether to let the bitch whelp naturally, or whether to do a Cesarean section and incur all the associated costs and risks in order to save all the puppies. Each bitch and each whelping is an individual happening. It is sometimes very difficult to make the right decisions as to what to do.

**Puppy, five
weeks old.
Photo: S. Allen.**

If the owner jumps the gun and takes the puppies by C-section before the bitch's hormones have told her she is supposed to be a mother, the bitch will refuse to care for the puppies. Sometimes bitches are in so much pain from the prolonged whelping and milk-engorged teats that they destroy the source of their pain – their puppies. Some bitches really like their puppies, but can't count. They are so tired, and so desirous of staying still around their puppies, that as long as they see one puppy in front of them, they do not realize that they are lying on top of a whole bunch of screaming, soon to be smothered babies.

The biggest danger to Neo puppies in the first four weeks of life is their own mother. More puppies die from being squashed by their mother than from any other cause. For this reason, it is imperative to have a whelping box, and it is imperative that someone stay with the mother round the clock for the first two weeks after parturition. You will leave the mother alone for just two hours, and when you come back, there will be another squashed puppy. The anxiety caused in the owner of the pregnant and postparturient Neo mother is extraordinary. Sometimes it is unbearable.

During the whelping process, which can last for 24 hours, it is best to take the puppies away from the mother and put them on a heating pad to stay warm and dry. You can leave one with the mother to keep her calm. You will have to bottle-feed the puppies every two hours or allow them to suckle on the mother if she is quiet enough to allow them to do it while she is in labor. If the

Puppy, eight weeks old. One who made it. Owner: Karen Drager. Photo: S. Allen.

mother has mastitis, or develops mastitis, as is common with the Molossian breeds, you will have to take all the puppies away from the mother or they will die. Then you will have to bottle-feed them every two hours for the next three weeks.

Because keeping baby Mastini alive on their own mothers is routinely so difficult, the Italians plan ahead to have a surrogate mother of some mixed breed ready to put the puppies onto. Surrogates are certainly a lot easier than bottle feeding and cleaning puppies every two hours for three weeks, but they also have their drawbacks. Sometimes it is difficult to get a surrogate to take a puppy. They have been known to kill their foster children.

Of course some people will say that all I have said is incorrect, that their Mastino mothers are wonderful with the puppies. And certainly some are, or try to be very good mothers. Generally, it is the larger, more massive, more gentle, more laidback Mastino female that has the most problems during and after parturition. The lighter, smaller, more active and wiry bitches seem to have the least amount of trouble having the puppies. That is why it is easier to get the leaner, less typey Neos than it is to get the more impressive, massive, wrinkled Neos so desired by fanciers for their unusual look. It is a simple fact that greater numbers of the less typey Neos get pregnant and give birth to more of the same type puppies. This fact then brings us back to the philosophical question of whether we should be perpetuating a breed type that has such low viability that it needs a lot of human assistance. Some

people say that the more natural dog, the one can do it all by itself and raise puppies to weaning age, should be the only ones we should allow to breed. If we followed this line of reasoning, we would have none of the specialized breeds we have today that have been cultivated through the centuries for a particular purpose or style.

This question is more routinely addressed with regard to the Neapolitan Mastiff in the United States precisely because our society is more impressed by athletic prowess as a measure of excellence than it is with any other single characteristic. If athletic prowess and stamina are what people want most in a dog, then the massive, wrinkled, loose-skinned, enormous-jowled, relatively sedentary Neapolitan Mastiff is not the dog for them.

As the duties required of the Mastino have

Sound dog, attractive dog, but not much head or body type. A generic Neapolitan Mastiff. Photo: S. Allen.

evolved throughout the ages, man has had to modify the breed in order for it to fit into today's society. Initially prized for its monstrous ferociousness and power, the Mastino, to be allowed to exist in our more pacifistic society, has had to trade off to a degree its physical ferocity for an aesthetic ferocity. Its appearance has evolved to fit the concept of the primitive guardian that Mastino fanciers covet. And, yes, the looks and softer temperament have been cultivated by man, and the dogs take some work to maintain. As a specialized dog, actually the antithesis of the normal "family" dog, the Neo takes some extra care to keep it healthy and reproducing.

To select for a sound dog that is practically maintenance free can be done. The dogs would still be Neapolitan Mastiffs in name, but not the sort that are the standard in Italy today. They would have less skin, dewlap, lips, wrinkle, bone mass and facial expression than those Neapolitan Mastiffs coveted today. It is safe to say that they will be more vigorous, which is what dog owners in the United States want. It is a fact, however, that along with that vigor, which is always associated with the survival of the fittest, is an outrageous power that is part of the

Sound dog, but with the head and body of a Neapolitan Mastiff. Lisandro, three-year-old male. Owner: R. Barani. Photo: S. Allen.

Mastino's genetics, and that is unfathomable to those people who are not experienced with the breed. This is not bad, per se, as long as the owner can control this power.

It is understandable that the novice will be confused by differences in appearance and type that exist in Neos all over the world today. It is certain that discussions will be vehement between owners and breeders of the different types of dogs. It may be that in the future, the Neapolitan Mastiff will evolve differently than it has to date. What one breeder may consider to be improvements to the breed, another may consider a detriment.

At this time, however, it would be safer for

Ironstone Diogenes, five weeks old. Breeder: S. Allen. Owner: C. Costello. Photo: S. Allen.

all who have dealings with the Neapolitan Mastiff to keep their dogs and ideas in tune with the type that the Italians consider their dog to be.

One thing is sure – that the Italian Mastino Neapolitano has an individuality of temperament and looks that distinguish it easily from all other breeds. To allow it to revert back to a generic Molossian would be to lose a breed of dog. To enhance the soundness of the Neo while trying to maintain its unusual appearance is admirable. To denigrate those dogs that are the modern-day concept of the ultimate home guard as too problematic to deal with is to destroy a breed for the sake of ease of production, maintenance and, consequently, salability.

Attila, 12-week-old male. Owner: R. Evans. Photo: S. Allen.

Six-month-old bitch bred by the author after generations of selecting primarily for soundness of all individual body parts and systems. She is tall, lean, has a long nose to accommodate all her teeth, and a plain face that goes along with her tight-skinned body type. She was bred down from very typey dogs, but each consecutive progeny was selected for soundness above all. The result is a very sound, active dog that races with the Greyhounds, leaps over fences, has boundless energy, and does not have the body shape, mass or facial features of a typey Neapolitan Mastiff.

It is actually only in the United States, where we have such a fast-growing population of Mastini with no one central organization to govern the standard, that these problems with type are even a question. The rest of the world has a fixed idea of what the Neapolitan Mastiff is in type, personality and use.

Feeding Puppies and Weaning

If you have to bottle-feed puppies, pasteurized goat's milk is excellent. If you do not have goat's milk, evaporated milk mixed with equal amounts of water is fine. To this I usually add a liquid vitamin supplement. I have also used human infant formulas, both milk and soy products. The soy products reduce the incidence of diarrhea that can occur with the milk-based formulas. The most important consideration when trying to get puppies to drink a bottle is that the milk be warm enough. It should be about 100 degrees Fahrenheit. If the milk is not warm enough, the puppies will not suck.

Even if the mother is nursing the puppies, there are occasions when the puppies may need supplemental bottle feeding. If the bitch has a large litter, the puppies may not all be able to get enough mother's milk to sustain them. In some cases, the bitch may simply not make enough milk to feed whatever size litter she has. You must examine the puppies several times daily to make sure each one is getting enough to eat, and if not, supplement them.

At five to six weeks of age, the puppies can also start eating ground, cooked meat or pressure-cooked whole chicken added to the soaked kibble. I feed them three to four times daily. At six weeks, I leave dry kibble out for them to eat whenever they want, and feed regular meals of the soft, soaked kibble and meat three times daily.

Puppy, four weeks old. Photo: S. Allen.

Teodata del Vittoriale, two-and-a-half-year-old female. Breeder: G. Mira. Owner: R. Barani. Photo: S. Allen.

By seven weeks, I add the soupy meat mixture to the dry kibble. I continue this feeding program until the pups are about 10 weeks old, when they are cut back to feeding two times per day. I feed them twice daily for the rest of their lives. I know some people who have great success feeding their dogs once a day. I like to feed smaller quantities more frequently so as not to risk bloat.

Neo puppies have voracious appetites. The art in raising puppies is to feed them enough so that they grow to their maximum genetic potential, but not to overfeed them. Allowing them to get too fat will cause stress on their bones and joints, which may lead to orthopedic problems later on in life.

Sansone, one-and-a-half-year-old male. Breeder and owner: Umberto Miranda. Photo: A. Spiriev. This dog was bred for type by a breeder who has a clear idea of what qualities are needed to produce the correct Mastino type. He is magnificent. He may need more care to maintain his looks and health.

Four-week-old puppy. Photo: S. Allen.

Ironstone Ischia, six weeks old. Owner: K. Drager. Photo: S. Allen.

Care and Health Care of Puppies

The proper care of puppies starts with the care given to the mother before they are even conceived. Before the mother even comes into heat, she should be up to date on her vaccinations against distemper, hepatitis, leptospirosis, parainfluenza, bordetella, canine parvovirus, canine coronavirus, rabies and Lyme disease. She should be on a regular heartworm preventative program, and she should be dewormed at regular intervals. Putting the mother on milbemycin, given monthly year round, will satisfy the requirements for deworming of nematode worms and heartworm prevention. Tapeworms have to be removed with other products such as epsiprantel or praziquantel.

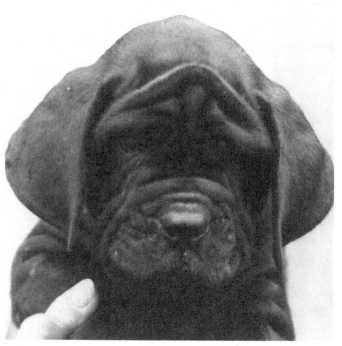

Puppy, five weeks old Photo: S. Allen.

Of course, there are many other products on the market for the control of these parasites, and many other regimes that can be used. As new vermifuges are developed, other deworming protocols may be recommended.

Of course, the mother will also be kept free of fleas, mites and ticks, all of which are

Stonehenge Alexandra, seven-week-old puppy. Photo: S. Allen.

very destructive by themselves but also are vectors for other diseases such as tapeworm infestation, bubonic plague, Lyme disease, etc.
Even though the mother has been dewormed

since puppyhood, the life cycle of the roundworm (Toxocara canis) is such that she will always be carrying roundworm larvae encysted in her muscles. During pregnancy, the larvae become active and start migrating to her intestines and also to the developing fetuses. The baby Neos will, therefore, be born with a roundworm burden. The roundworm larvae will continue to be passed to the puppies in the mother's milk. The larvae will grow into adult worms in the puppies' intestines, where they will reproduce and lay eggs that will pass in the puppies' feces. The mother will ingest more roundworm larvae when she cleans the puppies and eats their feces. The cycle is never ending.

The deworming medications on the market today kill the adult worms, but not the migrating larvae. It takes about two and a half weeks for an infective larva to develop into an adult worm. To keep up with the life cycle of the worm, puppies will have to be dewormed frequently, preferably at two-week intervals from the age of three weeks on. The deworming products that should be used should kill hookworms and whipworms as well, because many bitches could be infested with these worms. If fleas get on the puppies, they will have to be dewormed for tapeworms, because fleas are vectors for tapeworms.

Deworming of the puppy should not be stopped until two months after he has been taken to an environment where there has been no dog feces around for the past three years, and where he will absolutely not be able to step in his own feces. As long as the

Trucker, 10-week-old male. Owner: K. Drager. Photo: K. Drager.

puppy can come into contact with dog feces, he can acquire worms. Since it is almost impossible to keep a puppy from stepping in or finding deg feces on the ground, wherever he is, monthly dewormings with any of the numerous worm preparations on the market are a must.

As an aside, it is interesting to note how nature has ensured the success of reproduction of worms in dogs. Watch your young puppy the next time he defecates. Puppies defecate; then, instead of walking forward away from the feces, they take a step backward and turn around on their haunches before walking off. This ensures that they will step in their own feces, smearing it on their feet and legs, from where they will acquire more worm larvae when they later lie down to groom themselves.

Along with proper deworming, puppies must receive specific vaccinations to protect them against the potentially fatal diseases they can contract. Vaccination schedules are based on scientific research that has revealed the optimum times when puppies can be protected with the vaccines developed to combat the various potentially fatal diseases to which puppies are susceptible. In spite of the guidelines, every veterinarian you talk to will have developed his or her own protocol,

Marlena, six weeks old. Photo: S. Allen.

based in part on the successes or failures experienced with different protocols in different regions of the country. My specific protocol for vaccinating Neos will probably be different from you veterinarian's. I present as a guideline the schedule that has worked in the past for me.

Vaccination Schedule for Puppies

THREE WEEKS – Intranasal bordetella (kennel cough) vaccine. Deworm with a commercially available product containing milbemycin or pyrantel. Deworm the mother also.

SIX WEEKS – Parvo vaccine. Deworm.

SEVEN WEEKS – Distemper, hepatitis,

Marlena, nine months old. Photo: S. Allen.

parainfluenza vaccine. Crop the ears if it is going to be done.

EIGHT WEEKS – Parvo vaccine. Deworm both puppy and mother.

NINE WEEKS – Distemper, hepatitis, parainfluenza, leptospirosis vaccine.

12 WEEKS – Parvo vaccine. Deworm.

16 WEEKS – Distemper, hepatitis, parainfluenza, leptospirosis, parvovirus, coronavirus vaccine. Deworm.

FOUR TO FIVE MONTHS – Rabies vaccine.

Deworm routinely. Use a heartworm preventative all year round. Some heartworm preventatives are also vermifuges for nematodes so you can deworm and prevent heartworm with a single monthly pill.

After the dog is one year of age, continue a vaccination schedule protocol with your veterinarian.

Physical development of the Neapolitan Mastiff

While looking for that massive, majestic, substantial masterpiece of Neodom, an owner must be patient. Neapolitan Mastiffs are born adorable, and a prize Mastino prospect can usually be identified by an experienced breeder during the first few weeks of its life. The puppies remain cute until about 12 weeks of age. Then they start to fall apart as far as looks go. They loose their wrinkles and go through a plain, weedy, gangly stage until about two years of age. You begin to wonder why you ever spent any money or time on this ugly piece of scrub.

Marlena, one year old. Photo: S. Allen.

Ironstone Big City Dude, eight weeks old. Photo: S. Allen.

Big City Dude, seven months old. Photo: S. Allen.

Then suddenly, around two years of age, like Cinderella, the dogs transform almost overnight into that wonderful dream you wanted to acquire. Between two to three years of age, the head appears to broaden miraculously. The chest becomes wide, and the bone is suddenly heavy and thick. The wrinkles come back, and continue to become more and more prominent the older the dog becomes. What is anathema to middle-aged humans becomes the Neo's crowning glory.

So be patient. Let your Neo be thin while he is a teenager. His immature bones and joints won't be so stressed by massive weight. Remember, your Mastino is Italian, and by middle age, he or she will gain in girth! If the puppy was beautiful when it was a baby, and it has the right genes behind it, you must have faith that eventually it will be beautiful again.

Using dogs that I have raised as examples, I would like to illustrate how a Neo metamorphosizes.

1. MARLENA. Born from excellent parents, Ironstone Attila x Marchesina, she was beautiful as a puppy. At nine months, she was gawky, but very structurally correct. By a year of age, she was already broadening out and gaining substance.

2. BIG CITY DUDE had a huge wrinkled head when he was a baby. I felt he would grow to be something special. At seven months of age, he was narrow bodied, tight skinned, and had a huge, wrinkle-free head. At 10 months of age he had good skeletal conformation but he seemed so light boned,

Big City Dude, nine months old. Photo: S. Allen.

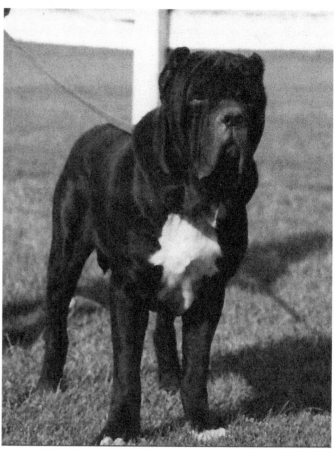

Big City Dude, 23 months old. Photo: S. Allen.

Big City Dude, 21 months old. Photo: S. Allen.

Big City Dude, three years old. Photo: S. Allen.

Big City Dude, 34 months old. Photo: S. Allen.

Islero del Bonrampino, eight weeks old. Breeder: G. Maja. Owner: S. Allen. Photo: S. Allen.

Islero del Bonrampino, 16 weeks old. Photo: S. Allen.

Islero del Bonrampino, 16 weeks old. Photo: S. Allen.

Islero del Bonrampino, 24 months old. Photo: S. Allen.

Islero del Bonrampino, 22 months old. Photo: S. Allen.

Islero del Bonrampino, 24 months old. Photo: S. Allen.

Islero del Bonrampino, six years old Photo: S. Allen.

Ironstone Nerone, 18-month-old son of Islero del Bonrampino. Compare him with the photo of Islero at 24 months old on the opposite page. Owner: B. Romano. Photo: S. Allen.

Ironstone Isadora, 24-month-old daughter of Islero. Compare her head with Islero's, and her body with his at 22 months old. Owner: H. Booker. Photo: S. Allen.

Lavinia del Bonrampino, eight months old
(above) **and three and a half years old** *(below).*
Breeder: G. Maja. Owner: S. Allan. Photo: S. Allen.

and his head appeared too large for his body. The only thing I could say for him was that he was sound, and moved like no other Neo I had ever seen – he seemed to float when he trotted. I sold him. Almost a year later I bought him back, as I felt I had been too hasty in selling him. At 23 months of age, he suddenly blossomed. His chest got wide, his body filled out, and his skin became wrinkled. At three years old, he was a very impressive-looking dog.

3. ISLERO DEL BONRAMPINO was actually always quite handsome and very broad. As a puppy, he had so much loose skin that it hung in folds all over his body. But as he grew, his head just got wider and wider, until it seemed to cause an unfolding of the skin to accommodate the ever expanding cranium. By 22 months of age, he was structurally very correct, still broad, but a little lanky looking. At 24 months, he suddenly developed body mass, and the facial wrinkling began to appear on his broad face. At six years of age, he looked

like the noble sage that comes to mind when we think of the Mastino. Finally, at seven years, the lips are hanging longer, the face is starting to gray, the wrinkles are becoming more flaccid, and the expression reflects what he has become – the patient guard who watches over his property and charges.

4. LAVINIA DEL BONRAMPINO. This dog, who was a lanky teenager at eight months of age but blossomed beautifully by three and a half years, explains why Mastinari do not regularly show their Neos until three years of age. Though dogs may be shown for championship points in the U.S. from the age of six months on, it is apparent that the Neo is not really fit for being shown until two to three years. A puppy like Lavinia may have correct body conformation as a young dog. But a Mastino is judged on more than conformation. A Mastino is judged on its presence and the emotions it evokes in the onlooker.

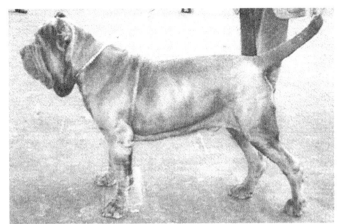

Intoccabile del Nolano, two-year-old male. Breeder: M. de Falco Jovane. Owner: A. van Doremalen. Photo: G. De Nisi. Body substance will increase for another year.

Frazier della Grotta Azzurra. *Above:* Two years old. *Below:* Four years old. Top dogs like Frazier only get better with age. Breeder: G. Siano. Owner: G. Mira. Photo: S. Allen.

Intoccabile del Nolano, three years old. His body is more substantial at this age. Photo: M. Rogen.

Poseidon of the Thatch Roof, two-year-old male. Son of Intoccabile, very similar to his dad at this age. Breeder: A. van Doremalen. Owner: C. Dedmon. Photo: S. Allen.

Coat Color in Neapolitan Mastiffs

One of the questions most commonly asked by breeders of Neapolitan Mastiffs is how to produce puppies of a certain coat color. Breeders want to know what color parents should be bred

Neapolitan Mastiffs come in four basic colors. Each breed has its own particular term for describing the colors. The basic colors as referred to in scientific language are black, blue, brown and isabelle. Doberman

Black male, Barone, owner not identified. Photo: Zimmerman.

together to get puppies of a particular color. The following is a little treatise on coat color in Neapolitan Mastiffs.

Like Dobermans and Newfoundlands,

Opposite page: **Gray male. Photo: J.P. Dupuis.**

breeders describe their dogs as black, blue, red and fawn. Newfoundland breeders describe their dogs as black, gray, bronze and champagne. Labrador Retriever fanciers refer to their dogs as black and chocolate. The Neapolitan Mastiff terminology is black, gray, mahogany and tawny, or blonde. The colors in each breed have the same genetic reasons for the production of a particular hue. The dominant colors named according to the type of melanin producing them are black and brown. The recessive colors that are produced by a dilution-factor gene are blue, in the case of black coats, and isabelle, in the case of brown coats.

Coat color in mammals is affected by several different genes at different loci on the chromosomes, in various combinations with one another.

There are two pigments that impart color to the tissues and hair coat of mammals:
1. Eumelanin, which is black or dark brown.

2. Pheomelanin, which is yellow.

The genes for coat color in the dog are as follows:

Mahogany puppy, darker brown shade. Photo: S. Allen.

Mahogany puppy, redder shade. Photo: S. Allen.

The A locus: influences the relative amounts and location of dark pigment eumelanin (black or brown) and light pigment, pheomelanin (tan or yellow) in individual hairs and the coat as a whole. There are five of these A locus alleles: As, ay, aw, as, at. The A allele in Neapolitan Mastiffs is As, which allows distribution of dark pigment over the whole body. In contrast, a Doberman Pinscher would have an at, which produces bicolor varieties having tan points.

The B locus: determines whether the dark pigment (eumelanin) in the coat will be black or chocolate brown. The Bb gene pair produces color as follows:

B – dominant gene. Produces black coat color with black nose and foot pads.

B – recessive gene. bb allows a reduced degree of pigment formation observed in the chocolate brown (mahogany) coat color. Nose and foot pads are also brown.

A black Neo has at the B locus, Bb or BB. A mahogany Neo is always bb.

The C locus: influences the depth of pigmentation. There are five alleles at this locus – C, cch, ce, cb, ca. C is the most common allele, and allows for full depth of dark pigmentation. The allele ca, for instance, would indicate complete albinism.

The D locus: influences the intensity of pigmentation. The D gene is dominant and is responsible for the more common densely pigmented color of most dogs. The d gene produces a blue dilution. It is recessive to D, so dd in black (B) dogs causes a gray coat such as in blue Great Danes, blue Greyhounds, blue Dobermans, grey Newfoundlands. In mahogany (bb) dogs, the dd combination causes a silvery brown color such as fawn Dobermans or Weimaraners.

Therefore, combinations of the Bb gene locus and the Dd gene locus give us the following colors in Neos:

BB or Bb with DD or Dd = black, dominant color.

BB or Bb with dd dilutes black to recessive gray (blue).

bb with DD or Dd = brown (mahogany).

bb with dd dilutes mahogany to tawny

Mahogany male, Leone. Breeder: L. Del Prete. Owner: J. Hospodar. Photo: J. Hospodar.

(isabelle, blonde).

The E locus: influences the distribution of dark pigment throughout the coat. It interacts with the A locus series. There are four of these alleles: Em, E, ebr, e. E causes the formation of dark pigment over the entire coat as in a black Labrador Retriever. The allele ebr is recessive to E, but causes the striping or brindling in the Neo.

The S series causes white spotting.

There are four different S allele patterns of white: S, Si. sp, sw. The si allele, called Irish spotting, puts white on the muzzle, feet, chest, belly, throat or neck, and tail tip.

There are other loci called the P series, T series, M series, G series and H series. But

Tawny male, Guaglione. Breeder: R. Scognamiglio. Owner: G. Mira. Photo: S. Allen.

these do not have alleles that affect the Neapolitan Mastiff.

From the above descriptions of the various genes affecting coat color, we can write genetic descriptions (genotypes) of the different coat colors in our breed. We can then use the Punnett-square method to plot genetic combinations of alleles from two parents, with the resulting phenotypes (coat color appearance) of the offspring.

For example, the coat colors of genotypes of Neos are as follows:

1. The genotype of a black Neo must be by definition BBDd or BBDD or BbDD or BbDd.

2. The genotype of a blue Neo must be by

Tawny female, Dolumbia de San Basile. Breeder: A. Aiello. Owner: F. Lanz.

definition BBdd or Bbdd.

3. The genotype of a mahogany Neo must be bbDd or bbDD.

4. The genotype of a tawny Neo is only bbdd.

Therefore:

1. Blue is a dilute black and recessive to it.

2. Mahogany is recessive to black.

3. Tawny is a dilute mahogany and recessive to it.

Another principle of genetics is that a heterozygous dominant such as a black BbDd could produce recessive colored dogs, bbdd (tawny) or Bbdd (blue). But a homozygous recessive, bbdd (tawny) or Bbdd, BBdd (blue) can never produce more dominant color if mated with another recessive dog.

When people ask me if two blue (gray) dogs can produce black puppies, the answer is no. The principles of genetics as we have discussed say no. As we have shown, the blue dog must have the homozygous recessive dd alleles to be blue. Two recessive genes can't produce a dominant genotype. Calculating the offspring's genotype and phenotype when the genotype of both parents is known can be easily done by the Punnett squares.

A blue phenotype dog can have genotype of Bbdd or BBdd.

1. If we breed Bbdd to Bbdd, we get:

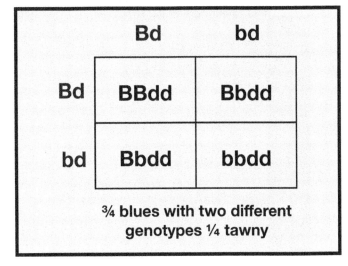

¾ blues with two different genotypes ¼ tawny

2. If we breed BBdd to BBdd, we get:

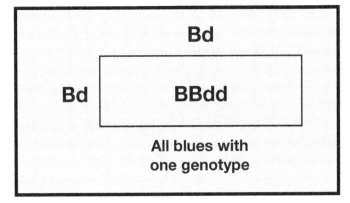

All blues with one genotype

3. If we breed BBdd to Bbdd, we get:

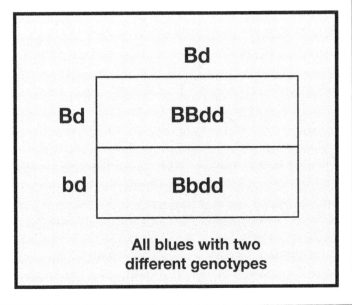

All blues with two different genotypes

	BD	Bd	bD	bd
BD	**BBdd** *black*	**DBDd** *black*	**BbDD** *black*	**BbDd** *black*
Bd	**BBDb** *black*	**BBdd** *blue*	**BbDdbl** *black*	**Bbdd** *blue*
bD	**BbDD** *black*	**bBDd** *black*	**bbDD** *mahogany*	**bbDd** *mahogany*
bd	**BbDd** *black*	**bBdd** *blue*	**bbDd** *mahogany*	**bbdd** *tawny*

9/16 black

3/16 mahogany

3/16 blue

1/16 tawny

Breeding blue to blue will never give black, but it may give tawny.

Breeding tawny to tawny will always produce tawny.

Breeding black to black or to any of the other colors can produce all four colors, depending on genotypes involved.

One example of heterozygous black to heterozygous black: BbDd to BbDd.

We can continue to plot the various color combinations, and we can make some interesting observations:

Black bred to black, mahogany, blue or tawny can produce all four colors, depending on the genotype of the blacks.

Mahogany bred to blue can give all four colors, depending on the genotype of the two individuals.

Blue bred to blue can produce blue or tawny, depending on the genotype, but blue bred to blue will never make black or mahogany.

Tawny bred to tawny will never make any color other than tawny.

References:

Burns, Marca, and Frazer, M.N.: Genetics of the Dog, J.B. Lippincott Co., Philadelphia, 1966.

Hutt, Frederick B. Genetics for Dog Breeders, W. H. Freeman & Co., San Francisco.

Little, Clarence C: The Inheritance of Coat Color in Dogs, Howell Book House, New York, 1984.

This dog's phenotype is black, but, her genotype, and that of the dog she is bred to, will determine the color possibilities for her offspring.

Patterson, D.T.: Notes from University of Pennsylvania School of Veterinary Medicine, Vet. Med. Genetics 7051, 1985-1986.

Roberson, Roy: Genetics for Dog Breeders, Pergamon Press.

Ironstone Islero, 22 months old. Breeder: S. Allen. Owner: H. Booker. Photo: S. Allen.

Showing the Neapolitan Mastiff

Dog shows give the proud breeder a place to show off his or her work. They give the proud new owner a place to show what he or she as been able to raise and train. Dog shows provide a place where people who have a common interest – the dog – can socialize. They provide a forum where breed fanciers can examine the creations of other breeders, and compare and discuss the attributes of other dogs within that breed.

Dog shows provide intense thrills and highs for breeders sometimes, and intense disappointment at other times. It is at dog shows that the public can easily examine a breed that interests them. Most truly serious breeders attend dog shows regularly so that they can keep up with the news and trends concerning their breed.

The protocol for showing a dog is determined by the rules and regulations of each organization that is sponsoring a particular show. In the United States, the AKC is the largest national cynologic organization, and the only internationally recognized cynologic organization. Dogs must be of a breed recognized by and registered with the AKC in order to be shown at AKC shows. There is a specific system for judging dogs and awarding dogs

Caligola di Ponzano, four-year-old male, winning Best of Breed at the World Dog Show in Dortmund, Germany, 1991. Breeder: M. Querci. Owner: A. Pegoli. Photo: G. De Nisi.

Neither wind nor rain shall keep them from their task. Tri States Working Dog Association Rare Breed Show, Hightstown, N.J., 1993. Borgia's Capo di Valtor and V. Valerio; Hannibal di Alaric and R. Monaco.

French National Specialty for Neapolitan Mastiffs, Chartres, Sept. 6, 1993. M. Patrick Salomon standing back, showing off his dog. Photo: S. Allen.

Trophies to be awarded at the Neo Specialty at Chartres. My young son was more impressed with the shining trophies that he was with the dogs. He had to take this picture. Typically, lovely trophies such as these are presented to the winners of shows held in Europe. Photo: J. Yarmush.

Typical stance used in showing off one's Neo, while the judge is at the right, looking on. Unfortunately, the owner and lovely bitch were unidentified. Photo: S. Allen.

The Mastino Napoletano Club Nederland Show. The fanfare associated with winning is typified in this photo of Bonny van Hadimassa going Winners Bitch at the show. Photo: K. Zimmerman.

Mastino specialty in Naples in 1986. The Mastini are lined up, while the judge to the right is observing. Photo: K. Rossé.

points toward obtaining an AKC-recognized championship.

Likewise, every other country in the world has its own major kennel club, which has its own specific rules for showing and judging dogs. Whereas most dog shows held in the United States follow AKC protocol, most dog shows held in the rest of the world follow FCI protocol for showing and judging dogs.

member countries, a dog registered with an FCI-member country can show and win points in any other FCI country. AKC-registered dogs can also show at dog shows in most FCI-member countries. Dogs born in the United States that are not registered with the AKC cannot usually show in most other FCI shows in other countries. They can show with other organizations in the United States designated as "rare breed"

French Neapolitan Mastiff Specialty at Chartres. Dogs being gaited at the end of the class after each dog has been judged individually. Mme. Sicre and Fantos de San Basile. Photo: S. Allen.

Except for England and perhaps a few other countries, the kennel clubs of most of the other countries are part of the FCI, and as such, follow the FCI format for holding international shows.

Because of this reciprocity among FCI-

organizations or clubs.

The style of showing Neapolitan Mastiffs differs greatly between FCI countries and the United States, where most shows are organized according to AKC protocol, even if the clubs are not AKC recognized. To

When Mastini are gaited in Europe, they are allowed to trot on a loose lead, their heads outstretched in their natural way of moving. Photo: S. Allen.

USNMC annual rare-breed show and Neapolitan Mastiff Specialty, Mullica Hill, New Jersey, June 5-6, 1993. Dogs being set up in line by their handlers. Ironstone Diva and R. Evans, Polly Pi Bella and C. Shmidthiser. Photo: S. Allen.

be sure, there are also kennel clubs in the U.S. that have adopted the FCI protocol for judging dogs. Even at these shows, the dogs are handled by their owners and "set up" much as they are done at AKC shows.

In Europe, the Neos are shown in a more relaxed fashion. While all the contestants in

the dog to gait, the owner usually just trots the dog back and forth a little bit in front of the judge.

While the judge is examining each dog, he is also dictating his findings on the dog to a secretary. A very detailed critique in writing then becomes part of public record for each

Bitch being set up in show position by owner, E. Schiavo. Ironstone Cara Mia. USNMC Mullica Hill, N.J., show.

one class are standing in a circle along the border of the ring, the dog to be judged and its handler walk to one end of the ring where the judge is standing. The owner (or handler) stands in back of the dog, allowing the dog to wander around or strike its own pose as the judge stands back and scrutinizes him. Judges do not routinely go up to and touch the dogs. When showing the Neo's teeth, the owner often straddles the dog, makes it sit down , or even makes it lie down while he is opening the mouth. When the judge asks for

dog judged. The judge spends quite a long time standing back from the dog, looking, thinking and dictating.

In the United States, the showing of the dogs is more formal and stylized. The dogs are led in a line in front of the judge, where they are all set up facing the judge's left, in a perfectly square stance. The dog's head is placed by the handler so that it is held high. The dog should maintain its stance and not move while the judge is examining the whole class

Above: **Puppy bitch in show stance. Breeders and owners: B. and V. Gagnon. USNMC Mullica Hill, New Jersey, show. Photo: S. Allen.**

Below: **J. Caponetto setting up Langia Mia, eight-month-old female. Breeders and owners: J. and D. Mullusky. USNMC Mullica Hill, New Jersey, show. Photo: S. Allen.**

together.

The judge then goes to each dog individually and examines it carefully while touching it all over. Often the judge will try to open the dog's mouth to look at the teeth. It is best with Neos, however, if the judge stands back and asks the owner to show the teeth. The dog is to remain standing and still while the handler shows the teeth.

After examining a dog while it is standing still, the judge asks the handler to trot the dog in a particular pattern, and then to return to a standstill in front of the judge. At this point, the judge observes the dog's expression, reaction and natural stance. After all, the dogs have been examined individually in this manner, the judge asks all the dogs to

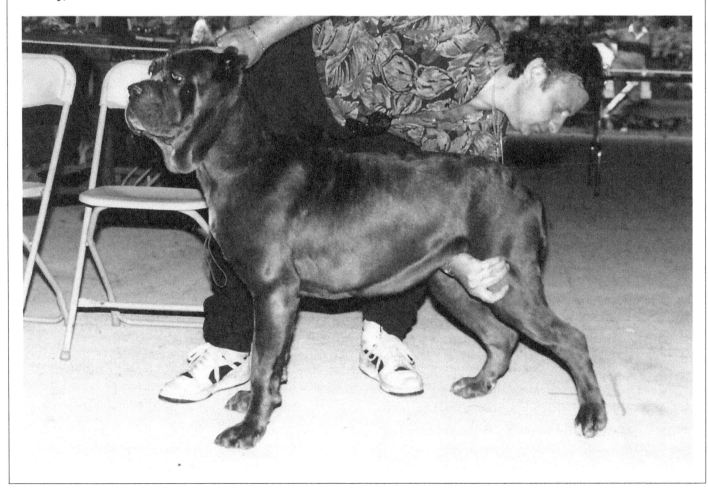

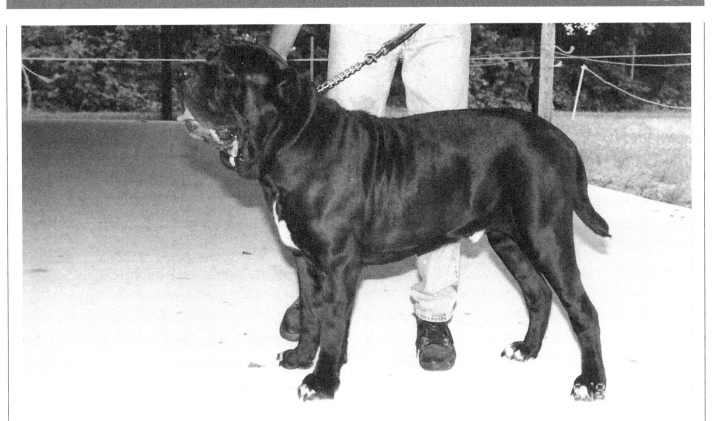

Young male in nice show stance. Bellotti's Drusus Busineou. Breeder: S. Costello. Owners: A. and B. Rivolta. Photo: S. Allen.

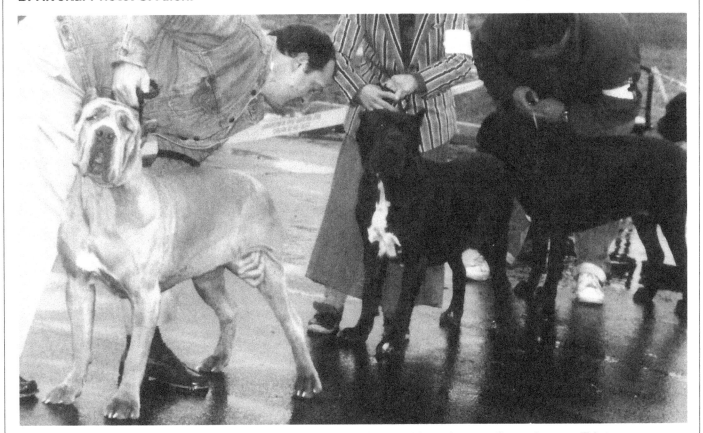

Handlers positioning their bitches in the rain, Hightstown, New Jersey. Stonehenge Tristezza, Ironstone Cassiopeia, Borgia's Briana of Forest Edge. Photo: S. Allen.

Puppies waiting their turn before going out in the rain, Hightstown, N.J. Blancho's Nina, three-and-a-half-month-old female on left. Breeders and owners: J. and D. Mullusky. On right, Cesare von der Somerweide, 10-month-old male. Breeder: F. Palmeri. Owners: J. and D. Mullusky. Photo: S. Allen.

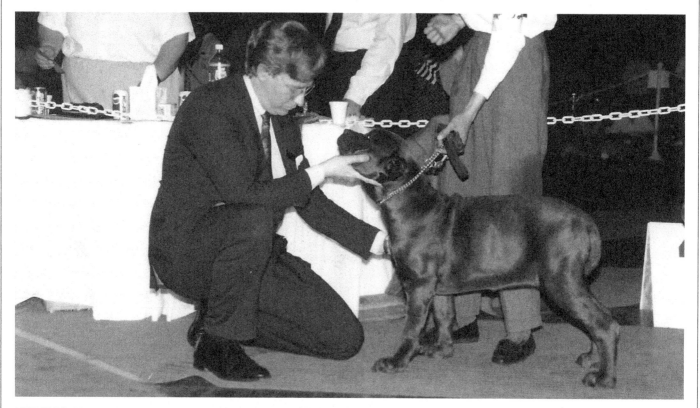

USNMC Neapolitan Mastiff Specialty held at the ARBA show in Washington, D.C., May 1, 1993. Judge Christofer Habig is examining a puppy according to AKC protocol. He is up close and touching it. Ironstone Themis, four months old, and owner E. Schiavo. Photo: S. Allen.

gait around the ring together.

In contrast to the natural gaiting done in Europe, dogs in the U.S. are traditionally trotted with their heads held very high. This is difficult with a Neo, as the Neo naturally wants to hold his head low or level with his topline. Trying to get a Neo to hold his head high while trotting is sometimes exhausting for the handler. The members of the Neo clubs should decide whether they would

FCI rules, but the style of showing is more like that in the United States. Actually, the Mexicans have embellished even more on the flashiness of the show ring. Their dogs move around the ring at very fast speeds, with their heads up very high. When setting their dogs up, the handlers hold the head and tail both very high. The judges like to see a very high-spirited, flashy dog.

Those American owners of Neapolitan

Proper gaiting technique according to AKC custom. Handler John Camponetto and Langia Mia. USNMC show. Photo: S. Allen.

like to mount an instructional campaign to inform judges that Neos gait better with their heads held on a line with the back, rather than up. This will be a philosophical question to be decided in the future.

In Mexico and other countries of South America, dogs are shown according to

Mastiffs who would like to show their dogs in the United States or elsewhere must learn the rules, regulations and style of showing for the particular show or country in which they want to show. Other than that bit of information, the only other remarks I can give you as far as showing Neos is concerned have come from my non-Neo-owning associates who have watched me over the years in my efforts to show my dogs. They came to these conclusions all by themselves, from simple observations or from firsthand experience when I was still able to bribe them to come to a show with me. Now they have learned better, and as soon as I mention the word "show," everyone disappears. Their words of wisdom are as follows:

1. Although the judges' decisions are the unknown factor at a dog show, the one certain constant is that the weather is either too hot, or it is raining. So be prepared either to freeze to death and come home with a cold, or else be prepared to sweat to death while you are spending the whole day trying to keep your Neos from expiring in the heat.

2. Take plenty of water with you for them. It is the commodity you will use most at a show, and usually the only item not available on the show premises.

3. Neos do not like to run around show rings. Make sure they are in a good mood before you take them to a show, and make sure they have gotten a good night's sleep the night before. There is nothing quite so embarrassing for the handler as to have your Neo lie down in the middle of the ring and refuse to move. It happens.

4. Do not feed them the afternoon before you are going to travel to a show. You can guess why.

Neo being gaited. Note the high head carriage, which is customary in showing in the U.S. Dog unfortunately unidentified. Photo: S. Allen.

Ch. Ironstone Menelaus being gaited at USNMC show, Mullica Hill, New Jersey. Owners: Z. Najdovsky and F. Layton. Note owner has dog on a loose lead, so, being a Neapolitan, he carries his head low. Photo: S. Allen.

5. Bring chairs; there is never any place to sit down at a dog show, and you spend a lot of time waiting.

6. Do not forget the towels for wiping off the slobber.

7. Always park in the shade.

Going to a dog show with Neapolitan Mastiffs is always an adventure. A lot of preparation is required ahead of time. A large vehicle is needed to transport them. In the very large vehicle should be placed very large crates, either plastic or wire crates that are at least 30 inches inches tall by 42 inches deep, and preferably are the 36 inch by 48 inch size.

How many dogs you can take to the show depends on how many crates you can fit into your vehicle. Of course, once you get to the show, if you park in the shade, you can leave the dogs inside the crates inside the vehicle. If you are not able to park in the shade, you must take the crates and dogs out of the vehicle and set them up somewhere under a tree.

You have to figure out what to do with your Neo so that you can get the crate out of the vehicle. If the show happens to be inside a building, you have to get both dog and crate, times the number of dogs you wanted to show, set up inside the building. Usually, buildings have stairs. You are beginning to get the picture.

Count on having two people for each Neo you intend to bring to the show.

In addition to crates, dogs, water, towels, chairs and paper towels, you may need to bring dog food and dishes if the show is far away or more than a one-day show. You need

leashes, proper collars, trash bags, shredded paper to put in the crates. You need properly trained Neos.

Training the dog to stand up for the judge, to show its teeth, to allow itself to be touched by a stranger, and to gait properly around the ring must start as soon as you acquire him. You must practice with him several times a week or more, to perfect your handling technique and the dog's presentation. Neapolitan Mastiffs do not look their best until they are at least two years of age, so it may take a while before your dog wins any shows. In the meantime, it is good to take him to shows and enter him just for the

Ch. Diva della Guardia del Vesuvio, four-year-old female. Breeder and owner: H. Boxoen. Photo: G. De Nisi.

Show in Mexico, Vanguard's Lucky, two-year-old female. Breeder: G. Schaffer. Owner: Enrique Dada. Photo: courtesy Dada. Dog set up by professional handler in proud stance typical in Mexico.

experience. Remember, Neos do not like surprises or new things. You must teach your Neo that shows are routine and something he not only has to get used to, but must also like. Then, by the time he is 18 months to two years of age, he may be ready to show and actually win.

If you take a Neo to a show, your undivided attention must be with the dog constantly. You must make sure he is not getting too hot. You must continue to cool him off with water if he is getting too hot. While he is outside of the crate, he must be on a leash at all times and away from other dogs. At dog shows, dogs are stressed and their tempers flare. If one dog of any breed starts to bark or attack another dog, the Neos will get excited and

ARBA Cherry Blossom Classic, Washington, D.C., 1992.
G. Schaffer and Vanguard's Alana, S. Allen and Ironstone
Atlas, E. Schiavo and Ironstone Honky Tonk Woman, K.
Rossé and Ironstone Authority. Photo: L. Allen.

want to jump into the fray. Your dog may be perfectly well behaved, but if you get it too close to another dog, the other dog could be the one to attack your dog.

If you are holding your Neo on a lead, you must always be aware of what he is doing. At dog shows, many owners are so engrossed in chatting with one another that they do not pay attention to what is happening on the other end of the lead in their hand.

It is common practice at dog shows for owners of a particular dog to pay a professional handler to show their dog for them. I do not recommend this procedure with Neapolitan Mastiffs. They are too attached to their owners to begin with, and will not work well for another handler for a few minutes in the ring. Most incidences of the mastiff breeds turning on their handlers in a show-ring situation occur when the handler of the dog is not the dog's respected owner. One exception to this rule is with puppies. Puppies may be able to be shown by anyone, including children. An adult male is best and most safely shown only by his owner.

Because of the nature of adult male Neapolitan Mastiffs, I cannot stress enough the importance of not asking anyone but someone whom the dog considers to be his master to show him. Also, never try to show a newly acquired adult male Neo. To show an adult male Neo, the handler must be fully in control and must be considered by the dog to be the dominant one in the pair. This is the nature of Neapolitan Mastiffs. To show them, you must be prepared to accept this fact.

In a way, it is perhaps fortuitous for the breed that they will not show well for anyone but their owner. This personality trait, unless modified in the future by breeders, will keep them working companions of man, and not a commodity to be commercially exploited. As I have said repeatedly in this book, I believe that Neapolitan Mastiffs are not a breed for everyone. It takes a person who has an innate understanding of animals and an ability to communicate on the animal's level to be able to successfully own a Neo.

Please do not conclude that I am saying Neos are bad dogs. I am saying that Neos are simply dogs. They are dogs in the sense that dogs used to be. They are still, now, that powerful guard and master of their personal space that man wanted in times when they were the most powerful weapon human beings had. Now dogs have been replaced by the Uzzi and Tech 9. Neapolitan Mastiffs just do not happen to know that.

To be sure, Neapolitan Mastiffs may be gentler today than they were in Roman times, but then so are we. Comparatively speaking, they are still physically stronger than we are. Whereas modern-day man has lost to an extent the art of the physical bluff, animals have not. People who have, in modern terminology, alpha personalities, will be able to own these dogs, which are in themselves alpha personalities. Owner and dog would then be properly physically matched. They would both have the same mental attitudes as well. Who then becomes master is only a matter of who exercises the higher intelligence.

Bruno della Vecchia Roma. Breeder: Thierry Paratore. Owners: Janice Wolf, DVM, and Tony Gurrola.

Epilogue

Having read this book, some of you may say, "Weren't you a little harsh at times? You profess to love the breed, so why did you say bad things about it?" My response is that I did not say "bad" things about Neapolitan Mastiffs, I only told it the way it is. I have tried to portray the dogs as I have observed them to be. I have tried not to pass judgment on the breed or on those associated with the breed. I believe the only subjective statements I have made regard why the breed has changed or is changing in countries other than Italy.

The statements that judges who do not know the breed will invariably choose a dog that is not correct in type are not criticisms or denigration of anyone. They are statements of fact, meant to stress how important it is for judges to know this breed before trying to judge it.

The emphasis I have placed on recognizing that Neos have dominant personalities is not a criticism of the breed. It is telling it how it is. It is not a conclusion I have come to after having dealt with a few individual Neapolitan Mastiffs. I have had dogs from practically every Mastino line in Italy.

Other sellers of Neos in this country will contradict me, saying, "My dogs are all sweet. I have never had a problem. She must just have aggressive dogs." To this I reply that I have never had a problem with any of my Neapolitan Mastiffs either. Mine are all sweet

to me also. I have acquired adult dogs and I have raised dogs from puppies. I believe that I know how to act around them and handle them, and I believe that those breeders who say they have never had a problem also know how to handle their dogs. The anecdotes I have recounted in this book, and many hundreds more that I have not, have taught me the nature of the Neapolitan Mastiff. They have shown me what these dogs can become when they are handled by those who have not had experience with them.

I believe that all dogs must be watched around children. It is not that I am deprecating dogs. But as I tell my children, all animals bite. Little children bite, little dogs bite, and big dogs bite bigger. The fact is that many people do not understand this, and that is why accidents happen. That is not a criticism; it is a fact. These people may have a problem dealing with Neapolitan Mastiffs. The blame for any problems will then be put on the dog. The ensuing step would be for Neapolitan Mastiffs to get a "bad name" and be put on the ever-expanding vicious dog breed list. I have spent so much time recounting the personality of these dogs in an attempt to prevent this from happening. Neapolitan Mastiffs are "cool" looking. They are a conversation piece, and everyone who sees a good specimen comes away impressed and infatuated. Many people immediately want one. This may be good. All I say is, avoid compulsive buying. Know the dog and yourself and your family situation before

The author with Islero and his daughter Isadora.

rushing to get one. Already, Neapolitan Mastiffs are ending up in shelters all across the country. This is a sad situation for a breed that has been relatively unknown and traditionally has sold for rather high prices.

I can only attribute this increased incidence of throwing away Neos to an increase in breeding the dogs by those seeking profit, and an increase in purchasing them by people who do not understand the breed. As I said earlier, a good-quality Neapolitan Mastiff is extremely difficult to breed and produce. The abundance of throw-away Neos has to then come from the poorer-quality

stock that reproduces more easily and which often has a higher incidence of physical and mental problems.

Because I do respect and love the breed, I do not want to see it ruined by inappropriate breeding through ignorance or profit seeking. I hope that those who have succumbed to their infatuation with the breed will engage in ownership of the Mastino with educated wisdom and genuine concern for this special breed. Thank you.

– Sherilyn Allen

Addendum: 2016

Here is a photo gallery of Neapolitan Mastiffs that have been bred since 1995, the original publication date of this book. It gives the reader a chance to see what is popular within the breed today.

AKC Champion Vincent de BluHouse, CGC. I like this dog. He has good conformation, strong rear, sound looking but with enough skin for type and correct wrinkles and beautiful head. He looks athletic, not fat and floppy. In my opinion, this is a good type to breed for. Owners: Gay and Mike McDonald. Breeders: Robin and David White, BluHouse Mastini.

This is the type of dog I was breeding in 2007. I liked soundness, harmony of proportions, and a pretty head. At the time, the more overdone dogs were wanted by the breeders.

Gonfiezza Rasmussen, an exceptionally beautiful dog. He had plenty of type and he was sound, an overall happy and nice-minded dog. Breeder and owners: Patti and Scott Care.

On most healthy specimens like this one, the skin is thick, not thin and hanging in wrinkles all over the body. On this Belgian-bred bitch, 22-month-old Multi-Ch. Numa Lucia, the dewlap and muzzle wrinkles are plump and defined, with thick skin, not flimsy and overdone. Her lines are clean, indicating good health and strength, with evident muscle. Breeder/owner: Sonja Smidova.

Another very pretty bitch, Relics from the Past Bella Giavanna, around six years old, bred and owned by Tom Bell. She has a beautiful face with correct wrinkles and enough dewlap for a female but not too much. Her conformation is very strong and her skin, though loose, is not sagging all over her body. She is very athletic and was a natural whelper. No C-section for her, as should be the case in sound and healthy dogs. There are always some specialized instances when animals need help in breeding because of various circumstances which have occurred outside of genetic traits. But in general, a breed should be able to reproduce without the aid of man and science, or it would simply become extinct on its own.

Dogs exhibited at the United States Neapolitan Mastiff Club national specialty in 2009. This was the height of the emphasis on "overdoneness" in the breed.

Ironstone Islero II at the beach in 2007. Another son of Islero del Bonrampino by frozen semen. I really like the athleticism of this dog. He is not overdone, but he has a classic, pretty face and head, and his body is very strong.

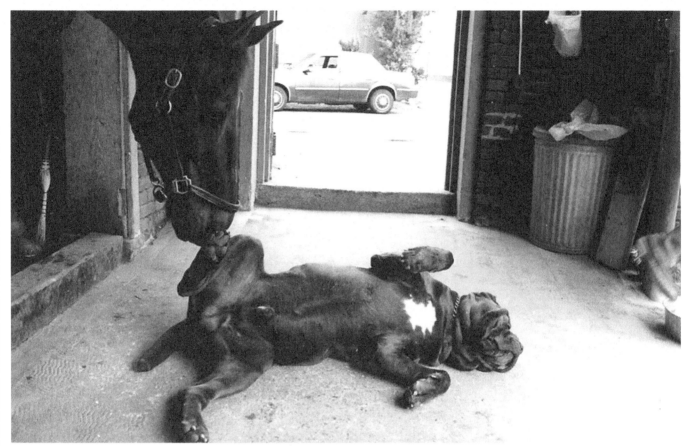

Granus the horse rubbing Orso's belly. Photo: S. Allen.

Above left: **Leah Kinzinger, who is legally blind, and her guide dog, Ironstone Rooster Cogburn - proof that Neos can be service dogs.** *Above right:* **Magnufi Nellina, nine months, owned by Lorene Cantarella, and Ch. Magnufi Francesca, two and a half years, owned by Uberto Gasche of Bengasche Mastini, Italy. Both bred by Lorene Cantarella. Photo: Cantarella.**

Doowneerg Usi. Breeder and owners: Kim Slater and Mateaki Mafi, United Kingdom.

GCh. Ironwood's Paparrazi, five and a half years old. Bred by Jim Deppen and Mimi Winkler. Owned by Jim Deppen and Susan Vann-Spruill.

The AKC standard for the Neapolitan Mastiff in America was writtten in 1988 and 1990 and went into effect in 2004. We tried to keep the pertinent parts of the 1991 FCI standard that was in force at the time, while condensing it into the format and language at the AKC wanted. Below is the AKC version of the Neapolitan Mastiff standard.

American Kennel Club Standard of the Neapolitan Mastiff
Effective May 1, 2004

General Appearance: An ancient breed, rediscovered in Italy in the 1940s, the Neapolitan Mastiff is a heavy-boned, massive, awe-inspiring dog bred for use as a guard and defender of owner and property. He is characterized by loose skin, over his entire body, abundant, hanging wrinkles and folds on the head and a voluminous dewlap. The essence of the Neapolitan is his bestial appearance, astounding head and imposing size and attitude. Due to his massive structure, his characteristic movement is rolling and lumbering, not elegant or showy.

Size, Proportion, Substance: A stocky, heavy-boned dog, massive in *substance*, rectangular in *proportion*. Length of body is 10 to 15 percent greater than height. Height: Dogs 26 to 31 inches, bitches 24 to 29 inches. Average weight of mature dogs 150 pounds; bitches 110 pounds; but greater weight is usual and preferable as long as correct proportion and function are maintained. The absence of massiveness is to be so severely penalized as to eliminate from competition.

Head: Large in comparison to the body. Differentiated from that of other mastiff breeds by more extensive wrinkling and pendulous lips which blend into an ample dewlap. Toplines of cranium and the muzzle must be parallel. The face is made up of heavy wrinkles and folds. Required folds are those extending from the outside margin of the eyelids to the dewlap, and from under the lower lids to the outer edges of the lips. Severe Faults - Toplines of the cranium and muzzle not parallel. Disqualifications - Absence of wrinkles and folds. *Expression* - Wistful at rest, intimidating when alert. Penetrating stare.

Eyes - Set deep and almost hidden beneath drooping upper lids. Lower lids droop to reveal haw. Eye Color - Shades of amber or brown, in accordance with coat color. Pigmentation of the eye rims same as coat color. Severe Faults - Whitish-blue eyes; incomplete pigmentation of the eye rims.

Ears - Set well above the cheekbones. May be cropped or uncropped, but are usually cropped to an equilateral triangle for health reasons. If uncropped, they are medium sized, triangular in shape, held tight to the cheeks, and not extending beyond the lower margin of the throat.

Skull - Wide flat between the ears, slightly arched at the frontal part, and covered with wrinkled skin. The width of the cranium between the cheekbones is approximately equal to its length from occiput stop. The brow is very developed. Frontal furrow is marked. Occiput is barely apparent. Stop - Very defined, forming a right angle at the junction of muzzle and frontal bones, and the sloping back at a greater angle where the frontal bones meet the frontal furrow of the forehead. Nose - Large with well - opened nostrils, and in color the same as the coat. The nose is an extension of the topline of the muzzle and should not protrude beyond nor recede behind the front plane of the muzzle. Severe Faults - Incomplete pigmentation of the nose.

Muzzle - It is ⅓ the length of the whole head and is as broad as it is long. Viewed from the front, the muzzle is very deep with the outside borders parallel giving it a "squared" appearance. The top plane of the muzzle from stop to tip of nose is straight, but is ridged due to heavy folds of skin covering it. Severe Faults - Top plane of the muzzle curved upward or downward. Lips - Heavy, thick, and long, the upper lips join beneath the nostrils to form an inverted "V." The upper lips form the lower, outer borders of the muzzle, and the lowest part of these borders is made by the corners of the lips. The corners turn outward to reveal the flews, and are in line with the outside corners of the eyes. *Bite* - Scissors bite or pincer bite is standard; slight undershot is allowed. Dentition is complete. Faults - More than 1 missing premolar. Severe faults - Overshot jaw; pronounced undershot jaw which disrupts the outline of the front plane of the muzzle; more than 2 missing teeth.

Neck, Topline, Body: *Neck* - Slightly arched, rather short, stocky and well-muscled. The voluminous and well-divided dewlap extends from the lower jaw to the lower neck. Disqualification - Absence of dewlap. Body

Ironstone Grace, 1999. Bred by S. Allen, later owned by David Zoni. Photo: S. Allen.

- The length of the dog, measured from the point of the shoulder to the point of buttock is 10 to 15 percent greater than the height of the dog measured from the highest point of the shoulder to the ground. Depth of the ribcage is equal to half the total height of the dog. Ribs are long and well sprung. Chest - Broad and deep, well muscled. Underline and tuckup - The underline of the abdomen is practically horizontal. There is little or no tuckup. Back - Wide and strong. Highest part of shoulder blade barely rising above the strong, level *topline* of the back. Loin - Well-muscled, and harmoniously joined to the back. Croup - Wide, strong, muscular and slightly sloped. The top of the croup rises slightly and is level with the highest point of the shoulder. *Tail* - Set on slightly lower than the topline, wide and thick at the root, tapering gradually toward the tip. It is docked by 1/3. At rest, the tail hangs straight or in slight "S" shape. When in action, it is raised to the horizontal or a little higher than the back. Severe Faults - Tail carried straight up or curved over the back. Kinked tail. Disqualification - Lack of tail or short tail, which is less than 1/3 the length from point of insertion of the tail to the hock - joint.

Forequarters: Heavily built, muscular, and in balance with the hindquarters. Shoulders - Long, well-muscled, sloping and powerful. Upper arms - Strongly muscled, powerful. In length, almost 1/3 the height of the dog. Elbows - Covered with abundant and loose skin; held parallel to the ribcage, neither tied in nor loose. Forelegs - Thick, straight, heavy bone, well muscled, exemplifying strength. About the same length as the upper arms. Set well apart. Pasterns - Thick and flattened

from front to back, moderately sloping forward from the leg. Dewclaws - Front dewclaws are not removed. Feet - Round and noticeably large with arched, strong toes. Nails strong, curved and preferably dark-colored. Slight turnout of the front feet is characteristic.

Hindquarters: As a whole, they must be powerful and strong, in harmony with the forequarters. Thighs - About the same length as the forearms, broad, muscular. Stifles - Moderate angle, strong. Legs - Heavy and thick boned, well - muscled. Slightly shorter than thigh bones. Hocks - Powerful and long. Rear pasterns (metatarsus) - Heavy thick bones. Viewed from the side, they are perpendicular to the ground. Viewed from the rear, parallel to each other. Rear dewclaws - Any dewclaws must be removed. Hind feet -Same as the front feet but slightly smaller.

Coat: The coat is short, dense and of uniform length and smoothness all over the body. The hairs are straight and not longer than 1 inch. No fringe anywhere.

Color: Solid coats of gray (blue), black, mahogany and tawny, and the lighter and darker shades of these colors. Some brindling allowable in all colors. When present, brindling must be tan (reverse brindle). There may be solid white markings on the chest, throat area from chin to chest, underside of the body, penis sheath, backs of the pasterns, and on the toes. There may be white hairs at the back of the wrists. Disqualifications: White markings on any part of the body not mentioned as allowed.

Ironstone Lillian, a bitch with a lovely head and tight, firm wrinkles. Owned and bred by Deb Kinzinger in conjunction with Sherilyn Allen.

Gait: The Neapolitan Mastiff's movement is not flashy, but rather slow and lumbering. Normal gaits are the walk, trot, gallop, and pace. The strides are long and elastic, at the same time, powerful, characterized by a long push from the hindquarters and extension of the forelegs. Rolling motion and swaying of the body at all gaits is characteristic. Pacing in the show ring is not to be penalized. Slight paddling movement of the front feet is normal. The head is carried level with or slightly above the back.

Temperament: The Neapolitan Mastiff is steady and loyal to his owner, not aggressive or apt to bite without reason. As a protector of his property and owners, he is always watchful and does not relish intrusion by strangers into his personal space. His attitude is calm yet wary. In the show ring he is majestic and powerful, but not showy.

Faults: The foregoing description is that of the ideal Neapolitan Mastiff. Any deviation from the above described dog must be penalized to the extent of the deviation.

Disqualifications: *Absence of wrinkles and folds. Absence of dewlap. Lack of tail or short tail, which is less than the length from point of insertion of the tail to the hock. White markings on any part of the body not mentioned.*

FCI Standard N 197 of the Mastino Napoletano
December 17, 2015

TRANSLATION: Mrs. Peggy Davis. Revised by Renée Sporre-Willes.

ORIGIN: Italy.

DATE OF PUBLICATION OF THE OFFICIAL VALID STANDARD: 13.11.2015.

UTILIZATION: Protection and guard dog.

FCI-CLASSIFICATION: Group 2 Pinscher and Schnauzer, Molossoid breeds and Swiss Mountain- and Cattle Dogs. Section 2:1 Molossoid breeds, Mastiff type. Without working trial.

BRIEF HISTORICAL SUMMARY: The Neapolitan Mastiff is a descendant of the great Roman Mastiff described by Columelle in the first-century A.D. in his book de re rustica. Widespread all over Europe by the Roman legions, with which he has fought, he is the ancestor of numerous mastiff breeds in other European countries. The breed has survived for many centuries in the countryside at the foot of the Vesuvius Mountain and in general in the region of Naples. The Neapolitan Mastiff has been re-selected since 1947, thanks to the tenacity and devotion of a group of dog lovers.

GENERAL APPEARANCE: Large, heavy and massive dog with a bulky appearance. The length of body to exceed the height at the withers.

IMPORTANT PROPORTIONS: The length of the body is 15 percent more than the height at the withers. The ratio skull-muzzle is as 2 to 1. Length of head is about 3.8/10 of the height at the withers. Neck is rather short. The circumference of the thorax is ample.

BEHAVIOUR/TEMPERAMENT: Steady and loyal, not aggressive. Guard dog of property and its inhabitants, always vigilant, intelligent, noble and majestic.

HEAD: Short and massive, with the skull wide at the level of the zygomatic arches; Ample skin with wrinkles and folds, the most typical and best marked goes from the outer palpebral angle down to the lip angle. The upper longitudinal axes of the skull and the muzzle are parallel.

CRANIAL REGION:
Skull: The skull is broad and flat, particularly between the ears, seen from the front it is slightly convex in its fore part. The zygomatic arches are very prominent, but with flat muscles. The protuberances of the frontal bones are well developed; the frontal furrow is marked; the occipital crest is barely visible.

Stop: Well defined.

FACIAL REGION:
Nose: Set in the prolongation of the muzzle, must not protrude beyond the outer vertical line of the lips; must be voluminous with large, well-opened nostrils. The colour is according to colour of the coat: black for black subjects, dark grey in dogs of other colours, and chestnut for brown coats.
Muzzle: Very broad and deep; the width is about equal to the length.
The length must be equal to a third of the length of the head. The lateral sides are parallel so that, seen from the front, the shape of the muzzle is practically square. The depth of the muzzle is about twice as much as that of the length.

Lips: Fleshy, thick and full. Upper lips, seen from the front, form an inverted "V" at their meeting point. The lower, lateral profile of the muzzle is shaped by the upper lips; their lowest part is the corner of the lips, with visible mucous membranes, situated on the vertical from the external angle of the eye.

Jaws/Teeth: Powerful with strong jawbones and dental arches joining perfectly. Lower jaw must be well developed in its width.

Teeth white well developed, regularly aligned and complete in number. Scissor bite, i.e. upper incisors closely overlapping the lower ones in close contact, set straight to the jaw, or pincer bite, i.e. upper incisors meet edge to edge with the lower incisors. The external margin of the upper incisors must be in close contact to the internal margin of the lower incisors. Reverse scissors bite tolerated.

Eyes: Set well apart on an equal frontal level; rather round in shape but never protruding or too deep set. Colour of iris usually darker than coat colour, except in coats of diluted shades where the eye colour is lighter. Skin folds never to interfere with the eyes.

Ears: Small in relation to the size of the dog, of triangular shape, set above the zygomatic arch, flat and laying close to the cheeks. The ears are natural.

NECK: The upper profile is slightly convex. Rather short and conical trunk shaped, well muscled. Lower profile of the neck is well endowed with loose skin which forms a double dewlap well separated, but not exaggerated; dewlap starts at level of the lower jaw and does not reach below middle of the neck.

BODY: The length of the body exceeds by 15% the height at the withers.

Top line: Top line of the back is straight.
Withers: Wide, long and not very prominent.

Back: Broad and in length about 1/3 of the height at the withers. The lumbar region must be harmoniously united with the back and muscled and well developed in width.

Loin: Broad, strong and well muscled. The hipbones are prominent to the extent of reaching the top lumbar line.

Chest: Broad with well-developed chest muscles. The ribcage is ample, with long and well-sprung ribs. The circumference of the thorax is ample. The tip of the sternum is situated at the level of point of shoulder.

TAIL: Broad and thick at the root; strong, tapering slightly towards the tip. In length it reaches the articulation of the hock. At rest it is carried hanging and curved in sabre fashion, in action lifted horizontally or only slightly higher than the top line.

LIMBS
FOREQUARTERS:
General appearance: The forelegs, from the ground to the point of the elbow, seen in profile and from the front, are vertical with strong bone structure in proportion with the size of the dog.

Shoulder: Long and well laid back, the muscles are well developed, long and well defined.

Upper arm: Well angulated to shoulder blade and with significant musculature.
Elbow: Must be parallel to the median plane of the body, i.e. neither turned in nor out.

Forearm: Length is almost the same as that of the upper arm. Placed in perfect vertical position. Strong bone structurewith lean and

This is one of Garry Travers' original Neos year ago, Scugnizzio. He is a magnificent, totally typical Neo with correct head, body and bone.

well-developed muscles.

Carpus (Wrist): Broad, lean and without nodosity, continues the vertical line of the forearm.

Metacarpus (Pastern): Continues the vertical line of the forearm. Moderate angulation and length.

Forefeet: Of round shape, large, toes well arched and well knit. The pads are hard and well pigmented. The nails are strong, curved and of a dark colour.

HINDQUARTERS:
General appearance: On the whole they must be powerful and sturdy, in proportion with the size of the dog and capable of the required propulsion in movement.

Thigh: In length measuring 1/3 of the height at the withers and the obliqueness is about 60°. Broad with thick, prominent and clearly distinct muscles. The thighbone and the hipbone (femur and coxal) form an angle of 90°.

Stifle (Knee): The femoro-tibial angle is about 110°–115°.

Lower thigh: Length is slightly inferior to that of the thigh and of an obliqueness of

AKC and Intl. Ch. Leggenda Khersones Anfeya, bitch bred in Ukraine. Breeder: Larissza Darus. Owner: Lisa Hershberger. Photo: Herschberger.

an angle of 140°–145°.

Metatarsus (Rear pastern): Strong and lean, almost cylindrical in shape, perfectly straight and parallel and fairly low set.

Hind feet: Smaller than the forefeet, round with well-knit toes. Pads dry, hard and pigmented. Nails strong, curved and of dark colour.

GAIT / MOVEMENT: This constitutes a typical characteristic of the breed. At the walk, the gait is of feline type, like the steps of a lion. It is slow and also resembles that of a bear. The trot is distinguished by a strong thrust of the hindquarters and a good extension of the forequarters. The dog rarely gallops; usual gait is walk and trot. Pacing is tolerated.

SKIN: Thick, abundant and loose all over the body, particularly on the head where it forms numerous folds and wrinkles, and at the lower part of the neck where it forms a double dewlap. Never in abundance to the extent to interfere with the dog's health and well-being.

COAT

Hair: Short and hard, dense, of the same length all over. Uniform short length that measures 1.5 cm maximum. Must not show any trace of fringing.

Colour: Preferred colours are: grey, lead grey and black, but also brown, fawn and deep fawn (red deer). Permissible is a little white patch on the chest and/or on the tip of the toes. All these colours may be brindled; hazel, dove-grey and isabella shades are

50°–55°, with strong bone structure and well visible muscles.

Hock joint: The tibio-tarsal articulation form

tolerated.

SIZE AND WEIGHT:
Height at the withers: Males: 65–75 cm.
Females: 60–68 cm.
Weight: Males: 60–70 kg. Females: 50-60 kg.

FAULTS: Any departure from the foregoing points should be considered a fault and the seriousness with which the fault should be regarded should be in exact proportion to its degree and its effect upon the health and welfare of the dog.

SEVERE FAULTS:
• Pronounced undershot bite.
• Tail carried too high.
• Size bigger or smaller than the limits allowed.

DISQUALIFYING FAULTS:
• Aggressive or overly shy dogs.
• Any dog clearly showing physical or behavioural abnormalities shall be disqualified.
• Accentuated convergence or divergence of the cranio-facial axes.
• Topline of muzzle concave or convex or very aquiline (Roman nose).
• Total depigmentation of nose.
• Overshot bite.
• Entropion / ectropion.
• Wall eye; total de-pigmentation of both rims of eyelids; cross eyed.
• Absence of wrinkles, folds and dewlap.
• Absence of tail whether congenital or artificial.
• Extensive white patches; white markings on the head.

N.B.: Male animals should have two

Patronus delle Correnti, three-month-old male owned by Susie Schramm.

apparently normal testicles fully descended into the scrotum.

Only functionally and clinically healthy dogs, with breed typical conformation, should be used for breeding.

As soon as a standard is written, some fanciers want to immediately change it. The Italians had been talking about changing the standard since I was dealing with them in the 1990s. The Americans have been talking about changing the AKC standard since it was written in 1999. Whereas the FCI standard was overly specific in measurements, the AKC did not want specifics because any slight deviation would then be construed as a major fault. Also, judges are not going to be in the ring with tape measures to measure length of head to height of withers, and length of thigh to height at withers, length of back to height of withers, femoral-tibial angles, angle obliqueness of femur, tibia, humerus, etc. The AKC wants brevity, with specifics only in that they define the breed in all its peculiar traits.

Given the differences between the very detailed original 1971 FCI standard, the more condensed 1991 FCI standard, the very succinct 1999 AKC standard, and now the even more condensed 2015 FCI standard with all its new animal-rights initiated changes, it would behoove the Neo breeder in the U.S. to study all three standards so as to breed a Neo close to what the Italians have traditionally thought and now think its measurements should be.

While I am not going to go into a detailed discussion and comparison of all the standards, I will mention the more noteworthy points:

Proportions: Everyone is in accord that the Neo is a massive, heavy dog whose length of body exceeds the height at the withers. The issue with both Italian and now some American breeders is: "Exactly how much longer than tall is it supposed to be?"

The original standard said the dog is 10 percent longer from point of hip to point of shoulder than its height at the withers. However, as breeders began to choose for more mass and wrinkle, those recessive genes also included a sort of dwarfism of a mastiff, and the dogs came out just as long, but with shorter, heavier legs. This is what happened to Dachshunds, Corgis, Dandie Dinmont Terriers, Basset Hounds, etc. So now the dogs they were producing were longer than 10 percent of their height. Some breeders wanted the standard to read "length 15 percent greater than height," and some even wanted to go to 18 percent. They were coming out with some pretty long dogs, and the breed was changing to a more acromegalic type.

The same thing happened with some of the prominent American breeders. Their quest for massive bone and all the wrinkle led to short but long dogs. They wanted the standard changed. The AKC standard at least gives leeway to the measurements, stating 10 percent to 15 percent longer than tall. What judge is going to stand in the ring with a tape measure and take up time to measure a dog that is 12 percent longer than tall if the standard were to state only 10 percent, or only 15 percent?

Well, the new Italian standard does just that. It states in several places that the length of body of the dog is 15 percent more than the height at the withers.

What is going to happen in Italy in a show if a dog is 14 percent or 16 percent longer than tall? The judge should have an eye to be able to see pleasing proportions that fit in harmony with a powerful, sound, if perhaps lumbering movement. They are not going to measure dogs, and I do not advocate the breeding of Neos to produce longer and longer bodies. We would end up with large, wrinkled Dachshounds.

Ears: Originally and traditionally, the mastiff breeds had cropped ears. This may be seen in 400-year-old paintings and in millennia-old statues. As fighting dogs, their longish, floppy ears were subject to being grabbed by the big game they were chasing. The AKC standard was astute enough to allow dogs to be shown with ears cropped, or uncropped. But it states that if uncropped, "the ears are medium sized, triangular in shape, held tight to the cheeks, and not extending beyond the lower margin of the throat." Most Neos

I have seen can have some pretty long ears, which can get quite close to the lower margin of the throat. So, the 2015 Italian standard states that the ears must be natural (cropping is no longer allowed in most European countries), and are "small in relation to the size of the dog." Neos are not born with "small" ears. Therefore, this definition of ears is the standard is basically meaningless. If we are going to ignore some parts of the standard, and hold other parts of the standard as gospel, how is a person to know which is which?

Tail: The tail of the Neapolitan Mastiff has traditionally been docked as a puppy, leaving two-thirds its original length. The AKC standard states that one-third of the tail is docked. But now, since cosmetic surgery of any kind is banned in Europe, tail docking is not done there; however, the 2015 FCI standard states that the tail reaches the level of the hock. An undocked Neo tail is longer than the distance from root of the tail to the hock. Granted, in the breed there are many genetic tail defects – short tails and kinked tails as are seen in brachycephalic bulldog breeds – and these tails might not reach the hock. The standard does not specify that the tail cannot be docked, and by stating that the tail should, in length, reach the hock, maybe the authorities are leaving room for breeders to cut off one-third of the tail at birth or shortly thereafter, hoping no one will notice.

Movement: Each standard describes the movement of the Neapolitan Mastiff differently.

The 1971 FCI standard said the walking gait

Above: **Vanguard-Macas Molossus Golozo.** *Below:* **Ironstone Contessa, an almost-10-year-old female. Both owned by Susie Schramm.**

was like that of a bear, lanky and slow. The 1991 FCI standard said the movement is one of the typical characteristics of the breed, the walk being feline, like that of a lion. It said the trot or pace is slow and resembles that of the bear. This is because a bear paces, and Neos sometimes trot but mainly pace. (The gaits are walk, trot or pace, and gallop.) Both standards say the Neo rarely gallops. The AKC, in its standard, would not allow the dog's gait to be described as like that of a lion or a bear. Therefore we had to come up with a description of the gait as being not flashy, but rather slow and lumbering, with rolling motion and swaying of the body at all gaits. Slight paddling movement of the front feet is normal. In actuality, this is how lions walk and trot. So the AKC standard gives a pretty good word picture of the Neo's gait. The problem is that many American breeders try to tell the judges that irregularity of the gait is part of the picture, and it is not. Lumbering and swaying of the body does not mean limping!

The 2015 FCI standard got things confused in its description of the gait. It does not distinguish between walk and trot or pace, and so it takes parts of both the 1971 FCI standard and the 1991 FCI standard and states that the gait is "feline type, like the steps of a lion. It is slow and also resembles that of a bear." Reading this, no one would understand what the different gaits are supposed to look like. This is why the AKC did not want reference to other animal gaits.

Size and Weight: These differ in every standard. The 1991 FCI was lenient, in giving a tolerance of 2 cm above or below the stated height of dogs and bitches. The AKC standard, again, is more ambiguous for reason. And the new 2015 FCI standard is overly absolute in that it makes "size bigger or smaller than the limits allowed" a severe fault. Its stated heights and weights are dogma! Is every Neo supposed to be weighed in the ring now?

Disqualifying faults: The 2015 standard removed some important disqualifying faults such as sky-blue eyes (which are associated with wackiness in dogs that have them). But, under pressure from animal-rights people, it makes entropion/ectropion disqualifying faults.

On left, mahogany male Quirino Anvire of Tinus Baskervilium, bred by Tatiana Jayembayeva, and on right, gray female Anvire Belinda, bred by Irina Antipenko, who also owns both dogs. Photo: Antipenko.

By definition, entropion is a rolling in of the upper or lower eyelid, no matter how mild the inward roll. Ectropion is a hanging down and rolling outward of the lower eyelid, no matter how slight it may be. Bloodhounds are typical ectropion-afflicted dogs. Droopy eyelids are part of their picture. I don't know how they are allowed to be shown at Crufts.

That said, because of their excessive frontal wrinkles and heavy folds of skin down the sides of their faces, and the heavy dewlap pulling all the skin down from the face, Neapolitan Mastiffs all have ectropion to one degree or another. The tight-wrinkled ones may not have entropion, but they will certainly have a degree of ectropion.

Entropion is not a good thing. It certainly has the potential to damage the eyeballs. The problem is, it is caused in Neos' upper eyelids because of all the heavy wrinkles on the forehead pushing the skin and eyelids into the globes. Neo owners want wrinkles on their dogs.

So how is anyone going to get rid of entropion in Neos? Solutions: 1. Get rid of the wrinkles in the dogs. 2. Breed dogs with tighter, heavier skin with stronger connective tissue that allows it to remain attached to the skull. You can look at the photos in this book and see how the looser, lax skin makes for more serious entropion than does the harder, tight-wrinkled skin, which tends to stay in place on the dog's face better. I suggest people stop breeding the loose, baggy-skinned Neos. That eliminates about 75 percent or more of the current dogs and their gene pool. Search out dogs with better

Ironwood's Marcello Roman Luciano, two-year-old male. Breeders: James Deppen and Mimi Winkler. Owner: Susan Vann-Spruill.

connective tissue, stronger skin – not floppy, lax skin that falls in wrinkles because of its own weight – and breed these dogs.

In the meantime, what do people do to show their dogs in European shows? They have a veterinarian perform entropion surgery on their dogs and hope the veterinarian is a good plastic surgeon as well, so that the suture scars will not show. Is this legal? No.

So the Italian FCI standard of 2015 is effectively wiping out the showing of Neos in Europe, if the judges are paying attention to the standard. The AKC standard does not mention entropion/ectropion being a disqualification. However people still get surgery done on their severely affected dog

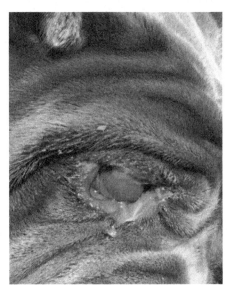

Above left: **This four-month-old female Neapolitan Mastiff has bilateral cherry eyes that cover her entire globe. No ophthalmologist is going to be able to tack these infected glands down under her third eyelids, where they belong. The connective tissue is too lax and the sutures and glands will just pop up and out again. The eyes are filled with pus. The upper eyelids are rolled inward with entropion because her very pretty, copious wrinkles are the soft, loose, connective-tissue kind. They can be flattened out by pressing on the skin. She also has severe lower lid ectropion because of the weight of the heavy lip folds and facial wrinkles and massive dewlap. Her face is certainly pretty to look at (without the cherry eyes). But it is the cause of all her eye problems.** *Above center:* **This picture shows the extent of her ectropion of the lower lids. She will need entropion surgery, but she is going to have to deal with the ectropion. Trying to repair this in a Neo will never work because of the too lax tissue, and the facial folds will pull it down.** *Above right:* **The puppy is lying on the ground, trying to rub the pus out of the left eye on the other side. You can see that the upper eyelid is rolled inward to the eyeball.**

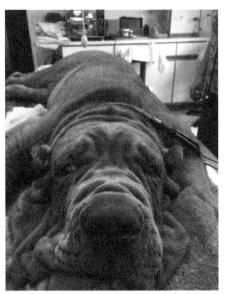

Above left: **The puppy is on the surgery table anesthetized. The photo shows the upper lid rolled into the eyeball.** *Above center:* **This picture shows me lifting out the rolled eyelid to reveal the wet lashes that were rolled underneath.** *Above right:* **On the anesthetized dog, the loose skin and wrinkles have flattened out. This would not happen on a dog with thicker, firmer skin and stronger connective tissue attaching skin to the cranium.**

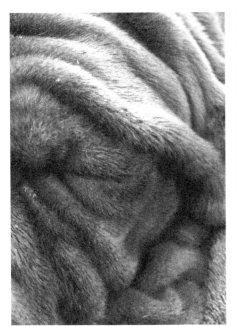 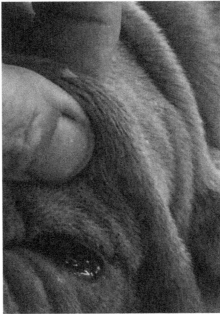 

Above left: **Lily's cherry eye has been removed. The upper lid is rolled in, touching the cornea of the eyeball now.** *Above center:* **This is how much skin has to be removed to eliminate the upper-lid entropion. You can see the eyelashes and eyelid margin are pulled out, but wet from being rolled inward to the eye.** *Above right:* **Here is a year-old male Neo with an ulcer in his right eye. He does not want to open either eye, as both eyes hurt him from the eyelashes irritating the cornea.**

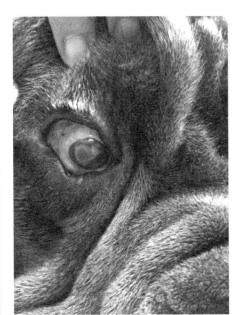 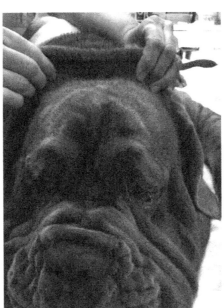 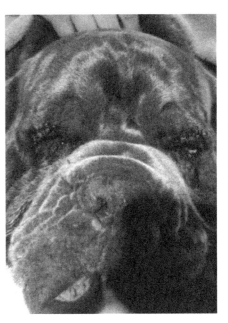

Above left: **The eyelids are parted on the anesthetized dog (he would not let me touch the eyes when awake), showing the deep ulcer, and the entropion of the lower lids as well as the upper lids. He does not have ectropion of the lower lids, as his facial folds are not as copious or loose as that of the previous puppy.** *Above center:* **See how much skin has to come off in order to get the upper eyelids to unroll the entropion.** *Above right:* **The dog after surgery of all four eyelids.**

The above case histories show why people want to eliminate entropion in Neos. The eyelids cause a major lifelong problem for the dog and the owner. The photos also show how difficult it is to get rid of the problem and still keep breed type.

This is a very large Neo. He is another one of Tom Bell's puppies, Relics from the Past Luigi, at two years of age. I tell Neo breeders to keep their puppies thin until they are mature at about three years of age. They need to grow muscle and keep their joints tight. Too much weight will pull them apart. So reluctantly, Tom is keeping his dogs lean until they have developed enough muscle to support their heavy body weight. I like this dog a lot. He has large size, heavy bone, totally athletic and defined muscle with clean lines and lots of energy. He has developed wrinkles and sufficient dewlap. This is what a Neapolitan Mastiff should be, in my opinion. It is a working dog, a guard dog, a dog to bring down intruders, not a fat, floppy, slobbering, low-intelligence caricature that looks fantastic in a photo, but has a hard time staying alive.

so that they do not end up with ulcers on the cornea and blindness. The AKC also bans the surgical correction of entropion/ectropion for showing. Do people still show dogs in the AKC that have had the surgery? You decide.

Ectropion comes in various forms of severity as well. All the heavy facial folds are going to cause pulling on the lower eyelids of Neapolitan Mastiffs. It is therefore a given that all Neapolitan Mastiffs are going to have ectropion of some degree or another if they have any breed type. Ectropion is not the problem for the dog's eyeballs that entropion is. If the ectropion is mild, and there is no entropion, such as may be seen in the dog on the cover of this book, there is no problem. However, if the Italian standard says ectropion is elimination fault, how can any Neo at all be shown in Europe?

If the ectropion is much more severe, and the lower eyelid hangs down much lower than what is seen on the dog on the cover of the book, it is because of the loose hanging skin and poor connective tissue. The upper lids then do not meet the lower lids when the eye is closed; the upper lids roll into the wet conjunctiva of the lower lid and get all goopy, and then get stuck onto the cornea, and more pus is made, The dog squints in pain, which causes the upper lid entropion to become a lot worse. The dog rubs the sore, gooped-up eyes, and then the cornea becomes scratched, infection gets into the scratch, and eventually an ulcer results. No one wants this to happen to a dog, especially their dog.

All this results in the idea or edict in the 2015 FCI standard attempting to get rid of eye problems in Neos. It is a great idea. It is practically impossible to do, but with care, some dog breeders will get tighter-eyed dogs. The dogs also will end up with less wrinkle, less mass, and be of a more normal dog type. The dogs will be sounder. They will be less typey. And this brings us back to the problem: You can breed for soundness or you can breed for type, but you won't have both to the extent that you are seeking.

A word of advice to breeders: Try your best to breed tighter-eyed Neos while keeping the type. You will have to eliminate from your program the dogs with excessive wrinkles and flimsy loose skin all over their bodies, especially their heads. This will mean you will have to remove a lot of dogs from your breeding program. But don't go trying to change the AKC standard on this. It is ideally nebulous on this matter, and any judge who knows dogs at all will not put up a dog with severe eye problems, anyway.

It so happens that a day after I wrote the above, a client brought in a four-month-old puppy with two cherry eyes for me to remove. I was able to get some great pictures illustrating how cherry eye can result from entropion, which occurs because of loose overabundant skin and wrinkles not attached well to the cranium, resulting in the skin rolling into the eyes of the dogs. The excessive ectropion occurs due to the weight of the overabundant thin loose skin pulling down on the eyelids.

That case history is illustrated on the previous two pages, along with another entropion surgery. The eyelids cause a major lifelong problem for the dog and owner.

The 2015 FCI standard is a lot of wishful thinking, though its intentions are good. Breeders have a difficult road ahead, and perceptions of "more overdone is better" may have to change.

In its idealism, the 2015 FCI standard of the Neapolitan Mastiff concludes with a goal for breeders: "Only functionally and clinically healthy dogs, with breed typical conformation, should be used for breeding." One would hope conscientious breeders would have this idea paramount to their program. It is odd to put it in a standard.

A last note is about the new disqualifying fault in the 2015 FCI standard: "Any dog clearly showing physical or behavioural abnormalities shall be disqualified." They are really trying to get the temperament problems with Neos under control. This is a good thing. The AKC has this problem covered in their regulations for showing. It does not have to be put into AKC breed standards. But the mere fact that the caveat is there in the 2015 FCI standard shows that the problem is out of control for dogs in today's society. I believe the overproduction of excessive type created by recessive genes goes along with mental dullness, shyness, and hence unjustified aggression in Neos. Breeding for mental health is as important as breeding for physical health (as the 2015 FCI standard states), and if all the requirements of the 2015 FCI standard are met, the Neo of tomorrow will not be the same dog as the Neo we are used to today.

Neos, like other normal animals, start out with infantile behavior, but eventually grow

Above left: **Ironstone Mafioso, first Neapolitan Mastiff to win Best of Breed at the Westminster Kennel Club Dog Show. Bred by S. Allen.** *Above right:* **Centurion Mastini's Romeo, bred by Bill and Anita Goetz and owned by Tom Bell. Photo: S. Allen.**

Caledonia Grazia, 2016 ATIMANA winner at two years old. Breeder/owner/handler Rachel G. Hosking. Photo: Mario Rodriguez.

up to be adults, evolving into a different behavior more characteristic of their use or job in society. I would hate to see Neos bred down to retaining the perpetual puppy behavior, as has been done with Golden Retrievers and Labs to a great degree. The attraction of Neos to many people is that they are a serious dog, thoughtful, able to react when needed to be a protector. They are not mindless, ever playful family pets. This is a hard task for breeders to address. If you get into Neos, be mindful of their ancient reason for being, and do not take their intelligence away from them.

Today, many of the people interested in breeding, showing and selling Neapolitan Mastiffs from 30 years ago are no longer in the breed. There are still a few diehards, and some new dedicated aficionados are on the scene. I said in the preface to this new edition that I haven't observed much change in the breed in the past 35 years, though many people today are trying to develop a healthier, sounder Neo. This is admirable, but obviously hard to do given the small gene pool. These breeders are to be commended for trying to address the challenge.

It will be interesting to see what happens in the future with this breed. It may go back to being a little-known treasure hidden by the country people in Italy and maybe in some parts of this large United States. Or breeders may succeed in creating a sounder, more popularized version of the Neapolitan Mastiff. Some people who have fallen in love with the spectacular appearance of the Neo might be better off collecting photos or statues and just staring at them every day. Some optimists who don't mind dealing with a plethora of physical ailments in a dog may be quite happy owning a live animal and paying the hefty upkeep. Those people who think owning a Neo is like owning any more modern breed of dog should not get involved with the breed because they will not be able to afford to deal with its physical issues or its temperament. They would then be doing a disservice to the dog in trying to keep it. More and more Neos are turning up in rescue; who would have thought this, given the initial investment it takes to procure one? But most Americans do not have the time, facilities or energy required to maintain a Neo. A true Neo is not a family pet in the American understanding of this term.

In writing about these feelings, I am not trying to be negative. It is because I love the breed that I am trying to protect it in a way. As a veterinarian, I have seen a lot of unintentional abuse done to these animals simply because people who bought them "did not know" or could not care for them properly. I have seen a number of people as well who have quite a few of them and could not live without them, or so they tell me, and their dogs are happy and doing fine. Sometimes I think that because this breed is not for everyone, it may be best kept as it has been for centuries, sort of hidden from the public, and guarded by those people who can understand it. It is hard to keep a relic as it was in our ever-changing modern society.

Breeders have quite a responsibility to maintain this magnificent breed while keeping it healthy. Just think how it survived

The author in October 2016 with Marcel Gordon and his puppy Khaleese, who just had her ears cropped.

all these hundreds of years without human interference in searching for overdone traits. Tobin Jackson, the famous and now deceased Mastiff and Neapolitan Mastiff breeder, told me years ago that his Mastiffs could breed by themselves and they had large litters. Then, as years went on, they started not being able to breed, they rarely got pregnant, and if they did, the litters were very small. Today, we have to think about the reasons this is happening. We may need to change our husbandry and our concepts of what we are trying to create with this breed. That is why this is a book of warnings as well as a book glorifying the Neapolitan Mastiff. It is a wonderful animal. Try to keep it what it was, in all of its Italian essence.

Index

CPSIA information can be obtained
at www.ICGtesting.com
Printed in the USA
BVOW05*2114241116

468814BV00008B/18/P

9 781943 824267